Nuevos Senderos

Nuevos Senderos

Reflections on Hispanics and Philanthropy

Edited by

Diana Campoamor,
Dr. William A. Díaz,
and Henry A. J. Ramos

Arte Público Press
Houston, Texas
1999

Recovering the past, creating the future

Arte Público Press
University of Houston
Houston, Texas 77204-2174

Cover illustration and design by Adelaida Mejia

Nuevos senderos : reflections on Hispanics and philanthropy / edited
by Diana Campoamor, William A. Díaz, and Henry A. J. Ramos.
   p.   cm.
   ISBN 1-55885-263-8 (alk. paper)
   1. Hispanic Americans — Charities. 2. Hispanic Americans —
Charitable contributions. I. Campoamor, Diana. II. Díaz, William A.
III. Ramos, Henry, 1959-.
HV91.N84   1998
362.84'068'073—DC21   98-38439
                                                          CIP

Portions of "A Statistical Profile of Latino Nonprofit Organizations in the
United States," by Michael Cortés, first appeared in *Nonprofit and Voluntary Sector
Quarterly*, vol. 27, pp. 437-458, copyright 1998 by Sage Publications.

♾ The paper used in this publication meets the requirements of the American National
Standard for Information Sciences—Permanence of Paper for Printed Library Materials,
ANSI Z39.48-1984.

9 0 1 2 3 4 5 6 7 8   10 9 8 7 6 5 4 3 2 1

Contents

Introduction

Part I
The State of the U. S. Latino Nonprofit Sector:
Its Makeup and Challenges

Part II
Expanding Latino Participation in U. S. Organized
Philanthropy: Best Practices and Evolving Models

Part III
Promoting Social Investment in Latin America: Emerging Issues and Lessons

Introduction

Hispanics in Philanthropy and the Nonprofit Sector: An Overview

Diana Campoamor and William A. Díaz, Ph.D.

It has been almost ten years since the publication of *Hispanics and the Nonprofit Sector*, a pathbreaking collection of papers edited by Herman Gallegos and Michael O'Neill. In the decade since that significant collection was published, the U.S. Latino[1] population has dramatically expanded its presence in American society and in the nonprofit sector. Now comprising some 15 percent of the national population, it is projected that Hispanics will constitute as much as 25 percent of the U.S. population (and become the nation's largest racial/ethnic minority) by the year 2050. Reflecting this growth, the Latino nonprofit sector has evolved to comprise more than 4,000 organizations. In addition, Latinos are increasingly active as foundation and nonprofit trustees and executive staff. Indeed Hispanics in Philanthropy (HIP), the independent sector's most significant national association of Latino philanthropic leaders, has grown more than fourfold during the past decade, increasing from roughly fifty individuals in 1988 to more than 350 individual and institutional members in 1998.[2] Still, there continues to be surprisingly little interest among nonprofit scholars relative to Latinos, their impact on the sector, or the sector's responsiveness to them.

During the past several years, HIP has focused growing attention on the need to expand research and dialogue on the status of Latinos in philanthropy and the nonprofit sector.[3] This collection reflects HIP's most recent efforts in the research field, focusing on leading issues affecting both U. S.- and Latin American-based institutions and constituencies. It is designed to advance public awareness and comprehension of emerging Latino community issues, needs, and contributions in the philanthropic arena. Several recent developments make this publication particularly timely. One is the developing role of Latinos as philanthropists themselves. Four articles in this volume address the phenomenon of expanded Latino community giving. Ana Gloria Rivas-Vázquez examines new pools of Latino wealth, the giving patterns of wealthy Latinos, and approaches for encouraging wealthy Latinos to give. Importantly, her research reveals that contrary to the myth that "Latinos don't give," Hispanic Americans have long-standing traditions of giving generously. Their patterns of giving, however, do not readily fit into conventional U. S. models of philanthropy. Rather, reflecting the Hispanic value of *personalismo* (personalism), giving by Latino donors is typically targeted to family members, extended family, and friends. Such giving establishes an informal social safety net around relatives and selected personal associates. In this way, it advances deep-rooted Hispanic cultural traditions, which emphasize the primacy of exercising care and responsibility in family and family-like relationships.

Rodolfo de la Garza, using a major national survey of Latinos, examines Latino giving and volunteering. He concludes that, controlling for socioeconomic status and citizenship, there is no statistically significant difference between Mexican Americans and Anglos (non-Hispanic whites) in their levels of giving and volunteering. Hence, neither culture nor ethnicity appears to impose effects on these levels. According to de la Garza, even recent immigrants, who demonstrate lower overall rates of giving and volunteering than native-born Latinos, learn predominant U. S. patterns of giving and volunteering within one generation. These important findings defy conventional wisdom about Hispanics' potential contributions to philanthropy as donors and volunteers by demonstrating that Latino community readiness to support the field is virtually the same as that of mainstream U. S. groups.

At every level, as U. S. foundations have sought to diversify their boards and staffs, the number of Latino foundation trustees and directors has risen sharply in recent years. As the article by Diane Sánchez and Rosie Zamora points out, those selected for these positions tend to be Latinos who are professionally distinguished with strong histories of community involvement. Although these individuals do not believe their ethnicity was the main reason for their selection, they are astute enough to realize that it could have been an important influencing factor. Interestingly, the more than thirty Latino trustees and directors interviewed by Sánchez and Zamora believe that education is the single most important issue facing the U. S. Hispanic population. In addition, the trustees and directors interviewed are concerned that there remain so few Latinos in the pipeline to succeed them as philanthropic and community leaders in the years to come.

Henry A. J. Ramos and Gabriel Kasper examine the rise of Latino community funds, locally endowed funds devoted to supporting Latino community-based nonprofits. These funds, when not freestanding institutions, typically operate under the auspices of community foundations or United Ways, but all are overseen by boards of local Latino community residents and professionals who lead development efforts and decide on grants. Ramos' and Kasper's evaluation of these funds is clearly mixed. The funds are strong on motivation, but not as clearly on philanthropic impact and "value added." The funds expand Latino participation in philanthropy and provide a training ground for Latino philanthropic leadership. However, their professionalism, long-term viability, and community support are still in question. Nevertheless, they represent a critical new stage in Latino-related philanthropy: the push for expanded development and control of the community's own philanthropic institutions.

A second major development in Hispanic philanthropy warranting broader examination has been the growth of the third sector in Latin America and the connection between that development and growing recognition of U. S. Latinos as a transnational population that provides a critical bridge between Latin America and the U. S., particularly at a time of expanding globalization. Two articles in this collection specifically focus on the nonprofit sector in Latin America. Rosa María Fernández Rodríguez, *et al.* examine the role of women in fundraising in Mexico. Similar to Rivas-Vázquez, they find that traditionally women's role in Mexico has relied on personal or voluntary initiative, using personal contacts to raise funds for particular projects. In the past, the majority of these women have come from Mexico's upper classes, allowing them to do volunteer work and fundraising. All this is now changing. In 1995-96, of 2,364 philanthropic institutions in Mexico, 812 (35 percent) were directed by women executives, compared to only about 30 percent in 1990. This expanding professionalization of women's role in Mexican philanthropy, according to the authors, is the result of increased education among women, as well as a growing civic consciousness *(conscuencia ciudadana),* sparked, in part, by Mexico's recent economic and political crises, as well as the earthquake of 1985.

The other article on Latin America's third sector, by Elba Luna, examines the social involvement of corporate foundations in Argentina. Luna finds that the growing tendency in Argentine corporate philanthropy to focus on social welfare issues builds on traditional patterns of assistance to well-known organizations in areas like education and health. While recognizing the value of expanding corporate giving in Argentina, Luna critiques the field for not being sufficiently bold, creative, and strategic. Luna also argues that philanthropic activity in Argentina is overly linked to corporate interests and control. Parenthetically, this situation seems similar to the ambiguous position of U. S. corporate foundations relative to management control.

The resiliency of traditional patterns that fail to adapt to changing needs, which Luna observes in Argentina, is also evident in the activities of many Latino nonprofits in the U. S. In Michael Cortés' statistical profile of Latino nonprofit organizations in the U. S., he notes that the most popular activities among these nonprofits include veterans' services, scholarship and educational programs, and the promotion of business and commerce. Pressing community needs for other nonprofit activities such as policy advocacy, community organizing, legal aid, and citizenship training and acquisition, are unfortunately rare.

Like the Latino population itself, the Hispanic nonprofit sector is still very young. Its major organizations, such as the National Council of La Raza (NCLR), the Mexican American Legal Defense and Educational Fund (MALDEF), and the Southwest Voter Registration/Education Institute are only thirty years old, at best. Organizations established at the local level to support frontline services, especially for newer Latino groups from Central America, are even younger and, therefore, more fragile. More than ever Latino organizations of all kinds must turn to philanthropy for the support they require to survive. Yet in doing so they must avoid a competition for scarce resources with more established African-American community groups that can be potentially destructive. The late Paul Ylvisaker, that courageous, forward-looking grantmaker who helped to establish modern philanthropy in Latino communities at the Ford Foundation, believed that the problems of African Americans and other disadvantaged groups would not receive sustained institutional attention unless the base of power and consensus among the disadvantaged was broadened. This message is reinforced in Arlene Scully's timely analysis of model initiatives that encourage positive interactions between Latinos and African Americans, why these models work, and how foundations can better support them. No issue is more thorny or important to the future of U. S. race relations than the implications of Latino population growth on America's historically black/white paradigm. Supporting constructive engagement involving Latino and African-American groups in collaborative problem-solving and community-building efforts is one of modern philanthropy's greatest responsibilities as we approach the twenty-first century.

The body of articles contained in this collection provides an important glimpse into the opportunities available to philanthropic leaders and practitioners to better involve and serve Latinos in the future. In the main, we can break these lessons down into five directives:

1. Support Expanded Research on Latino Issues in the Field.

In relation to population size and socioeconomic status, Hispanic groups throughout the United States are highly understudied. Only in recent years with the emergence of Latino university scholars and think tanks has basic research been undertaken that promises to better inform mainstream institutions and decision makers about Latino constituencies. Yet still relatively few foundations support this emerging work and/or the policy and practical innovations it typically seeks to inform.

Latinos are especially misunderstood where their particular service needs and philanthropic potentials are concerned. Unfortunately, identifying appropriate response strategies in these important areas is complicated by the absence of more accessible national data on Latino groups. Even IRS data upon which researchers typically rely to assess nonprofit participation and activity is largely unavailable for Latinos, owing to continuing shortcomings in government record keeping and classifications. As a result, more reliable conclusions about the size and characteristics of the Latino nonprofit sector, as well as effective response strategies designed to strengthen Latino service delivery and participation in the field, are difficult to produce.

The absence of more pertinent knowledge about Latinos in the independent sector is damaging not only to Latino interests, but also to the interests of the sector itself. Latino donor practices and giving potentials, for example, are often misunderstood by mainstream foundation and nonprofit executives owing to the failure of existing research and practice to account for the particularities of Hispanic culture, experience, and motivation. Accordingly, mainstream nonprofit leaders who increasingly need to look to Latinos for future sustaining support often miss opportunities to successfully engage them as donors and volunteers.

More concerted efforts by foundations to support expanded practical research designed to address Latino issues in philanthropy and the nonprofit sector would help to improve prospects for Latinos and the independent sector alike.

2.   Encourage Emerging New Models of Latino Giving and Philanthropy.

With nearly $350 billion in annual purchasing power in the United States alone—and uncounted billions in remittances sent each year to assist family members and others in their countries of origin, Latinos' potential to contribute resources to help expand the philanthropic pie is real and significant.4 Moreover, Hispanics want to bring new resources, ideas, and energy to charitable efforts that benefit their communities of interest. A 1996 Chronicle of Philanthropy report on Latino giving found that the average amount donated by contributing Hispanic households rose 22 percent from 1993 to 1995 after accounting for inflation.[5] New research and modeling efforts are needed to highlight exemplary ways to tap and direct this impressive potential for expanded Latino engagement in philanthropy through Latino community giving institutions, as well as community foundation efforts to develop Latino family funds and other giving instruments specifically tailored to Hispanic donors.

In addition, Latino community groups—some informed by their unique experiences in the U. S., others by their historical experiences in Latin America—are increasingly at the forefront of significant innovations in community building and service delivery. For example, Latino community development corporations are creating more family- and community-integrated housing models that incorporate on-site youth and senior services. They are promoting new models of community-based enterprise and job training in depressed urban corridors. And they are revolutionizing the naturalization and literacy fields through the use of informal networks called Talleres and popular education strategies.

Such efforts are helping to accelerate the civic participation and contributions of Latino groups in this country and elsewhere. They are also offering up important lessons for many non-Latino groups. Initiatives of this sort need support from more established mainstream philanthropies to bolster their prospects for success and to expand learning in the field regarding how Latinos and others can be more effectively integrated as philanthropic participants and innovators.

3. Facilitate Latino Trustee/Leadership Networking Efforts to Improve Organized Philanthropy's Reach in Latino Communities.

Only in recent years, as Hispanics have been appointed to foundation and nonprofit boards and senior staff positions, have private grantmaking institutions and larger mainstream civic organizations significantly expanded their institutional focus to include attention to Latino community concerns. Hispanics in Philanthropy has played a central role in this process by acting as an informal bridge between established mainstream institutions and emerging Latino leaders and groups. In this process, we have learned a great deal about the critical role networking and relationships play in informing changes in philanthropic perspective and practice that ultimately benefit Hispanic and other emerging constituencies.

Leadership development and networking activities that enable Latino and other independent sector executives to strengthen their knowledge and appreciation of one another are especially critical as Hispanic communities become more palatable to organized philanthropy. Hispanics in Philanthropy's work continues to focus largely on providing fora for more exchange of this sort to occur. Still, much more along these lines needs to be done at all levels of activity in the field. Leading foundations need to take greater initiative to encourage Latino leadership development and networking in the course of their own work and governance. The many nonprofit organizations they support, both large and small, need to do the same. Only in this way can these institutions forge the necessary relationships and information conduits to do relevant work in Latino and other minority communities.

4.   Promote Community Bridge-Building Efforts Involving Latino and Other
     Grassroots U. S. Constituencies.

     One of the greatest challenges facing emerging Hispanic communi-
ties and other U. S. groups is the danger associated with growing
intergroup conflict. Latinos are especially impacted by increasingly hostile sentiments about minorities, immigrants, and the poor that shape
contemporary policy debates and community relations. Such sentiments
lead to dangerous misperceptions about the goals and aspirations of
Latino people in the United States that ultimately contradict core
American principles.
     Foundations and nonprofit groups alike are uniquely situated to
promote community bridge-building efforts that engage Hispanics and
other grassroots community groups in mutual assistance activities
designed to address shared community problems while combating
stereotypes and misperceptions that are antithetical to the interests of
civil society. More commitment of attention and resources needs to be
brought forward by philanthropic leaders in this area, however.

5.   Foster Increased Exchange Between U. S. Philanthropic/Nonprofit
     Leaders and Their Latin American Counterparts.

     Finally, one of the greatest opportunities to expand philanthropic
impacts in the Americas resides in efforts to expand dialogue and sharing between United States and Latin American practitioners. Much
would be gained from increased Inter-American exchange. Latin
American philanthropy and civil society offer many exciting new models of social organization and investment. United States practitioners
would benefit immensely from opportunities to observe and adopt more
successful practices from Latin America. Conversely, emergent Latin
American foundations and nonprofit institutions would benefit
immensely from opportunities to tap U. S. experience and expertise in
areas ranging from nonprofit governance and strategic planning to communications and technology.
     To realize these many potential benefits, philanthropic leaders in
both the United States and Latin America need to make expanded sharing and partnership a greater priority than they have in the past.
Significant national institutions such as the Council on Foundations,
Independent Sector, and Hispanics in Philanthropy can all make contributions in this area from the U. S. side. What is needed are more regular

and focused interactions and coordination by these institutions with one another, as well as with appropriate counterpart institutions based in Latin America. Major U. S. funders with interests in Latin America could play an important role in instigating more dialogue and interaction of this sort through expanded support for periodic practitioners' conferences in the region, leadership exchange efforts, and (where warranted) special initiatives designed to encourage joint project initiatives.

Clearly, attention to the many challenges just contemplated will not alone solve all problems related to Latino participation in the independent sector, but their serious treatment by leaders and key institutions in the field will make a meaningful difference. It is important that we all work together in this direction. Organized philanthropy has unique means and insights to help address the challenges intelligently and effectively. Hopefully, the contents of this book can help to guide its response.

The research leading to this volume was commissioned from selected scholars, practitioners, and journalists both to inform the field generally as well as to help HIP inform its own strategic planning and programs. The overall project was guided by a research advisory committee of leading national experts on philanthropy and the nonprofit sector. Its members included:

Diana Campoamor
President, Hispanics In Philanthropy

Dr. William A. Díaz
Senior Fellow, University of Minnesota,
Hubert H. Humphrey School of Public Affairs,
Chairman, HIP Research Committee

Félix Gutiérrez
Senior Vice President and Executive Director,
The Freedom Forum, Pacific Coast Center

Virginia Hodgkinson
Research Professor,
Georgetown University Public Policy Institute
Center for the Study of Voluntary Organizations & Services

Dan Moore
Vice President for Programs,
The W.K. Kellogg Foundation

Dr. Michael O'Neill
Director,
University of San Francisco
Institute for Nonprofit Organization Management

Dr. Janice Petrovich
Director,
Education, Knowledge & Religion Program,
The Ford Foundation

Barbara Taveras
President,
The Edward W. Hazen Foundation

Each of the committee's members contributed mightily of their time and wisdom, helping to improve the quality of the research reflected herein and facilitating the overall project's completion. The project benefited especially from able editorial leadership provided by Henry A. J. Ramos of Mauer Kunst Consulting and Dr. Nicolás Kanellos of Arte Publico Press; without their attention to detail and their relentless encouragement, this book would not have been possible. Finally, we are most grateful for the generous financial support we received to produce this volume, from the Ford, Levi Strauss, C. S. Mott, S. H. Cowell, and Edward W. Hazen Foundations, and the Houston Endowment, Inc. We are indebted to these funders and their executive staff members not only for supporting this important project, but also for modeling the behavior and priorities we seek to institutionalize in the broader philanthropic field.

Notes

[1] Throughout we use the terms Latino and Hispanic interchangeably to refer to Americans of Spanish or Latin American descent.

[2] Hispanics In Philanthropy (HIP) is a national nonprofit organization dedicated to expanding private foundations' responsiveness to Latino issues through dialogue, public information, and advocacy. Its more than 350 individual and institutional members include leading foundation and nonprofit trustees and executives of the United States and various Latin American nations.

[3] In 1990, with support from the James Irvine and Edward W. Hazen Foundations, HIP developed a national research agenda that helped to inform several follow-up studies and foundation initiatives that have added valuable thinking and understanding to the field of philanthropy. Subsequently, HIP sponsored national and regional speaking events featuring various research experts, and published periodic working papers on selected topics of importance to Latino constituencies. Along the way, the organization has used its newsletters and annual conferences as information dissemination vehicles for this work.

[4] American Hispanics' buying power—that is, their after-tax income as a group—has grown 65 percent since 1990, from $211 billion to $348 billion. See *Money*, December 1997, p. 142.

[5] See Dundjerski, M., "Tapping the Wealth of Hispanics," *The Chronicle of Philanthropy*, October 31, 1996, p. 33.

Part I

The State of the U. S. Latino Nonprofit Sector: Its Makeup and Challenges

A Statistical Profile of Latino Nonprofit Organizations in the United States[1]

Michael Cortés

Private, nonprofit organizations are a leading force for civic, cultural, educational and social development and change in the United States. Societies that rely on competitive economic markets and that are governed by democratic institutions bear a constant risk of injustice and discrimination against relatively powerless interests. Throughout most of the history of the United States, the nonprofit sector has reduced the risks and mitigated the shortcomings of profit-driven economic behavior and majority rule. Society as a whole benefits from balances struck between profit-seeking business, representative government, and community values championed by the private, nonprofit sector.

The nonprofit sector is an especially important resource for relatively powerless racial and ethnic minority groups. The entire nation benefits when minority interests are respected. After all, everybody is a member of one minority or another. But discrimination poses greater problems for obvious ethnic and racial minorities. Private, voluntary associations and nonprofit corporations are a vital resource for economically and politically disadvantaged groups.

The nation's growing population of Latino minorities is an important case in point. Latino communities in the United States confront too many problems with too few resources. Statistics on the following pages will show that Latinos are poorly served by public education and other government institutions. In the nation's private sector, Latino labor market participation rates are well above average. Nevertheless, poverty rates among Latinos are especially high. It falls to the third sector—the world of private, nonprofit organizations and voluntary associations—to address whatever failures and inequities profit-oriented markets and democratic government visit upon Latino minorities. We look to the nonprofit sector to pursue those American social values that the other two sectors fail to implement. Of society's three sectors, the nonprofit sector provides our best hope of developing the innovative new programs and social change strategies needed for fuller integration of Latinos into U. S. economic and political institutions.

In short, nonprofit organizations are of vital importance to Latino communities. In a nation that values equal economic opportunity, democracy, and equal protection under the law, we must look to the nonprofit sector for leadership when addressing Latinos' problems and aspirations. But is the nonprofit sector really up to the task? Nobody really knows. There is surprisingly little information about nonprofits that respond to and serve Latinos. A small but promising body of research shows us that Latino nonprofits can play a pivotal role in fighting injustices and improving services in Latino communities (Gallegos and O'Neill 1991). This paper adds to that scant body of knowledge by offering a statistical overview of nonprofit corporations that specialize in responding to and serving Latino populations.

Defining Terms

Before describing Latino nonprofits, we should consider the terms we use. Let us begin by clarifying what we mean by (1) the nonprofit sector, (2) Latino nonprofits, and (3) prior research.

The Nonprofit Sector

The private, nonprofit sector of U. S. society goes by many names: the voluntary sector, the charitable sector, the independent sector, the tax-exempt sector, the third sector. The nonprofit sector is distinct from the private, profit-oriented business sector and from the government institutions that comprise the public sector.

Hall (1994) and O'Neill (1989) describe the nonprofit sector as an idea that has been emerging for more than a century. Even so, the boundaries separating the three sectors remain vague and ambiguous. Some private, nonprofit corporations are created or funded by government to serve public purposes. Other nonprofits are instruments of for-profit businesses, or vice versa.

The idea of a nonprofit sector is in large part an artifact of the U. S. Internal Revenue Code (I.R.C.). The I.R.C. exempts about 1.6 million religious, charitable, educational, and other types of legally incorporated organizations (qualifying under I.R.C. §501(c) or §521) from certain forms of taxation. About three-quarters of a million of those tax-exempt nonprofits serve the public (as opposed to private memberships) in various ways.[2] The combined annual income of public-serving nonprofits exceeds $416 billion. Compared to the for-profit and public sectors, the nonprofit sector represents a small but significant part of the nation's economy (Hodgkinson *et al.* 1993).

The nonprofit sector is also a residual catch-all category for unincorporated, informal, voluntary associations that are neither governmental nor profit-seeking, as the name "third sector" implies. Tax-exempt corporations, voluntarism, philanthropy, and informal community organizations together continue a distinctive civic, social, and political heritage noted as early as 1835 by the French observer Alexis de Tocqueville (1945) during his visits to the United States.

Latino Nonprofits

Latino nonprofits in the U.S. are organizations whose missions focus on Latino community problems or aspirations; they are controlled or led by Latino community members. In addition, Latino nonprofits are either (a) tax-exempt corporations governed by Latino directors or led by Latino chief executives, or (b) voluntary associations dominated by Latino members or constituents.

Latinos are defined for present purposes as Chicanos, Puerto Ricans, Mexican immigrants, Cuban refugees, Cuban-Americans, and other ethnic minorities of Spanish or Latin-American descent residing permanently in the U.S. There are 29,577,000 Latinos, 11 percent of all U. S. residents (U.S. Bureau of the Census 1997c). By the year 2005, Latinos will be the nation's largest minority. By the year 2050, one out of four U.S. residents will be Latino (U.S. Bureau of the Census 1997a). High birth rates in the United

States are the principal reason why Latinos' numbers are growing so rapidly (U.S. Bureau of the Census 1995).

Immigration has also contributed to Latino population growth. The nation's Latino population includes a large number of recent immigrants and their children. But the popular belief that most Latinos are illegal immigrants is wrong. A significant number of Latino families have been rooted in the southwestern U.S. for more than 400 years (Cortés 1980). The proportion of Latinos who are U.S. citizens is currently approaching 68 percent (U.S. Bureau of the Census 1997b).

Latinos are a population beset with a disproportionately large share of the nation's social problems and a disproportionately small share of U. S. society's benefits and opportunities. Despite their high labor force participation rates, Latinos' individual earnings are well below average. The Latino workforce is concentrated in low-skilled, low-paying, and often high-risk jobs. Twenty-nine percent live in poverty. Poverty rates are 39 percent for Latino children, 50 for Latino female-headed households, and 66 for Latino children in female-headed households (Borjas and Tienda 1985; Congressional Research Service 1985; Escutia and Prieto 1986; Federal Interagency Forum on Child and Family Statistics [FIFCFS], 1997; U.S. Bureau of the Census 1995).

Just 54 percent of Latino adults have a high school education (National Center for Education Statistics [NCES], 1996). Latino youth have the nation's largest high school dropout rates. Nearly one-third of all Latinos between sixteen and twenty-four years of age have dropped out of high school (NCES 1997). Their dropout rate is even higher in major U.S. cities, typically ranging between 40 and 60 percent (NCES 1980). Of those Latino young adults who *do* graduate from high school, only 16 percent go to college and earn a Bachelor's degree (FIFCFS 1997). The failures of public education will preserve Latinos' relative disadvantage in U.S. labor markets for the foreseeable future (Astin 1982; Orum 1985; Santos 1984).

Prior Research

Research on Latino nonprofits is scarce. Research to date generally falls into two categories. One is case studies of individual organizations. Many—perhaps most—of the growing collection of case studies have been performed by university graduate students (e.g., Castillo 1988;

Santiago 1978; Sierra 1984; Soto 1974). The other category consists of personal accounts and historical anecdotes gathered by scholars and participants (e.g., Martínez 1991; Nicolau and Santiestevan 1991; Urrutia 1984).

Statistical data on Latino nonprofits are hard to find. The best available statistics to date have been those provided by Estrada (1991). Estrada relied upon published directories in order to estimate the number of Latino nonprofits in the U.S. He examined organizations listed in the *Encyclopedia of Associations* (Gale Research 1988) and found that six-tenths of one percent (0.6%) included the terms Hispanic, Latino, Latin American, Puerto Rican or Cuban in their titles. Extrapolating to statistics based on Internal Revenue Service (IRS) data published by Independent Sector, Estrada estimated that at least 2,200 Latino nonprofits (excluding churches) existed in the United States at the time of the research.

Estrada's estimate appears questionable, for two reasons. First, the Independent Sector research used for the extrapolation looked only at organizations recognized under I.R.C. §§501(c)(3)-(4). Other nonprofits were not included. Second, biases affecting compilation of such directories are unknown. Representation of Latino nonprofits in the directory used by Estrada might have been disproportionately high or low. We therefore used a different research strategy to produce the statistical profile presented below.

Approach

The following pages present a statistical profile of Latino nonprofits that have applied to the IRS for recognition as tax-exempt organizations. IRS data offer the most comprehensive and inclusive set of data on nonprofit organizations in the United States. IRS data do not identify Latino organizations as such. Nevertheless, content analysis of IRS data allows us to estimate the number and characteristics of tax-exempt Latino organizations.

We began with data supplied by the Statistics of Income Division of the IRS from its Exempt Organizations Business Master File. We identified Latino organizations in the IRS Business Master File by examining organization names. A computer was used to identify organizations with names, including one or more words from a specially compiled list of 299 Latino search terms. The resulting list of organizations was then reviewed by hand, to eliminate non-Latino organizations that the computer identified by error. The details of this approach are described in a separate paper (Cortés 1997).

Findings

Insufficient Data on Churches

Churches are exempt from taxation under I.R.C. §501(c)(3), even if they do not apply to IRS for recognition.[3] Nevertheless, 804 churches were among the Latino nonprofits found in the IRS Exempt Organizations Business Master File (see Table 1).

Table 1		
Latino Churches That Applied to IRS for Recognition as Tax-Exempt Organizations		
TYPE OF EXEMPT ORGANIZATION	NUMBER OF LATINO NONPROFITS	PERCENT (%)
Churches Ruled Exempt Under I.R.C. §501(c)(3)	804	16.5
Other Nonprofits Ruled Exempt Under:		
I.R.C. §501(c)(3)	2,757	56.6
Other §501 subsections	1,311	26.9
Total Ruled Exempt	**4,872**	**100.0**

aPercentages are rounded to the nearest .1%.

We do not know why those 804 churches chose to make themselves known to the IRS. They may have applied for IRS rulings to make it easier to raise funds, to facilitate exemption from state or other taxes, to gain low-cost nonprofit postage rates, or for other reasons. The fact that IRS rulings are optional for churches poses a problem for this study. The extent of underrepresentation of churches in IRS data is unknown. Nearly 17 percent of the Latino nonprofits found in IRS data are churches, but the actual percentage of churches in the Latino nonprofit sector could easily be higher.

It is also hard to tell whether all of the 804 churches we found actually fit the definition of Latino nonprofits used for this study. Our definition requires that organizational missions focus on Latino community problems or aspirations, and that the organizations be controlled or led by Latino community members. It is difficult to tell which churches fit that definition, without learning more about the governance norms and conventions of each denomination represented.

Thus, our data on churches in the Latino nonprofit sector are inadequate in two important respects. We do not know how many churches fit our definition of Latino nonprofits. And we do not know the extent to which churches are underrepresented, since many—perhaps most—Latino churches do not bother to apply for official recognition of their tax-exempt status. For those two reasons, the scope of this paper has been narrowed to focus only on organizations that are not churches. (Religious organizations that are *not* churches remain part of this study.) By excluding churches, we can have more confidence in the following findings about nonchurch Latino nonprofits.

Most Latino Nonprofits Are Exempted Under §501(c)(3)

Of all the various types of tax exemptions available under the Internal Revenue Code, the most frequently used tax exemption is that reserved for charitable, educational, literary, religious, and scientific organizations, as well as organizations that work to prevent cruelty to animals or children, as authorized by I.R.C. §501(c)(3). Most Latino nonprofits exempted under subsection (c)(3) qualify as charitable. One-third (including some of the charitable organizations) also qualify as educational (Appendix A).

All organizations exempted under subsection (c)(3) must benefit the public at large in some way. Roughly 40 percent of the entire U.S. nonprofit sector is exempt under subsection (c)(3). But the proportion for Latinos is much higher. About two-thirds of all Latino nonprofits in the IRS Business Master File are exempted under subsection (c)(3) (see Table 2).

Among Latino nonprofits exempted under subsection (c)(3), about 63 percent receive a substantial part of their financial support from government or the general public (see Table 3). Ninety-five percent of Latino (c)(3)'s are classified by the IRS as "public charities"—as opposed to "pri-

Table 2

More Than Two-Thirds of Latino Nonprofits Are Exempted Under I.R.C. §501(c)(3)

I.R.C. SUBSECTION	TYPE OF EXEMPTION	NUMBER OF LATINO NONPROFITS[a]	PERCENT[b] (%)
(c)(2)	Organizations owning income property benefiting another §501(c) corporation	8	.2
(c)(3)	Charitable, educational, literary, religious, scientific, or preventing cruelty to animals or children	2,757	67.8
(c)(4)	Civic leagues and social welfare organizations engaging in social action, and local employee associations	675	16.6
(c)(5)	Labor unions and agricultural associations	30	.7
(c)(6)	Chambers of commerce, real estate boards, trade associations	327	8.0
(c)(7)	Social and recreation clubs	141	3.5
(c)(8)	Lodges and fraternities benefiting members or their families	47	1.2
(c)(9)	Union welfare funds and employee beneficiary associations	17	.4
(c)(10)	Lodges and fraternities doing charitable, educational, literary, religious or scientific work	16	.4
(c)(12)	Local nonprofit life insurance associations, and member-supported irrigation and telephone co-ops	2	.0
(c)(13)	Member-owned nonprofit cemeteries	2	.0
(c)(14)	Credit unions and mutual corporations	25	.6
(c)(15)	Small mutual insurance co-ops	1	.0
(c)(17)	Unemployment benefit trusts	1	.0
(c)(19)	Nonprofit war veteran organizations	18	.4
(c)(20)	Legal services organizations	1	.0
	Total	4,068	100.0

[a]Churches are not counted in this table.
[b]Percentages are rounded to the nearest .1%.

vate foundations"—because they depend primarily upon public support.[4] Public support, in this sense, includes government grants, grants from a variety of private funders, individual contributions from the general public, or a diversified funding base consisting of any or all of those sources.

Table 3			
Most Latino Nonprofits Exempted Under I.R.C. §501(c)(3) Are Supported Primarily by Government or the General Public			
IRS FOUNDATION CODE	TYPE OF CHARITIES AND FOUNDATIONS EXEMPT UNDER I.R.C. §501(c)(3)	NUMBER OF LATINO NONPROFITS[a]	PERCENT[b] %
PRIVATE FOUNDATIONS:			
2	Exempt from paying excise taxes on investment income	1	.0
3	Other operating foundations	7	.3
4	Non operating foundations	114	4.1
9	Suspense	24	.9
11	Schools	60	2.2
12	Hospitals and medical research programs	27	1.0
GOVERNMENT PROGRAMS:			
13	Organizations owned or operated by government to benefit a college or university	3	.1
14	Governmental units	3	.1
15	Organizations receiving a substantial part of their support from a governmental unit or the general public	1,722	62.5
16	Organizations receiving less than a third of their support from gross investment income and unrelated business income, and more than a third of their support from contributions or fees or other income generated by tax-exempt activities	757	27.5
17	Organizations created to benefit another §501(c)(3) organization described by one of the foundation codes 10-16, listed above	38	1.4
18	Public safety testing organizations	1	.0
	Total	**2,757**	**100.00**

[a]Churches are not counted in this table.
[b]Percentages are rounded to the nearest .1%.

Seventy Percent Can Receive Tax-Deductible Contributions

A principal advantage of exemption under subsection (c)(3) is the assurance it provides donors that their contributions are deductible on their individual or corporate tax returns (under I.R.C. §170). The (c)(3) exemption also makes it easier to raise funds from private foundations. However, under some circumstances, other types of tax exemptions besides the (c)(3) also allow nonprofits to confer tax deductibility upon their donors. This is the case with Latino nonprofits. While just 68 percent have (c)(3) exemptions, fully 70 percent of Latino nonprofits are eligible to receive tax-deductible contributions (see Table 4).

Table 4		
Donations to Most Latino Nonprofits Are Tax Deductible		
ELIGIBLE TO RECEIVE TAX-DEDUCTIBLE CONTRIBUTIONS	NUMBER OF LATINO NONPROFITS[a]	PERCENT[b] (%)
Eligible	2,853	70.1
Not Eligible	1,176	28.9
Uncertain	39	1.0
Total	4,068	100.0

[a]Churches are not counted in this table.
[b]Percentages are rounded to the nearest .1%.

Most Latino Nonprofits Are New

Compared to the rest of the nation's nonprofit sector, Latino nonprofits are largely a recent phenomenon. Sixty-eight Latino nonprofits, representing less than 2 percent of those found in the IRS Business Master File, were granted recognition of their tax-exempt status by an IRS ruling during the first half of the twentieth century. If we view IRS ruling dates as nonprofit birthdays, half of all Latino nonprofits are less than ten years old (see Table 5).

During and after the Second World War, the formation of new Latino nonprofits occurred at a rate ranging from 1 to 14 per year. The rate picked up in the 1960s to between 4 and 71 per year, with the dramatic exception of 1966. That year, 277 new Latino nonprofits were ruled

Table 5

Half of All Latino Nonprofits Are Less Than Ten Years Old

YEAR RULED TAX-EXEMPT BY IRS	NUMBER OF LATINO NONPROFITS[a]	PERCENT (%)	CUMULATIVE PERCENT[b]
1908-1966	516	12.8	12.8
1967-1971	277	6.9	19.7
1972-1977	411	10.2	29.9
1978-1983	420	10.5	40.4
1984-1986	326	8.1	48.5
1987-1989	422	10.5	59.0
1990-1991	369	9.2	68.2
1992-1993	554	13.8	81.9
1994	298	7.4	89.4
1995	324	8.1	97.4
January-April 1996	104	2.6	100.0
Ruling year unknown	47		
Total	**4,068**		

[a]Churches are not counted in this table.
[b]Percentages are rounded to the nearest .1%.

tax-exempt by the IRS. Rates continued to climb, on average, during the decades that followed. The 1970s saw an average of 67 new organizations formed per year. The average for the first half of the 1980s was 84 per year. From 1985 through 1989, the rate surged to 151 per year, and it has continued to increase ever since. Current rates exceed 300 per year (see Figure 1). While the number of new tax exemptions for the nonprofit sector as a whole also spiked during the War on Poverty and related social programs during the 1960s, and has grown at an increasing rate in more recent years, the growth of Latino nonprofits during those years has been well above average.

Limited Income and Assets

Most Latino nonprofits, like most other nonprofits, are not required to report their income and assets to the IRS each year. Only organizations that normally receive more than $25,000 annually are required to do so. Most nonprofits in the IRS Business Master File fall below that threshold (see Tables 6 and 7).

Table 6

Most Latino Nonprofits Have Too Little Income to Report

REPORTED ANNUAL INCOME	NUMBER OF LATINO NONPROFITS[a]	PERCENT (%)	CUMULATIVE PERCENT[b]
No reported income[c]	2,510	61.7	61.7
$1-$9,999	29	.7	62.4
$10,000-$24,999	8	.2	62.6
$25,000-$99,999	553	13.6	76.2
$100,000-$499,999	553	13.6	89.8
$500,000-$999,999	166	4.1	93.9
$1,000,000-$4,999,999	186	4.6	98.5
$5,000,000-$9,999,999	34	.8	99.3
$10,000,000-$49,999,999	24	.6	99.9
$50,000,000 or more	5	.1	100.0
Total	**4,068**	**100.0**	

[a]Churches are not counted in this table.
[b]Percentages are rounded to the nearest .1%.
[c]Nonprofits receiving less than $25,000 per year are usually not required to report their income to IRS.

Table 7

Assets of Most Latino Nonprofits Are Unknown

ASSETS SHOWN ON MOST RECENT ANNUAL RETURN	NUMBER OF LATINO NONPROFITS[a]	PERCENT (%)	CUMULATIVE PERCENT[b]
No reported assets[c]	2,544	62.5	62.5
$1-$9,999	203	5.0	67.5
$10,000-$24,999	182	4.5	72.0
$25,000-$99,999	425	10.4	82.4
100,000-$499,999	372	9.1	91.6
$500,000-$999,999	120	2.9	94.5
$1,000,000-$4,999,999	151	3.7	98.3
$5,000,000-$9,999,999	30	.7	99.0
$10,000,000-$49,999,999	24	.6	99.6
$50,000,000 or more	17	.4	100.0
Total	**4,068**	**100.0**	

[a]Churches are not counted in this table.
[b]Percentages are rounded to the nearest .1%.
[c]Nonprofits with incomes under $25,000 per year are usually not required to report their assets to IRS.

Legal Incorporation

More than three-quarters of the Latino nonprofits found in the IRS Business Master File are legally incorporated under the laws of their respective state. The proportion of other types of organizations, such as trusts and associations, is relatively small in Latino communities (see Table 8).

	TYPE OF TAX EXEMPTION				TOTAL[a]	
TYPE OF LATINO ORGANIZATION	§501(c)(3)		OTHER §501			
	Number	Percent	Number	Percent	Number	Percent
Corporation	2,489	90.3	648	49.4	3,137	77.1
Trust	14	.5	17	1.3	31	.8
Cooperative	7	.3	0	0	7	.2
Partnership	0	0	0	0	0	0
Association	238	8.6	646	49.3	884	21.7
Unknown	9	.3	0	0	9	.2
Total	2,757	100.0	1,311	100.0	4,068	100.0

Table 8

Most Tax-Exempt Latino Nonprofits Are Corporations

[a]Churches are not counted in this table.
[b]Percentages are rounded to the nearest .1%.

Lack of Affiliation

Latino nonprofits are more likely than other nonprofits to be independent organizations. Latino organizations tend not to affiliate with national, state, or regional umbrella groups. Latino organizations are less likely to be controlled by other organizations through interlocking boards of directors or other such arrangements (see Table 9).

Southwestern Concentration

Nearly half of all Latino nonprofits are located in the states of California, Texas, or New Mexico. Other jurisdictions with smaller but

Table 9

Most Latino Nonprofits Are Not Controlled By Other Organizations

IRS AFFILIATION CODE	TYPE OF AFFILIATION	NUMBER OF LATINO NONPROFITS[a]	PERCENT[b] (%)
1	Organization is the center of a national, regional, or geographic group of organizations, each with a separate tax exemption	16	.4
2	Organization is intermediate in a group of separately exempted organizations (e.g., state headquarters of a national group)	4	.1
3	Independent organization (or independent auxiliary) not affiliated with any national, regional, or geographic group	3,328	81.8
6	Parent of a group of organizations sharing one tax exemption under an IRS group ruling18	17	.4
7	Intermediate in a group of organizations sharing one tax exemption (e.g., state headquarters of a national group with an IRS group ruling)	0	0
8	Parent of a group of §501(c)(1) organizations sharing one tax exemption under an IRS group ruling	0	0
9	Subordinate in a group of organizations sharing one tax exemption (e.g., a local, separately incorporated affiliate of a national group with an IRS group ruling)	696	17.1
0	Affiliation unknown	7	.2
	Total	**4,068**	**100.0**

[a]Churches are not counted in this table.
[b]Percentages are rounded to the nearest .1%.
[c]IRS uses code 8, instead of code 6, for group parent organizations exempted under I.R.C. §501(c)(1).

significant concentrations of Latino nonprofits are (in declining order) New York State, Florida, Puerto Rico, Illinois, the District of Columbia, and Colorado (See Table 10).

Widespread Organizational Activities

The IRS Business Master File provides only limited information about the actual program activities of nonprofit organizations. When organizations apply for recognition of their tax-exempt status, the IRS asks them to provide information about their intended activities. Those intended activities have been classified with a wide variety of codes (Appendix B).

Table 10

Nearly Half of All Latino Nonprofits Are Located in California, Texas, or New Mexico

Location	Number of Latino Nonprofits[a]	Percent[b]	Location	Number of Latino Nonprofits[a]	Percent[b]
Alabama	7	.2	Nevada	9	.2
Alaska	2	.0	New Hampshire	1	.0
Arizona	171	4.2	New Jersey	83	2.0
Arkansas	4	.1	New Mexico	642	15.8
California	849	20.9	New York	270	6.6
Colorado	108	2.7	North Carolina	5	.1
Connecticut	41	1.0	North Dakota	0	0
Delaware	3	.1	Ohio	43	1.1
Florida	209	5.1	Oklahoma	27	.7
Georgia	15	.4	Oregon	24	.6
Hawaii	3	.1	Pennsylvania	55	1.4
Idaho	6	.1	Rhode Island	5	.1
Illinois	156	3.8	South Carolina	1	.0
Indiana	27	.7	South Dakota	0	0
Iowa	15	.4	Tennessee	6	.1
Kansas	39	1.0	Texas	473	11.6
Kentucky	13	.3	Utah	20	.5
Louisiana	21	.5	Vermont	1	.0
Maine	1	.0	Virginia	45	1.1
Maryland	44	1.1	Washington	48	1.2
Massachusetts	67	1.6	West Virginia	1	.0
Michigan	66	1.6	Wisconsin	35	.9
Minnesota	26	.6	Wyoming	9	.2
Mississippi	3	.1	District of Columbia	119	2.9
Missouri	22	.5	Puerto Rico	188	4.6
Montana	0	0	Virgin Islands	1	.0
Nebraska	24	.6	Unknown	15	.4
Total				**4,068**	**100.0**

[a]Churches are not counted in this table.
[b]Percentages are rounded to the nearest .1%.

A single organization may be assigned up to three different codes, or in some cases, no codes at all. It is therefore difficult to sum up nonprofits' proposed activities in any sort of precise, mathematical way. Nevertheless, some proposed activities are obviously widespread among Latino nonprofits. Chief among them are veterans' activities, awarding scholarships and educational activities, and promotion of business and commerce (see Table 11).

Table 11

Widespread Activities Among Latino Nonprofits[a]

ACTIVITIES PROPOSED BY ORGANIZATIONS SEEKING TAX EXEMPTION	Number of Latino Nonprofits[a]
Veterans' Activities	254
SCHOOLS, COLLEGES, AND RELATED ACTIVITIES: Scholarships Other school related activities	 108 178
BUSINESS AND PROFESSIONAL ORGANIZATIONS: Business promotion (chambers of commerce, business leagues, etc.) Professional association	 163 126
CULTURAL, HISTORICAL, OR OTHER EDUCATIONAL ACTIVITIES: Cultural performances Other cultural or historical activities Discussion groups, forums, panels, lectures, etc. Community service organization	 104 109 113 101
CIVIL RIGHTS ACTIVITIES: Defense of human and civil rights Elimination of prejudice and discrimination (based on race, religion, sex, national origin, etc.)	 89 28
SERVICES TO INDIVIDUALS: Supplying money, goods, or services to the poor Gifts or grants to individuals (other than scholarships) Grants, gifts, or loans to other organizations	 82 26 58

[a]Source: Appendix B, Table A2.
[b]Churches are not counted in this table.

Neglected Community Needs

Some other activities (as classified by IRS) are noticeably rare among Latino nonprofits. Proposed activities notably lacking among Latino organizations include emergency preparedness, consumer advocacy, endowments, environmental conservation, legislative and political activities, litigation and legal aid, fundraising, and advocacy attempting to influence public opinions about social problems or public policy (see Table 12).

It is not clear why those activities are neglected. Given the poverty and other problems facing Latino communities in the United States, as

Table 12

Rare Activities Among Latino Nonprofits[a]

Activities Proposed by Organizations Seeking Tax Exemption	Number of Latino Nonprofits[b]
Emergency or disaster aid fund	1
Consumer interest group	1
Endowment fund or financial services	2
CONSERVATION, ENVIRONMENTAL, AND BEAUTIFICATION ACTIVITIES:	
Preservation of natural resources (conservation)	3
Combating or preventing pollution (air, water, etc.)	2
Land acquisition for preservation	1
Preservation of scenic beauty	1
Garden club	3
Other conservation, environmental, or beautification activities	2
LEGISLATIVE AND POLITICAL ACTIVITIES:	
Propose, support, or oppose legislation	5
Voter information on issues or candidates	1
Voter education (mechanics of registering, voting, etc.)	5
Other legislative and political activities	5
FARMING AND RELATED ACTIVITIES:	
Farm bureau	1
Agricultural group	2
Horticultural group	1
Farmers cooperative marketing or purchasing	1
Breeders association	1
Other farming and related activities	5
MUTUAL ORGANIZATIONS:	
Mutual ditch, irrigation, telephone, electric company, etc.	9
Credit union	9
Reserve funds or insurance for domestic building and loan association, cooperative bank or mutual savings bank	1
Mutual insurance company	1
Other mutual organization	2
LITIGATION AND LEGAL AID ACTIVITIES:	
Public interest litigation activities	2
Other litigation or support of litigation	1
Legal aid to indigents	12
Fundraising	13
ADVOCACY ATTEMPTING TO INFLUENCE PUBLIC OPINION ON:	
Government aid to parochial schools	1
U.S. foreign policy	4
Pacifism and peace	5
Stricter law enforcement	1
Ecology or conservation	2
Medical care service	2
Welfare systems	3
Racial integration	1
Use of intoxicating beverages	1
Use of drugs or narcotics	4
Other matters	17

Table 12 (continued)	
Rare Activities Among Latino Nonprofits[a]	
ACTIVITIES PROPOSED BY ORGANIZATIONS SEEKING TAX EXEMPTION	NUMBER OF LATINO NONPROFITS[b]
HOUSING ACTIVITIES:	
Low-income housing	30
Low and moderate income housing	12
Housing for the aged	15
Instruction and guidance on housing	25
Other housing matters	25
YOUTH ACTIVITIES:	
Boy Scouts, Girl Scouts, etc.	70
Boys Club, Little League, etc.	7
FFA, FHA, 4-H, etc.	1
YMCA, YWCA, etc.	1
Camp	3
Care and housing of children (orphanage, etc.)	23
Prevention of cruelty to children	9
Combat juvenile delinquency	15
Other youth organization or activities	13

[a]Source: Appendix B, Table A2.
[b]Churches are not counted in this table.

described earlier in this paper, we might speculate that those seemingly neglected activities represent important unmet needs. In any event, reasons why those activities are rare are not readily apparent.

N.T.E.E. Classifications

Our description of activities pursued by Latino nonprofits relies on activity categories developed by the IRS. Unfortunately, that classification scheme leaves us in the dark about other activities in the nation's nonprofit sector, Latino and non-Latino alike. In an effort to learn more about nonprofit activities, an alternative set of activity codes was developed by Independent Sector. The new activity codes are called the "National Taxonomy of Exempt Organizations" (N.T.E.E.). They were developed by Independent Sector in cooperation with the IRS.

Unfortunately, the N.T.E.E. adds little to our understanding of Latino nonprofits, because only 875 Latino nonprofits have been assigned N.T.E.E. classifications (see Table 13). Of those classified, ninety-five were assigned N.T.E.E. "Common Codes" indicating types of services provided by Latino nonprofits to other elements of the nonprofit sector (see Table 14).

Table 13

**About One-Third of Latino Nonprofits Exempt
Under I.R.C. §501(c)(3)
Are Classified Under N.T.E.E.**

N.T.E.E. CODE	CLASSIFICATION	NUMBER OF LATINO NONPROFITS[a]	PERCENT	CUMULATIVE PERCENT[b]
MOST FREQUENT CLASSIFICATIONS:				
P84	Ethnic immigrant centers and services	79	2.9	2.9
A23	Cultural and ethnic awareness	40	1.5	4.3
B82	Scholarships and student financial aid services	39	1.4	5.7
P20	Multipurpose human services	27	1.0	6.7
L20	Housing development, construction, management	17	.6	7.3
X20	Christian[c]	16	.6	7.9
	Classifications with less than 15 Latino organizations apiece	657	23.8	31.8
	Unclassified Latino §501(c)(3) organizations	1,882	68.3	100.0
	Total	**2,757**	**100.0**	

[a]Churches are not counted in this table.
[b]Percentages are rounded to the nearest .1%.
[c]Although churches are not counted in this table, other religious organizations are.

Discussion and Conclusions

A Partial Profile

It appears that Latino nonprofits comprise less than four-tenths of a percent of all nonprofits listed in the IRS Exempt Organizations Business Master File. Analysis of IRS data on those 4,872 Latino nonprofits has provided us with a statistical profile of organizations in the United States. But we must remember that the profile presented here provides only a partial picture.

To complete the picture, we would have to look beyond the IRS files. We would have to learn more about Latino churches, most of which need never apply to the IRS for tax exemption (thanks to prevailing interpretations of the First Amendment to the U. S. Constitution). We would have to learn more about the large majority of Latino nonprofits whose income is less than $25,000 per year, and who therefore need not report their income and assets to the IRS. We would have to learn more about Latino community organizations, voluntary associations, and small non-profit corporations bringing in less than $5,000 annually, none of which are required to apply to the IRS for their tax exemptions.

And finally, we would have to learn more about the vast, unorganized, uncounted individual and family donations of time, money, love, and civic responsibility toward the betterment of Latino communities, to the benefit of us all. Anyone who has worked extensively with Latino nonprofit organizations can tell that this statistical profile, like other previous research, has hardly scratched the surface of the Latino nonprofit sector.

Table 14

Latino §501(c)(3) Nonprofits Serving Other Nonprofits

N.T.E.E. COMMON CODE	SERVICE TO OTHER NONPROFITS	NUMBER OF LATINO NONPROFITS[a]	PERCENT	CUMULATIVE PERCENT[b]
A	Alliance organization	0	0	0
B	Management and technical assistance	12	.4	.4
C	Professional societies and associations	14	.5	.9
D	Regulation, administration, and accreditation services	0	0	.9
E	Research institutes and services	2	.1	1.0
F	Public policy research and analysis	1	.0	1.1
G	Reform	0	0	1.1
H	Ethics	0	0	1.1
I	Single organization support	10	.4	1.4
J	Fundraising or fund distribution	11	.4	1.8
K	Equal opportunity and access	1	.0	1.9
L	Information and referral	6	.2	2.1
M	Public education (increasing public awareness)	29	1.1	3.1
N	Volunteer bureaus	5	.2	3.3
P	Formal/general education	4	.2	3.5
Z	Unknown	778	28.2	31.7
	Not classified	1,884	68.3	100.0
	Total	**2,757**	**100.0**	

[a]Churches are not counted in this table.
[b]Percentages are rounded to the nearest .1%.

Statistical profiles based on IRS data are partial profiles at best. The rest of the Latino nonprofit sector remains unmeasured. Scholars who would help Latino communities know themselves, have much more research to do.

Why Are Latino Nonprofits So Young?

The number of new Latino nonprofits is surprisingly high. One of the most interesting and important unanswered questions emerging from this research is, Why are Latino nonprofits so young? Like the people they serve, the average age of Latino nonprofits is lower than for the rest of the nonprofit sector. Speculation about the reasons why suggest two hypotheses that should be tested by future research. One hypothesis attributes growth to spin-offs by older Latino nonprofits. The other hypothesis attributes growth to the nation's growing Latino population.

The spin-off hypothesis has its roots in the much maligned "War on Poverty" launched by President Johnson's ill-fated Economic Opportunity Act of 1964. The Act and its successor programs are proclaimed failures by observers who fault federal policies of the 1960s and 1970s for not eradicating poverty. On the other hand, one of the most important and lasting legacies of the War on Poverty is the civic infrastructure of nonprofit organizations created of, by, and for members of low-income and oppressed communities in the United States. An underlying assumption of War on Poverty strategists was that long-term solutions to poverty required social, economic, and political empowerment of the poor. Creation of new community-based organizations was a fundamental component of that strategy.

Our findings show a dramatic spike in the creation of new Latino nonprofit organizations in 1966, as the new War on Poverty was being implemented. The rate remained somewhat elevated thereafter. The spin-off hypothesis would argue that creation of a critical mass of Latino nonprofits leads eventually to the creation of new nonprofits, as organizational growth and learning leads to expansion and diversification of the Latino nonprofit sector. Theoretical rationales would come from the multidisciplinary literature on organization theory.

An alternative to the spin-off hypothesis is the population growth-driven hypothesis. The growth-driven hypothesis would argue that Latino nonprofits are formed in reaction to growing needs and markets for their services. Our findings show a steadily growing surge in new nonprofits formed in the late 1980s and into the '90s. The surge parallels (and lags only a few years behind) the recent surge in Latino immigrant populations in the United States. Theoretical rationales for the growth-driven hypothesis would come from economic theories of nonprofit organization.

Further analysis of IRS data could test the competing hypotheses by learning more about new Latino organizations arriving on the scene over the past ten years. What demographic variables best predict the location of new Latino nonprofits? Do they tend to be geographically proximate to existing Latino nonprofits, especially those formed during the War on Poverty? Or are new nonprofits concentrated instead in geographic regions newly populated by Latinos, where no prior infrastructure of Latino nonprofits existed?

Implications for Organizers

The question of competing hypotheses is not merely academic. If new Latino populations in the United States are concentrated in geographic areas where few, if any, Latino nonprofits exist, there may be growing unmet needs for new services in those areas. The results of such an analysis would have important strategic implications for community organizers and risk-preferring funders. Those who hope to minimize the social costs of our nation's failures at economic and political integration of Latino minorities would want to focus their organizational start-up efforts in those underserved geographic areas.

Implications for Funders

Possible mismatch in the geographic distributions of Latino nonprofits and Latino populations should concern socially responsible funders. So, too, should the possibility that Latino nonprofits are more poorly supported than other nonprofits. Additional analysis of IRS data should draw comparisons between Latino nonprofits and the rest of the United States nonprofit sector. Companion research using other data sets should explore whether needy and disadvantaged Latino populations are well served by non-Latino nonprofits.

Our present findings also challenge funders' program priorities. Veterans' activities, awarding scholarships and educational activities, and promotion of business and commerce are relatively well established within the Latino nonprofit sector. But what of other, more neglected community needs? There appears to be a relative absence of such activities as consumer advocacy, environmental conservation, and legislative and political advocacy to defend Latino minority interests in public policy debates within representative government. Litigation and legal aid, and development of more community-oriented fundraising campaigns and endowments, also appear to be rather rare.

IRS data on Latino nonprofit activity are not conclusive. The only activities we know about from IRS data are the ones proposed on forms 1023 or 1024 at the time Latino nonprofits applied for tax exemptions. Some of these seemingly rare activities are probably more commonly performed in ways incidental to organizations' main missions. The neglect is probably not quite as bad as IRS data suggests.

Nevertheless, our findings about neglected community needs do comport with informal but extensive anecdotal reports and personal experience. The activities rarely undertaken by Latino nonprofits are related to the social, economic, and educational problems facing Latino minorities described at the beginning of this paper. For example, the failures of public education in Latino communities correspond to the relative absence of legislative and political activities among Latino nonprofits. Better public policy advocacy is prerequisite to better education policy.

In Conclusion

The introduction to this paper began with the rather hopeful assertion that nonprofits "are a leading force" for development and change in the United States. Published histories of the nonprofit sector bear this out. But almost nothing has been published about Latino nonprofits. Is the nonprofit sector a "leading force" for improving the role and prospects of Latino populations in United States society? Can we look to the Latino nonprofit sector for solutions? Researchers know too little to say.

Our initial statistical profile of the Latino nonprofit sector relies on an inadequate data base, which happens to have the only data available. Our results are both encouraging and discouraging. The good news is that Latino nonprofits exist in substantial numbers. The bad news is that they seem too often to look the other way, instead of attacking Latino communities' most difficult problems.

Why do Latino nonprofits look the other way instead of doing more to address the serious problems confronting Latinos in the United States? The data presented here leaves that question unanswered. We can only speculate about reasons why, until more research is done.

We can speculate that the real blame for problem avoidance by Latino nonprofits lies with people who support those organizations. The Latino nonprofit sector is not well endowed with money. It seems Latinos have very few private foundations of their own. Resist though they might, "public charities" are drawn to program priorities that donors favor. In a society troubled by increasing disparities of income, it would behoove those who control wealth to mind what they do with it. Reluctance to fund Latino nonprofits, to tackle the difficult roots of Latino community problems, might ultimately imperil us all.

Notes

[1] Research for this paper was supported in part by Hispanics in Philanthropy and the Ford Foundation. This paper does not necessarily represent the views of either organization.

The author is indebted to Dr. David Stevenson at the National Center for Charitable Statistics, and Mr. Eric Crutchfield at Independent Sector, both in Washington, D.C., for their kind assistance and advice. Computer programming by Dr. Laura Appelbaum and data collection assistance by Ms. Joanne Barnett, both of the University of Colorado Graduate School of Public Affairs, are gratefully acknowledged. Thanks are also due to Dr. Michael O'Neill at the University of San Francisco Institute for Nonprofit Organization Management and Mr. Henry A. J. Ramos of Mauer Kunst Consulting for their helpful comments on earlier versions of this paper. The author alone is responsible for any remaining errors. Portions of this paper also appear in M. Cortés, "Counting Latino Nonprofits: A New Strategy for Finding Data," submitted to *Nonprofit and Voluntary Sector Quarterly*.

[2] By corporations that "serve the public," we mean nonprofit corporations exempted from taxation as educational or charitable organizations under I.R.C. §501(c)(3). Thus, we have adopted Salamon's (1992, pp. 13-15) concept of "public serving" nonprofits, as opposed to "member serving" which are exempted under other I.R.C. subsections.

[3] Applicants completing IRS form 1023 are instructed that they "will be considered tax-exempt under section 501(c)(3) even if they do not file Form 1023 [if they are] churches, their integrated auxiliaries, [or] conventions or associations of churches."

[4] Private foundations are defined by the Tax Reform Act of 1969, which added new language to I.R.C. §170 and §509. The Act creates a new distinction between "private foundations" and "public charities." Private foundations differ from public charities, primarily because they depend largely upon income from a single body of investments, owned either by the foundation itself or a principal benefactor.

Bibliography

Astin, A. W. (1982). *Final Report of the Commission on the Higher Education of Minorities*. Los Angeles: Higher Education Research Institute.

Borjas, G. J., & Tienda, T. (Eds.). (1985). *Hispanics in the U. S. Economy*. New York: Academic Press.

Castillo, L. F. (1988). *An Exploratory-Descriptive Study of the Historical Development of Independent Fundraising in the Los Angeles Chicano Community*. Unpublished M.S.W. thesis, University of California, Los Angeles.

Congressional Research Service (1985). *Hispanic Children in Poverty*. Washington, D.C.: Government Printing Office.

Cortés, C. E. (Ed.) (1980). *Latinos in the United States: An Original Anthology*. New York: Arno Press.

Cortés, M. (1997). *A Statistical Profile of the Latino Nonprofit Sector in the U. S*. Paper presented at the meeting of the Association for Research on Nonprofit Organizations and Voluntary Action, Indianapolis, IN.

Escutia, M. M., & Prieto, M. (1986). *Hispanics in the Work Force*. Washington, D.C.: National Council of La Raza.

Estrada, L. F. (1991). Survival Profiles of Latino Nonprofit Organizations. In H. E. Gallegos & M. O'Neill (Eds.), *Hispanics and the Nonprofit Sector* (pp. 127-137). New York: Foundation Center.

Federal Interagency Forum on Child and Family Statistics (1997). *America's Children: Key National Indicators of Well-Being*. Washington, D.C.: Author.

Gale Research (1988). *Encyclopedia of Associations* (22d ed.). Detroit: Author.

Gallegos, H. E., & M. O'Neill (Eds.). *Hispanics and the Nonprofit Sector*. New York: Foundation Center.

Hall, P. D. (1994). Historical Perspectives on Nonprofit Organizations. In R. D. Herman and Associates (Eds.), *The Jossey-Bass Handbook of Nonprofit Leadership and Management* (pp. 3-43). San Francisco: Jossey-Bass.

Hodgkinson, V.A., & Weitzman, M.S. (1989). *Dimensions of the Independent Sector: A Statistical Profile* (3rd ed.). Washington, DC: Independent Sector.

Hodgkinson, V. A., Weitzman, M. S., Noga, S. M., & Gorski, H. A. (1993). *A Portrait of the Independent Sector: The Activities and Finances of Charitable Organizations.* Washington, D.C.: Independent Sector.

Immigration and Naturalization Service (1994). *Annual Report.* Washington, D.C.: Government Printing Office.

Martínez, V. (1991). Hispanic Advocacy Organizations. In H. E. Gallegos & M. O'Neill (Eds.), *Hispanics and the Nonprofit Sector* (pp. 67-82). New York: Foundation Center.

National Center for Educational Statistics (1980). *The Condition of Education for Hispanic Americans.* Washington, D.C.: Government Printing Office.

National Center for Educational Statistics (1996). *Digest of Education Statistics: 1996* (NCES 96-133). Washington, D.C.: Government Printing Office.

National Center for Educational Statistics (1997). *Dropout Rates in the United States: 1995* (NCES 97-473). Washington, D.C.: Government Printing Office.

Nicolau, S. O., & Santiestevan, H. (1991). Looking Back: A Grantee-Grantor View of the Early Years of the Council of La Raza. In H. E. Gallegos & M. O'Neill (Eds.), *Hispanics and the Nonprofit Sector* (pp. 49-66). New York: Foundation Center.

O'Neill, M. (1989). *The Third America: The Emergence of the Nonprofit Sector in the United States.* San Francisco: Jossey-Bass.

Orum, L. S. (1985). *The Education of Hispanics: Status and Implications.* Washington, D.C.: National Council of La Raza.

Salamon, L. M. (1992). *America's Nonprofit Sector: A Primer.* New York: Foundation Center.

Santiago, I. (1978). *A Community's Struggle for Equal Educational Opportunity: Aspira v. Board of Education.* Unpublished doctoral dissertation, Fordham University.

Santos, R. (1984). *Hispanic Youth: Emerging Workers.* New York: Praeger.

Sierra, C. M. (1984). *The Political Transformation of a Minority Organization: The National Council of La Raza 1965-1980.* Unpublished doctoral dissertation, Stanford University.

Soto, J. M. (1974). *Mexican-American Community Leadership for Education.* Unpublished doctoral dissertation, University of Michigan.

Tocqueville, A. de (1945). *Democracy in America.* (H. Reeve, Ed.). New York: Alfred A. Knopf.

U.S. Bureau of the Census (1995). *Population Profile of the United States: 1995* (Current Population Reports, Series 23-189). Washington, D.C.: U.S. Government Printing Office.

U.S. Bureau of the Census (1997a). *Facts for Hispanic Heritage Month* (Memorandum CB97-FS.10, Sept. 11).

U.S. Bureau of the Census (1997b). *The Foreign-Born Population: 1995.* Current Population Survey Report, PPL-58, (http://www.census.gov/population/socdemo/foreign/95/95tab-1.txt), April 8.

U.S. Bureau of the Census (1997c). *Resident Population of the United States: Estimates, by Sex, Race, and Hispanic Origin, with Median Age* (http://www.census.gov/population/ estimates/nation/intfile3-1.txt), Dec. 24.

Urrutia, L. (1984). An Offspring of Discontent: The Asociación Nacional México-Americana, 1949-1954. *Aztlán, 15,* pp.177-184.

Appendix A

Types of Exemptions Enjoyed by Latino Nonprofits

Table A1. Latino Nonprofits Have Qualified For
Most Types of Tax Exemptions
Allowed Under I.R.C. § 501

I.R.C. SUBSECTION	REASON FOR TAX EXEMPTION	NUMBER OF NON-CHURCH LATINO NONPROFITS	
(c)(2)	Owns income property benefiting another nonprofit	8	
(c)(3)	Charitable	2,093	
	Educational	921	
	Literary	19	
	Prevents cruelty to animals	2	
	Prevents cruelty to children	7	
	Conducts tests for public safety	0	
	Religious	99 *	
	Scientific	8	
	Total exempted under § 501(c)(3)	3,157	2,757**
(c)(4)	Civic league engaging in social action	434	
	Local association of employees	14	
	Social welfare organization engaging in social action	290	
	Total exempted under § 501(c)(4)	738	675 *
(c)(5)	Agricultural organization	10	
	Horticultural organization	3	
	Labor organization	17	
	Total exempted under § 501(c)(5)	30	30 *
(c)(6)	Board of trade	134	
	Business league	149	
	Chamber of commerce	46	
	Real estate board	1	
	Total exempted under § 501(c)(6)	330	327 *
(c)(7)	Pleasure, recreational or social club	141	

I.R.C. SUBSECTION	REASON FOR TAX EXEMPTION	NUMBER OF NON-CHURCH LATINO NONPROFITS	
TABLE A1—CONTINUED			
(c)(8)	Fraternal lodge, society, order or association benefiting members or their families		47
(c)(9)	Nongovernmental employee union welfare fund or beneficiary association	17	
	Governmental employee union welfare fund or beneficiary association	0	
	Total exempted under § 501(c)(9)		17
(c)(10)	Domestic fraternal society, association or lodge doing charitable, educational, literary, religious or scientific work benefiting society at large		16
(c)(11)	Teachers retirement association		0
(c)(12)	Local benevolent life insurance association	0	
	Member-supported ditch or irrigation company	1	
	Member-supported cooperative telephone company	1	
	Other similar member-supported cooperatives	0	
	Total exempted under § 501(c)(12)		2
(c)(13)	Burial association	1	
	Member-owned nonprofit cemetery	1	
	Total exempted under § 501(c)(13)		2
(c)(14)	Credit union	23	
	Other mutual corporation or association	2	
	Total exempted under § 501(c)(14)		25
(c)(15)	Small mutual insurance association that does not provide life or marine insurance		1
(c)(16)	Finances crop operations		0
(c)(17)	Supplemental unemployment compensation plan		1

TABLE A1—CONTINUED

I.R.C. SUBSECTION	REASON FOR TAX EXEMPTION	NUMBER OF NON-CHURCH LATINO NONPROFITS	
(c)(18)	Employee funded pension trust created before June 25, 1959		0
(c)(19)	War veterans post or organization		18
(c)(20)	Legal service organization		1
(c)(21)	Black lung trust		0
(c)(22)	Multi-employer insurance plan		0
(c)(23)	Veterans association formed before 1880		0
(c)(24)	Trust authorized by Employee Retirement Insurance and Security Act § 4049		0
(d)	Apostolic and religious		0
(e)	Provides services for cooperating hospitals		0
(f)	Provides services for cooperating educational institutions		0
(k)	Child care organization		0
	Total Non-Church Latino Nonprofits	4,274	3,941

*Churches are not counted in this table.

**The sum of all reasons given for tax exemption exceeds the total number qualifying for this particular subsection of the Internal Revenue Code, because some organizations were exempted for multiple reasons.

Appendix B

PROPOSED ACTIVITIES

Table A2. Activities Proposed By Latino Nonprofits
Seeking Tax Exemption

I.R.S. ACTIVITY CODE	PROPOSED ACTIVITIES	NUMBER OF NON-CHURCH LATINO NONPROFITS
Religious Activities:		
001	Church	*
002	Religious order	1
004	Church auxiliary	5
005	Mission	12
006	Missionary activities	32
007	Evangelism	22
008	Religious publishing activities	6
029	Other religious activities	37
Schools, Colleges and Related Activities:		
030	School, college, trade school, etc.	28
031	Special school for blind, handicapped, etc.	5
032	Nursery school	3
033	Faculty group	2
034	Alumni association or group	12
035	Parent or parent-teachers association	6
036	Fraternity or sorority	18
037	Other student society or group	2
040	Scholarships	108
041	Student loans	1
042	Student housing activities	1
043	Other student aid	3
044	Student exchange with foreign country	3
046	Private school	36
059	Other school related activities	178

TABLE A2—CONTINUED

I.R.S. ACTIVITY CODE	PROPOSED ACTIVITIES	NUMBER OF NON-CHURCH LATINO NONPROFITS
Cultural, historical or other educational activities:		
060	Museum, zoo, planetarium, etc.	19
061	Library	3
062	Historical site, records or reenactment	8
063	Monument	2
064	Commemorative event (centennial, festival, pageant, etc.)	39
065	Fair	6
088	Community theatrical group	34
089	Singing society or group	3
090	Cultural performances	104
091	Art exhibit	11
092	Literary activities	13
093	Cultural exchanges with foreign country	14
094	Genealogical activities	4
119	Other cultural or historical activities	109
Other instruction and training activities:		
120	Publishing	21
121	Radio or television broadcasting	6
122	Film production	2
123	Discussion groups, forums, panels, lectures, etc.	113
124	Non-scientific study and research	17
125	Giving information or opinions	14
126	Apprentice training	4
149	Other instruction and training	44
Health services and related activities:		
150	Hospital	11
151	Hospital auxiliary	1
153	Care and housing for the aged	7
154	Health clinic	30
155	Rural medical facility	2
158	Rescue and emergency service	2
159	Nurses register or bureau	1
160	Aid to the handicapped	25
161	Scientific research on diseases	15
162	Other medical research	1
163	Health insurance (medical, dental, optical, etc.)	1
165	Community health planning	7
166	Mental health care	16
167	Group medical practice association	2
179	Other health services	31

TABLE A2—CONTINUED

I.R.S. ACTIVITY CODE	PROPOSED ACTIVITIES	NUMBER OF NON-CHURCH LATINO NONPROFITS
199	Scientific research activities	6
	Business and professional organizations:	
200	Business promotion (chamber of commerce, business league, etc.)	163
201	Real estate association	2
202	Board of trade	1
203	Regulating business	1
204	Promotion of fair business practices	1
205	Professional association	126
211	Underwriting municipal insurance	1
213	Tourist bureau	1
229	Other business or professional group	18
	Farming and related activities:	
231	Farm bureau	1
232	Agricultural group	2
233	Horticultural group	1
234	Farmers cooperative marketing or purchasing	1
237	Breeders association	1
249	Other farming and related activities	5
	Mutual organizations:	
250	Mutual ditch, irrigation, telephone, electric company or like organization	9
251	Credit union	9
252	Reserve funds or insurance for domestic building and loan association, cooperative bank or mutual savings bank	1
253	Mutual insurance company	1
259	Other mutual organization	2
	Employee or membership benefit organizations:	
260	Fraternal beneficiary society, order or association	25
261	Improvement of conditions of workers	6
262	Association of municipal employees	2
263	Association of employees	20
264	Employee or member welfare association	11
265	Sick, accident, death or similar benefits	11
269	Vacation benefits	1
279	Other services or benefits to members or employees	35

TABLE A2—CONTINUED		
I.R.S. ACTIVITY CODE	PROPOSED ACTIVITIES	NUMBER OF NON-CHURCH LATINO NONPROFITS
Sports, athletic, recreational and social activities:		
280	Country club	3
281	Hobby club	13
282	Dinner club	1
283	Variety club	2
284	Dog club	1
285	Women's club	6
286	Hunting or fishing club	1
287	Swimming or tennis club	1
288	Other sports club	14
296	Community center	22
297	Community recreational facilities (park, playground, etc.)	6
298	Training in sports	6
299	Travel tours	1
300	Amateur athletic association	20
301	Fundraising athletic or sports event	3
317	Other sports or athletic activities	12
318	Other recreational activities	21
319	Other social activities	50
Youth activities:		
320	Boy Scouts, Girl Scouts, etc.	70
321	Boys Club, Little League, etc.	7
322	FFA, FHA, 4-H club, etc.	1
324	YMCA, YWCA, etc.	1
325	Camp	3
326	Care and housing of children (orphanage, etc.)	23
327	Prevention of cruelty to children	9
328	Combat juvenile delinquency	15
349	Other youth organization or activities	13
Conservation, environmental and beautification activities:		
350	Preservation of natural resources (conservation)	3
351	Combating or preventing pollution (air, water, etc.)	2
352	Land acquisition for preservation	1
354	Preservation of scenic beauty	1
356	Garden club	3
379	Other conservation, environmental or beautification activities	2

I.R.S. ACTIVITY CODE	PROPOSED ACTIVITIES	NUMBER OF NON-CHURCH LATINO NONPROFITS
TABLE A2—CONTINUED		
Housing activities:		
380	Low-income housing	30
381	Low and moderate income housing	12
382	Housing for the aged	15
398	Instruction and guidance on housing	25
399	Other housing activities	25
Inner city or community activities:		
400	Area development, redevelopment of renewal	9
401	Homeowners association	1
402	Other activity aimed at combating community deterioration	18
403	Attracting new industry or retaining industry in an area	3
404	Community promotion	16
405	Loans or grants for minority businesses	3
406	Crime prevention	3
408	Community service organization	101
429	Other inner city or community benefit activities	29
Civil rights activities:		
430	Defense of human and civil rights	89
431	Elimination of prejudice and discrimination (race, religion, sex, national origin, etc.)	28
432	Lessen neighborhood tensions	1
449	Other civil rights activities	3
Litigation and legal aid activities:		
460	Public interest litigation activities	2
461	Other litigation or support of litigation	1
462	Legal aid to indigents	12
Legislative and political activities:		
480	Propose, support or oppose legislation	5
481	Voter information on issues or candidates	1
482	Voter education (mechanics of registering, voting, etc.)	5
509	Other legislative and political activities	5

TABLE A2—CONTINUED		
I.R.S. ACTIVITY CODE	PROPOSED ACTIVITIES	NUMBER OF NON-CHURCH LATINO NONPROFITS
Advocacy attempting to influence public opinion concerning:		
517	Government aid to parochial schools	1
518	U.S. foreign policy	4
520	Pacifism and peace	5
528	Stricter law enforcement	1
529	Ecology or conservation	2
531	Medical care service	2
532	Welfare systems	3
535	Racial integration	1
536	Use of intoxicating beverages	1
537	Use of drugs or narcotics	4
559	Other matters	17
Services to individuals:		
560	Supplying money, goods or services to the poor	82
561	Gifts or grants to individuals (other than scholarships)	26
563	Marriage counseling	4
564	Family planning	4
566	Job training, counseling or assistance	41
568	Vocational counseling	3
569	Referrals to social service agencies	19
573	Rehabilitating alcoholics or ex-convicts	23
574	Day care	12
575	Services for the aged	13
Services to community programs and agencies:		
600	Community Chest, United Way, etc.	3
601	Booster club	2
602	Gifts, grants or loans to other organizations	58
603	Non-financial services or facilities for use by other organizations	13

I.R.S. ACTIVITY CODE	PROPOSED ACTIVITIES	NUMBER OF NON-CHURCH LATINO NONPROFITS
TABLE A2—CONTINUED		
Miscellaneous activities:		
900	Cemetery or burial activities	3
901	Perpetual care fund (cemetery, columbarium, etc.)	1
902	Emergency or disaster aid fund	2
904	Government instrumentality or agency	1
906	Consumer interest group	1
907	Veterans activities	254
908	Patriotic activities	51
910	Domestic organization with activities outside the U.S.	10
911	Foreign organization	7 **
912	Title holding corporation	5
913	Prevention of cruelty to animals	2
914	Achievement prizes or awards	4
915	Erection or maintenance of public buildings or works	2
917	Thrift shop, retail outlet, etc.	2
918	Book, gift or supply store	2
920	Association of employees	1
921	Loans or credit reporting	7
922	Endowment fund or financial services	2
923	Indians (tribes, cultures, etc.)	1
927	Fundraising	13

*Churches are not counted in this table.

**Foreign organizations are beyond the scope of this study. The seven shown here were included in error. All other foreign organizations were removed from our data set before it was tabulated.

Explorations into Latino Voluntarism

Rodolfo O. de la Garza
with Fujia Lu

This article examines Latino organizational participation. It focuses on the type and the extent of Hispanic organizational involvement, and the factors associated with that behavior. It also evaluates how that participation affects becoming involved in a wide range of electoral and nonelectoral political activities. The purpose of the report is to gain an insight into the role that organizations play in Latino society and the extent to which organizations help link Latinos to national political life.

The report is divided into three sections. It begins with a brief discussion addressing two issues: the significance that organizational participation has for sociopolitical life in the United States and the role that organizations have played among Latinos in U. S. society. The second draws on two national surveys to examine and explain Latino organizational involvement.[1] The concluding section evaluates the results of that analysis and the issues it raises.

Organizational Participation and American Society

Voluntarism has long been considered the foundation of American democracy.[2] Moreover, Americans are much more likely than citizens of other nations to voluntarily create and join organizations.[3] Indeed, the recent apparent decline in this pattern has given rise to concern about the future of American democracy.[4]

The origins of American voluntarism are rooted in the history of the nation. These include the view that individuals must look to themselves rather than to the government for their well-being. A related notion includes a fundamental distrust of government and a societal commitment to limited government. A third factor stems from the nation's patterns of historical growth. Immigrants from different backgrounds came to North America and worked together to charter new territories and create new communities without the support of the extant U. S. government. By the time these areas became incorporated as American states, the autonomous character of their civil society was already well established. The continuing strength of those traditions of autonomy is suggested by the anti-federal sentiments currently voiced in the West and other parts of the nation.

The significance of this voluntarism to the character of American society is difficult to overstate. First, it is the foundation of the nation's civil society. Voluntarism organizes and maintains a wide range of societal activities from sports leagues to charities to educational and cultural programs. This not only reduces the scope of governmental involvement in daily life, it also integrates society. For example, immigrants create their organizations to pursue group-specific goals. In time, many of these groups join with nonethnic organizations to pursue objectives that transcend ethnic boundaries, and many individual ethnics also join nonethnic organizations to work with people from different backgrounds to pursue common goals.[5]

A third and equally significant aspect of voluntarism is its impact on political life. Voluntarism per se is apolitical. That is, there is no inherently political consequence resulting from individuals joining together to establish a soccer league or a church choir. Often, however, participating in such organizations affects individuals in ways that impact on their political consciousness and participation. For example, participating in a group may teach social skills, increase substantive knowledge on topics unrelated to the group's functions, and increase an individual's ability to work with people from distinct backgrounds. Additionally, group activities may increase an individual's political knowledge and interest by bringing the members into contact with government agencies and officials. Depending on the experience, this could mobilize or alienate the individual. Also, individuals may learn leadership skills as a result of group activities. Thus, regardless of the group's purpose, group participation is likely to increase an individual's knowledge of social and political processes, and related leadership skills. All of this will increase a sense of efficacy, which will increase the likelihood of becoming politically involved.[6]

The extent to which Latinos share in the nation's voluntaristic patterns is unclear. Historically, numerous studies asserted that cultural factors such as exaggerated individualism and familism prevented Latinos from establishing organizations. Such claims reflected an ignorance of Mexican-American organizational achievements especially around labor and civil rights issues,[7] and they ignored how factors such as poverty, low educational attainment, and discrimination impeded more extensive organizational development.

The existence of such organizations does not, however, effectively refute the assertion that Latinos are not given to high rates of organizational participation. It is unclear, for example, to what extent Latinos established and participated in civic organizations beyond mutual aid societies and labor unions, nor is it clear how widespread the membership in these organizations became.[8] In more recent decades, for example, the first major survey of Mexican Americans found that in 1965-1966 a majority of respondents in Los Angeles had never heard of most Mexican-American organizations, including the League of United Latin American Citizens (LULAC), the oldest national Mexican-American group, the Arizona-based Alianza Hispana-Americana, the largest Mexican-American mutual aid organization, and California's Mexican American Political Association. In San Antonio, the only organizations that a majority of respondents had heard of were LULAC and the American GI Forum, both of which are Texas-based, and 15 and 8 percent, respectively, were members of these groups.[9]

The patterns that define the nation's voluntarism, then, may not characterize Latinos. While the nation as a whole is highly involved in a wide range of organizations, Latinos appear to be more likely to participate in a narrow range of groups that are limited in membership, narrow in focus, and unknown to most of the Latino population. The following section tests these propositions.

Contemporary Latino Organizational Participation

Organizational participation is defined along two dimensions, making contributions and being a member. These are independent activities with no necessary relationship. Together, however, they capture the ways individuals may associate with a group. Individuals may contribute money or goods, or they may volunteer their labor or expertise. To gain a complete picture of giving, both types of activities must be measured. Being a member of an organization may also involve several dimensions related to levels of involvement (e.g., not very active, active, being an officer) and organization type (local vs. national). Here, membership will be examined only at its most basic level, i.e., whether or not an individual is a member of an organization.

It is also important to emphasize that, from the perspective of how voluntarism affects individuals and shapes the character of civil society, joining an organization is significantly different from contributing to one. Joining any type of formal group is likely to enhance an individual's sense of personal efficacy, interpersonal skills, and knowledge and thus increase the probability of an individual becoming politically involved via voting and other activities. Individuals who limit their involvement to making financial or other types of contributions are unlikely to experience these consequences.

Latino Giving

There are no systematic studies analyzing what types of individuals contribute to organizations. Instead, there are aggregate-level studies and anecdotes that together suggest that Latino immigrants have more developed patterns of giving than do the native-born. The clearest evidence of the former are analyses of the remittances that immigrants send home which in many cases amount to over 10 percent of the annual earnings of Latino immigrant households.[10] Although most of this money is sent to relatives and thus cannot be considered the equivalent of contributions to organizations that serve the community in general,[11] that proportion of remittances that goes to charities[12] and community development projects[13] is evidence of voluntarism.

Anecdotes are the best evidence we have regarding giving among the native-born, and these suggest that there is little willingness among them to contribute financially to Latino organizations and causes. Several years ago, for example, then president of the Mexican American Legal Defense and Education Fund (MALDEF) Juaquín Avila voiced frustration at the lack of widespread financial support that MALDEF received from the Mexican-American community (personal conversation with the author). In the 1980s a campaign to raise funds from Mexican-American alumni of the University of Texas to endow a professorship in the name of George I. Sánchez failed to reach its goal. Similarly, organizations such as the Institute for Puerto Rican Policy in New York and the Southwest Voter Registration Education Project of San Antonio regularly encounter significant financial problems, in part because they do not benefit from regularized widespread contributions from their Latino constituents. And, at the 1995 annual meeting of NALEO (National Association of Latino Elected Officials), County Supervisor Gloria Molina of Los Angeles decried the low response she received from Latino attorneys in California when she requested contributions to support an anti-Proposition 187 effort.

The Latino National Political Survey (LNPS) and the Survey of Giving and Volunteering provide the first opportunity to examine the validity of these examples. Each of these focuses on distinct aspects of organizational involvement, but together they enable us to determine the factors that explain Latino organizational participation and the independent effects that ethnicity has on Latino giving.

LNPS respondents[14] were asked to identify any organizations or associations that they belonged to or had given money or goods to in the past twelve months that were:

1) unions, associations, or groups associated with work, business, or professions;
2) charities, religious organizations, or other organizations that look after people such as the elderly, handicapped children, or similar groups;
3) concerned with social issues such as reducing taxes, protecting the environment, promoting prayer in schools, or any other cause;
4) sports, recreation, community, neighborhood, school, cultural or youth organizations;
5) Hispanic organizations.

A variety of social characteristics could affect the responses to these questions. Respondents were therefore grouped in terms of national origin, nativity, gender, and education to illustrate the relationship between these characteristics and giving.

The results indicate that, overall, Anglos are much more likely than Latinos to contribute to organizations. While 58 percent of Anglos make some kind of contribution to at least one organization, only 31 percent of Mexicans, 29 percent of Puerto Ricans, and 27 percent of Cubans do so (Table 1). Furthermore, among those who contribute, Anglos are also the most likely to contribute to more than one organization. This is indicated in that the percentage of Anglo contributors is greater than 100 percent. This could only occur if individuals contribute to more than one organization.

Table 1
Respondents Who Contribute to Organizations
by Types of Organizations and National Origin[1]

TYPE OF ORGANIZATION	ANGLO %	MEXICAN %	PUERTO RICAN %	CUBAN %
Charity	63	34	26	32
Work	23	14	9	9
Social	20	4	3	6
Community	27	11	8	9
Total Contributors	260	456	479	1546
Total Respondents	171	589	183	679

[1] Respondents may contribute to more than one organization.

Examining memberships by nativity and gender yields additional insights into contribution patterns (Tables 2 and 3). Overall, regardless of ethnicity, gender, and nativity, respondents are most likely to be involved with charitable organizations. Also, regardless of gender and nativity, Latinos are much less likely to be involved with social organizations than with other groups. Finally, overall, men report slightly higher rates of giving than do women. Table 2 reveals two additional patterns. Native-born Mexicans and Cubans are much more likely to contribute to groups than are their immigrant counterparts. However, even U. S.-born Mexicans and Cubans are much less likely to do so than are the Anglo native-born (the number of foreign-born Anglos is too small for comparisons to be meaningful).

Table 2
Percent of Respondents Who Contribute to Organizations by Type of Organization, National Origin, and Nativity[1]

Type of Organization	Anglo Native-born %	Anglo Foreign-Born %	Mexican Native-born %	Mexican Foreign-born %	Puerto Rican Native-born %	Puerto Rican Foreign-Born. %	Cuban Native-born %	Cuban Foreign-born %
Charity	63	70	45	24	25	27	45	30
Work	23	25	15	12	8	9	15	8
Social	21	8	6	2	5	2	17	4
Community	27	30	17	6	8	9	27	6
N	248	12	298	187	57	116	51	135

[1] Respondents may contribute to more than one organization.

Table 3
Percent of Respondents Who Contribute to Organizations by Type of Organization, National Origin, and Gender[1]

Type of Organization	Anglo male %	Anglo female %	Mexican male %	Mexican female %	Puerto Rican male %	Puerto Rican female %	Cuban male %	Cuban female %
Charity	64	63	32	37	26	27	32	31
Work	27	19	19	7	15	4	9	9
Social	22	19	3	5	4	2	6	5
Community	30	25	12	10	10	7	10	9
N	137	121	266	214	922	787	103	83

[1] Respondents may contribute to more than one organization.

These patterns indicate that Latinos and Anglos differ in their giving patterns. It is unclear, however, whether ethnicity or other factors such as income, nativity, and education are the source of these differences. In other words, are there differences in the giving patterns of Latinos and Anglos who are native-born and have the same education and income? We use data from the Survey of Giving and Volunteering (SGV) to answer this. SGV asks two questions regarding giving. One asks if any money or property has been given to various types of private organizations for charitable purposes; the second asks if any volunteer work has been done for these private organizations. The latter is likely to constitute occasional contributions of resources such as time and labor instead of money and thus are unlikely to have the same effect on an individual that joining an organization does. Therefore, here we consider volunteering as equivalent to giving money. It should also be noted that the Mexican-origin population is the only Hispanic group in the SGV large enough to yield statistically reliable results when analyzed.

The patterns for giving and volunteering of SGV respondents are similar to those of LNPS respondents. As Table 4 illustrates, foreign-born Mexicans are the least likely to give money, volunteer, or give money and volunteer. Mexican Americans (native-born Mexicans) are less likely than Anglo Americans or African Americans to give money, but they have higher volunteer rates than blacks. However, as Table 5 illustrates, those U. S.-born Mexicans who volunteer have higher rates of voluntarism in support of organizations that provide education, recreation, youth services, and human services than do Anglos or Blacks.

Table 4

Percentage of Respondents Who Give Money and Volunteer

	GIVE MONEY	VOLUNTEER	GIVE MONEY & VOLUNTEER	ONLY GIVE MONEY	ONLY VOLUNTEER	NEITHER GIVE MONEY NOR VOLUNTEER
Native-born Mexican	56	48	38	18	10	34
Foreign-born Mexican	33	25	15	18	10	57
Anglo	78	56	51	27	5	17
Black	63	42	38	25	5	32

Table 5
Percentage of Respondents Who Have Been Volunteers during Past 12 Months, by Nativity and Type of Organization[1]

TYPE OF ACTIVITY	NATIVE-BORN MEXICAN	FOREIGN-BORN MEXICAN	U.S.-BORN BLACK	U.S.-BORN ANGLO
Health	11	1	10	14
Education	20	3	11	16
Religious	27	10	30	27
Human Services	14	5	9	13
Environment	3	.3	2	10
Public/ Social	3	.1	5	7
Recreation	10	0	5	7
Art, Culture	7	1	4	7
Work-related	7	0	5	7
Political	3	0	3	5
Youth Development	19	2	14	16
Private Foundation	2	1	2	2
International	5	1	1	2
Informal (not officially organized)	34	1	12	26
Others	2	0	1	3

[1] Totals may exceed 100% because individuals may volunteer with more than one organization.

Two factors may help explain these patterns. The first is the levels of trust that individuals have in organizations. Lower trust levels should result in lower levels of giving and volunteering. In keeping with this prediction, foreign-born Mexicans report the lowest trust (1.90) of the four groups, and the difference between them and Mexican Americans is statistically significant (p = .001). Contrary to expectations, however, Mexican Americans report higher trust than do Anglos (2.29 vs. 2.17, p = .06) 15 listed in Table 5 (1 = very little trust, 2 = some trust, 3 = a lot of trust, 4 = a great deal of trust).

Income could also affect these rates of contributions. Individuals who have less disposable income will have less to contribute, and they may spend so much of their time trying to increase their earnings that they might also have less time for volunteering. Mexicans, including immigrants and the native-born, have lower incomes than Anglos and therefore as a group we would expect them to contribute less than Anglos, as they do.

To determine whether individual Anglos and Mexicans who are similarly situated have similar patterns of giving and volunteering, the data were analyzed using multiple regression.[16] The results indicate that, after controlling for nativity, income, and education as well as how confident an individual is in an organization, there are no statistically significant differences between Mexican-Americans and Anglos. In other words, "ethnic culture" appears to have no significant impact on rates of giving and volunteering. It should be noted, however, that the native-born, be they Anglo, Mexican-American, or African-American, have higher rates of giving and volunteering than do the foreign-born. This suggests that "immigrant culture" rather than "ethnic" or "racial" culture affects giving patterns.

Latino Organizational Participation

As has been noted, the LNPS provides the first opportunity to systematically analyze Hispanic organizational participation. The only measure of organizational participation used here is membership in an organization.

Membership patterns of LNPS respondents resemble their patterns of giving (Table 6). Anglos have much higher membership rates and are much more likely to be members of multiple organizations than Latinos. There are, moreover, relatively slight differences in membership rates among Mexicans, Cubans, and Puerto Ricans.

Table 6
Organizational Membership by National Origin

TOTAL MEMBERSHIPS	ANGLO %	MEXICAN %	PUERTO RICAN %	CUBAN %
0	43	69	71	73
1	29	20	22	19
2	17	7	5	5
3	11	4	3	4
N	456	1546	589	679

Gender and nativity are also associated with distinct membership patterns. Among Mexicans and Cubans, the native-born have much higher membership rates. Indeed, native-born Cubans and Anglos have comparable membership rates, but native-born Mexicans and Puerto Ricans lag substantially behind (Table 7). Within each national origin group, men are more likely than women to be members and to hold multiple memberships (Table 8).

Table 7 Organizational Memberships by National Origin and Nativity								
Memberships	Anglo Native-born %	Anglo Foreign-born %	Mexican Native-born %	Mexican Foreign-born %	Puerto Rican Native-born %	Puerto Rican Foreign-born %	Cuban Native-born %	Cuban Foreign-born %
0	43	45	61	76	72	70	45	77
1	29	18	24	16	19	23	34	17
2	16	37	10	5	6	5	11	4
3	12	0.00	5	3	4	2	10	3
N	435	21	765	781	202	387	92	587

Table 8 Organizational Memberships by National Origin and Gender								
Memberships	Anglo women %	Anglo men %	Mexican women %	Mexican men %	Puerto Rican women %	Puerto Rican men %	Cuban women %	Cuban men %
0	49	37	71	67	76	65	76	69
1	29	28	20	20	18	26	14	24
2	12	22	7	8	4	7	6	3
3	10	13	3	5	2	3	4	4
N	238	218	739	807	327	262	346	333

The types of organizations that respondents join also vary by national origin, gender, and nativity. In general, respondents are most likely to join charitable groups (Tables 9-10). Again, native-born Cubans strongly resemble native-born Anglos in the types of groups they join. Also, it is noteworthy that only native-born Cubans and Anglos report even moderately high memberships in social organizations.

Table 9
Respondents Who are Members of Organizations by National Origin, Nativity and Type of Organization[1]

Type of Organization	Anglo Native-born %	Anglo Foreign-born %	Mexican Native-born %	Mexican Foreign-born %	Puerto Rican Native-born %	Puerto Rican Foreign-born. %	Cuban Native-born %	Cuban Foreign-born %
Charity	31	44	25	12	12	18	35	13
Work	22	25	14	12	7	10	15	8
Social	13	8	3	2	4	2	11	4
Community	20	15	11	6	11	6	25	5
N	248	12	298	187	57	116	51	135

[1] Respondents may be members of more than one organization

Table 10
Respondents Who are Members of Organizations by National Origin, Gender, and Type of Organization[1]

Memberships	Anglo women %	Anglo men %	Mexican women %	Mexican men %	Puerto Rican women %	Puerto Rican men %	Cuban women %	Cuban men %
Charity	29	35	21	17	16	15	16	15
Work	17	28	7	18	5	14	7	11
Social	11	14	2	2	2	3	5	5
Community	17	22	7	10	5	10	8	8
N	121	137	214	266	78	92	83	103

[1] Respondents may be members of more than one organization

The differences between Anglos and the three Latino groups considered here, and between the native, and foreign-born, could be rooted in educational factors. That is, the reason that Anglos have higher rates of participation than Mexicans, Puerto Ricans, and Cubans is that they have higher educational attainment. Similarly, since the native-born are more educated than the foreign-born, they too are likely to have higher participation rates. To control for the effects of education, therefore, it is necessary to compare membership rates for similarly educated groups.

As Table 11 illustrates, one highly significant pattern emerges when education level is controlled: individuals with higher education are more likely to be members of organizations, and this is especially the case for Anglos and Cubans. Conversely, as is most evident among Mexicans, less educated individuals are greatly underrepresented among those who join formal groups. Given that the less educated are a much higher proportion of Latinos, this appears to account for much of the difference in the membership rates between them and Anglos.

Table 11
Educational Characteristics of Members of Organizations by National Origin

Education	% Anglo sample	% Anglo members	% Mexican sample	% Mexican members	% Puerto Rican sample	% Puerto Rican members	% Cuban sample	% Cuban members
0-8 years	8	7	40	26	30	19	33	17
9-12	17	13	17	15	22	19	13	7
H. S. grad.	55	55	36	46	37	40	33	41
Post-H.S.	7	25	11	12	20	22	20	35
N	456	260	1515	479	571	171	659	183

These low rates of Hispanic membership may reflect participation in nonethnic rather than ethnic organizations. It is possible, as the literature on Hispanic organizations suggests, that Latinos have high rates of organizational involvement in their own groups, and thus their participatory rates should not be evaluated in terms of membership in mainstream groups. As Table 12 indicates, however, as measured either by contributions or memberships, very few Latinos are involved with Hispanic organizations. This is true for both the native- and foreign-born (Table 13).

Table 12
Percent of Respondents Who Participate in Hispanic Organizations by Type of Participation and National Origin

TYPE OF PARTICIPATION	MEXICAN %	PUERTO RICAN %	CUBAN %
Give Money	2	4	5
Member	2	3	3
N	1546	589	679

Table 13

Participation in Hispanic Organizations by Type of Participation, National Origin, and Nativity

Type of Activity	Mexican Native-born %	Mexican Foreign-born %	Puerto Rican Native-born %	Puerto Rican Foreign-Born. %	Cuban Native-born %	Cuban Foreign-born %
Contribution	4	1	3	4	1	5
Membership	4	1	3	3	2	3
N	765	781	202	389	92	587

Furthermore, among the small number of those who are members, the more educated Latinos are more likely to join ethnic organizations (Table 14). Consequently, the less educated are even more underrepresented among Hispanic groups than they are among mainstream groups. Moreover, few Latino citizens, those who are most likely to be familiar with Hispanic organizations, are able to identify any specific Latino organization that looks out for their interests (Table 15). This is despite the fact that the great majority of respondents indicate that ethnic organizations are the ones most likely to "look out for their interests" (Table 16).

Table 14

Educational Characteristics of Members of Hispanic Organizations by National Origin[1]

EDUCATION	% MEXICAN	% PUERTO RICAN	% CUBAN
0-8 years	4	3	2
9-12 years	0	3	3
High school graduate	4	3	2
Post-high school	7	8	3
N	1515	571	659

[1] This table indicates that 4% of Mexicans with 0-8 years of education are members of Hispanic organizations.

Table 15
Organizations that Look Out for Interest of Respondent's Group by National Origin[1]

ORGANIZATION	% MEXICAN	% PUERTO RICAN	% CUBAN	TOTAL %
LULAC	98	2	0	100
Cuban American National Foundation	0	0	42	42
Asociación Cubano America	0	0	24	24
United Farm Workers / other farmworkers' organizations	22	0	0	22
Aspira, Inc.	0	15	0	15
Institute for Puerto Rican Policy	0	15	0	15
American GI Forum	15	0	0	15
U. S. Hispanic Chamber of Commerce	11	2	1	14
National Association for Latino-Americans	10	2	0	12
National Council of La Raza	12	0	0	12

[1] Includes only organizations named by ten or more respondents.

Table 16
Types of Organizations That Look out For Respondent's Concerns by Respondent's National Origin[1]

TYPE OF ORGANIZATION	% MEXICAN	% PUERTO RICAN	% CUBAN
National origin	78	82	83
Latino/Hispanic	8	6	8
Work/business	2	2	1
Charities	5	2	5
Social2	1	1	
Sports/youth	3	5	0
Government related	3	3	2
N	1038	408	525
% identifying no organization	33	31	20

[1] Includes only native-born and naturalized citizens.

These membership patterns create an anomaly. If the majority of Latinos think Hispanic organizations best represent their interests, why are their membership rates in these organizations so low? One answer is suggested by the types of organizations identified in Table 15. Only two of these, LULAC and the American GI Forum, are community-based membership organizations. The others are service providers, advocacy groups, or business and professional organizations. Thus, it would seem that either there are few Hispanic community-based membership organizations available for Latinos to join or that these do not defend the interests of their members. Another possibility is that individuals may be members of organizations that are functionally but not nominally ethnic. For example, most of the members of a particular chapter of groups such as the Veterans of Foreign Wars may be Latino, but the organization is not Hispanic per se. This pattern is suggested by the fact that 93 percent of Mexican and Cuban-origin citizens and 87 percent of Puerto Ricans indicate that half or more of the membership in the organizations to which they belong consists of co-ethnics (Rodolfo O. de la Garza, et. al, *Latino Voices*, p. 67). Whatever the case, it is clear that Latino organizations are not especially salient to Latinos. As has been indicated, organizational participation is important as an end in and of itself, but also as a means for spurring political participation. Table 17 illustrates the latter point. Among all Hispanics and Anglos, higher organizational membership is associated with higher levels of participation in the following political activities: signing a petition, contacting an editor or public official about issues, attending public meetings, wearing campaign buttons, attending political meetings, working for a political party or candidate, or contributing money to a candidate or party.

Table 17
Total Political Participation by National Origin and Total Organizational Participation[1]

National Origin	Political Activities	0 Memberships	1 Membership	2 Memberships	3 Memberships
Anglos N=447	0	46	36	22	18
	1-3	53	57	59	48
	4-7	2	8	19	34
Mexicans N=1545	0	76	53	28	14
	1-3	22	40	45	57
	4-7	2	6	26	29
Puerto Ricans N=589	0	75	40	29	25
	1-3	22	48	59	50
	4-7	3	12	12	25
Cubans N=680	0	83	53	27	14
	1-3	16	35	69	57
	4-7	1	11	4	29

[1] This table indicates that 46 percent of Anglo respondents with 0 memberships engage in no political activities, compared to 18 percent of those with three or more memberships who engage in 0 political activities.

The relationship between organizational involvement, registering to vote, and voting is equally clear. As Tables 18 and 19 illustrate, registration rates and voting rates increase as memberships increase. Indeed, the differences between Anglo and Latino registration and voting rates disappear and may actually reverse themselves at higher levels of community organizational engagement (i.e., Latinos who are members of two or more groups report higher rates of registering and voting).

Table 18
Percent of Citizens Registered to Vote in 1989
by Total Organizational Participation and National Origin

Registered Voters	0 Memberships/ % Registered	1 Membership/ % Registered	2 Memberships/ % Registered	3 Memberships/ % Registered
Anglos N=437	88	90	92	100
Mexicans N=687	68	83	96	94
Puerto Ricans N=431	70	87	83	67
Cubans N=268	54	66	89	100

Table 19
Percent Who Voted in 1988 by Total Organizational Participation
and National Origin

% Voted	0 Memberships/ %	1 Membership/ %	2 Memberships/ %	3 Memberships/ %
Anglos N=391	63	76	81	100
Mexicans N=686	40	61	85	56
Puerto Ricans N=425	41	75	84	83
Cubans N=268	57	71	68	100

The impact of organizational memberships on electoral participation is more clearly indicated by the results of analysis that measure the independent effects of memberships after controlling for age, gender, and education. In other words, are individuals who are not members of nonethnic or ethnic organizations, but are of the same sex and age and have the same levels of education more or less likely to register and vote? The answer is they are less likely to vote. Thus, it is clear: organizational memberships increase the likelihood that individuals will register and vote. Moreover, membership in Hispanic groups also increases the probability of registering and voting.[17] (Results are available upon request.) In other words, all else being equal, individuals who are members of organizations are more likely to register and vote. Furthermore, organizational membership boosts Latino electoral involvement more than it does Anglo registering and voting, and thus helps reduce the gap between Anglo and Latino electoral participation.[18]

Conclusion

Several patterns characterize Latino organizational participation. First, at the group level, Latino giving and volunteering is lower than that of Anglos. However, when analyzed at the individual level, there are no statistically significant differences between similarly situated Anglos and Mexican-Americans (the only Latino group we surveyed that was large enough to be analyzed separately). Thus, the group patterns reflect differences in characteristics, such as nativity and educational levels, rather than "ethnic" cultural characteristics. Immigrants, however, have lower rates of giving and volunteering than do the native-born. This suggests that such activities are more central to U. S. civil society than to Latin America's civil practices. Moreover, given that there are no significant differences between U. S.-born Anglos and Mexicans in these dimensions, it also seems clear that these behaviors are learned within one generation.

Second, although overall Hispanic membership rates are lower than those of Anglos, there are two noteworthy exceptions to this pattern. First, Latino underrepresentation is concentrated among the least educated, who also constitute a plurality of all Latino adults. Second, U.S.-born Cubans have participatory rates almost equal to those of Anglos.

A third pattern is that Hispanic organizations are of low salience to Latinos. Latinos report lower rates of involvement with Hispanic than with non-Hispanic groups, and few Hispanics can name an Hispanic organization. Given this pattern, it is especially noteworthy that the majority believe that Hispanic organizations "defend their interests."

Finally, participating in organizations boosts electoral involvement even more among Latinos than it does among Anglos. Low rates of organizational participation, therefore, are especially damaging to the ability of Latinos to realize their political potential.

What are the implications of these findings? First, they suggest that socioeconomic rather than ethnic characteristics explain Latino organizational participation. Latinos, in other words, have low rates of giving, volunteering, and joining, because they are relatively poor and less educated rather than because of ethnic values that discourage civic involvement. Nonetheless, these low rates of participation indicate that Hispanics, and the foreign-born in particular, are contributing to the apparent national decline in civic involvement.

These results also require rethinking the role that organizations, and Latino organizations in particular, play in Hispanic communities. As the Congressional Hispanic Caucus' *National Directory of Hispanic Organizations* and the *Anuario Hispano/Hispanic Yearbook*[19] document, there is no shortage of Latino organizations. Most of these provide very specific services to localized constituencies, and thus very few are well-known to most Hispanics. More significantly, few are membership-based and they do not offer the kinds of participatory opportunities that prepare citizens for effective involvement in community affairs. Nonetheless, because of the services that this plethora of organizations delivers, it appears that it is these types of groups that Hispanics have in mind when they state that they are well served by Latino organizations.

Regardless of how effective they are, however, it is essential to acknowledge that the existence of such service and advocacy organizations does not indicate that Latinos have developed a wide network of community-based groups that links average residents to each other or to mainstream society. Indeed, the evidence suggests that no such network exists. This void has two major consequences. It limits the ability of Latinos to address in a routine and satisfactory manner the issues that affect the quality of their daily lives and prevent them from becoming major problems. And, more significantly, it denies Latinos, and the foreign-born in particular, the opportunity to benefit from organizations in order to develop skills that are essential to successfully engaging the political system, skills which they are unlikely to learn on the job or in·school, as most Anglos do. Thus, the absence of a community-based organizational network exacerbates the problems that Latinos must overcome if they are to be full participants in American society.

It is beyond the scope of this paper to suggest how this void can be filled. Nonetheless, whatever strategy is developed needs to accommodate three realities. First, many Latinos are more likely to be involved with mainstream groups than with Hispanic organizations. It would seem possible, therefore, for funders to encourage the development of linkages between Latino and non-Latino civic associations so that together they may establish a network that will incorporate Latinos and provide the foundation for mobilizing to support Hispanic community interests.

Second, there are few Latino membership organizations within Latino communities. These are the groups most likely to incorporate working-class Hispanics, and it is therefore imperative that a network of such groups be developed. At a minimum, the mechanisms for doing so would include identifying leadership within established institutions such as churches, schools, and sports clubs, and working with them to establish more inclusive groups. It should be emphasized that whether or not these groups develop explicitly as ethnic groups, their membership will surely be overwhelmingly Hispanic. Therefore, every effort should be made to allow local interests to determine the focus and identity of such organizations.

Finally, there is a particular need to develop organizations in which immigrants play a major role. This will not only educate them in the skills that are essential to becoming full members of society, but it will provide them with the foundation for defending their interests in a political environment that is increasingly hostile to noncitizens.

Notes

[1] Rodolfo O. de la Garza, et. al, *Latino Voices: Mexican, Puerto Rican and Cuban Perspectives on American Politics.* Boulder: Westview, 1992; Independent Sector, *Giving and Volunteering in the United States,* Washington, D. C., 1992.

[2] Alexis de Tocqueville, *Democracy in America* (translated by George Lawrence). New York: Harper and Row, 1969.

[3] Gabriel Almond and Sidney Verba, *The Civic Culture.* Princeton University Press, 1963, p. 302.

[4] Robert Putnam, "Bowling Alone: America's Declining Social Capital," *Journal of Democracy,* January 1995, pp. 65-78.

[5] Lawrence H. Fuchs, *The American Kaleidoscope.* Hanover: Wesleyan University Press, 1990.

[6] Sidney Verba, Kay Lehman Schlozman and Henry Brady, *Voice and Equality: Civic Voluntarism in American Politics.* Cambridge: Harvard University Press, 1995, p. 272.

[7] Salvador Alvarez, "Mexican American Community Organizations," *El Grito,* V-IV, 2 (Spring, 1971), pp. 91-100.

[8] Ricardo Romo, "The Urbanization of Southwestern Chicanos in the Early Twentieth Century," *New Scholar,* VI, pp. 183-207.

[9] Leo Grebler, Joan W. Moore and Ralph C. Guzman, *The Mexican American People.* New York: The Free Press, 1970, pp. 542.

[10] Rodolfo O. de la Garza, Manuel Orozco, and Miguel Baraona, "Binational Impact of Latino Remittances: A Policy Brief," Claremont, CA: The Tomás Rivera Policy Institute, January 24, 1997.

[11] For an example of research that equates these two types of giving see Bradford Smith, Sylvia Shue, Jennifer Lisa Vest and Joseph Villarreal, *Ethnic Philanthropy.* Institute for Nonprofit Organization Management, University of San Francisco, 1994.

[12] Bradford Smith, et. al., *Ethnic Philanthropy*, pp. 53-134.

[13] Robert Smith, *"Los ausentes siempre presentes":The Imagining, Making and Politics of a Transnational Migrant Community between Ticuani, Puebla and New York City.* Ph.D. Dissertation, Columbia University, New York, 1995.

[14] The LNPS is the first and to date the only national political survey of Latinos. The respondents were a nationally representative sample of Mexican, Puerto Rican, and Cuban-origin Hispanics residing in the United States. See R. O. de la Garza, et. al. 1992.

[15] The scores are the mean responses regarding trust in each of the types of organizations.

[16] The independent variables include the categories of confidence in organizations, Mexicans, blacks, nativity, education, income, and interaction terms among ethnicity and nativity, education and income. The dependent variables are number of organizations to which money was given and to which the respondent volunteered. Results available from the author upon request.

[17] Furthermore, the analysis indicates that even if they are members of nonethnic groups, those who are also members of Hispanic groups are also more likely to register and vote.

[18] William A. Díaz, "Latino Participation in America," in *Hispanic Journal of Behavioral Sciences* 18 (2), May, 1966, pp. 154-174.

[19] T.I.Y.M. Publishing Company, Inc., McLean, Virginia, 1996.

Latinos and African Americans: Connecting

Arlene Scully[1]

"In the 1990s relationships between Blacks and Latinos are strained and rife with tension. These conflicts in the social, economic, education, and political arenas have created a competitive mindset—fighting for the same piece of the American pie . . . Common ground can be found by focusing on the systemic causes and society's refusal to accept responsibility for generational poverty and oppression experienced by Blacks and Latinos in this country . . . There are collaborations, grass roots and institutional, that have taken form and brought together multiracial groups around a [common] purpose . . ."

Edward Negrete, Jr. and Susan Shimizu Taira, Ph.D.

Introduction

This article examines the growing importance of Latino and African-American community relations for both funders and the communities they support. It does not pretend to be definitive, but rather seeks to spur discussion of the issues. This work builds on a survey of Latino and African-American grantmakers initiated by Hispanics in Philanthropy (HIP) in 1995, that underscored potentially divisive issues between Latinos and African Americans working in philanthropy. Interviews were conducted with program executives from both groups. Developed by Diane Sánchez (a trustee of the Oakland, California-based East Bay Community Foundation) and Ricardo Millett (director of evaluation at the W.K. Kellogg Foundation), the study revealed that:

1. Intergroup tension, if not conflict, does exist at the foundation level.

2. The tension typically stems from pressure exerted by community and foundation constituencies that benefit—either de facto or by design—from funding initiatives that target a specific racial or ethnic group.

Many of those interviewed expressed the need for more open discussion of these issues at the foundation and community levels.

Survey responses prompted further questions: Is there awareness, understanding and leadership within the foundation world around these issues? Are there projects that encourage interaction and discussion between African Americans and Latinos who work within foundations? Are there projects funded within Latino and African-American communities that investigate and/or address tensions between the two groups?

In order to pursue these questions, we interviewed foundation and community practitioners, as well as researchers involved in intergroup initiatives across the country.[2] We not only hoped to identify the key issues affecting African-American/Latino relations, but to determine best practices in addressing them. So little research or clear direction is available in this area, however, that we are largely left to use our own judgments in reaching conclusions about this complex topic. One of our main objectives is to determine the points of contention that seem most frequently to divide African Americans and Latinos and, more importantly, to identify the points at which their interests and needs coincide in mutually beneficial ways. By doing this, we hope in some small way to encourage a fruitful response from practitioners.

During the course of our research it became clear that, although Latinos and African Americans comprise the two largest minorities in the U.S., their issues cannot be isolated from the social nexus that necessarily involves many other groups, including whites. The history and interplay of racism, immigration, and class also play a significant role—a circumstance that is touched on here, but only to the extent that our limited space allows.

By addressing the critical challenges African-American/Latino tensions present to philanthropy, and by highlighting emerging initiatives designed to promote community dialogue and collaboration, which typically include other groups as well, this article seeks to underscore ways in which funders can exercise greater understanding and leadership in formulating appropriate programmatic responses.

Background and Objectives

The April 1996 issue of *Harper's* featured a discussion between noted scholars and social commentators, Cornel West and Jorge Klor de Alva. The exchange was suggestively titled *Our Next Race Question: The Uneasiness Between Blacks and Latinos.* Coincidentally that same year The Ford Foundation funded the Tomás Rivera Center and the Joint Center for Political & Economic Studies, leading Latino and African-American research centers, respectively, to collaborate on facilitating dialogue between Latino and African-American organizations.

This increased attention to African-American and Latino relations was a predictable response to the projection that, over the next twenty-five years, Latinos would surpass African Americans as the nation's largest minority group. For Latinos, this growth in population comes with the potential and push for dramatically expanded access to power and funds. But among African Americans it brings an increased uneasiness, given the prevailing sense that what one group gains the other loses. As the 1995 HIP study indicates, tensions between African Americans and Latinos in the foundation world, while largely unarticulated, reflect growing pressures from community constituencies. Whether based entirely on fact or not, the zero-funding juggernaut has caused conflict among different groups in the past and will continue to do so unless it is addressed.

The past decade has seen serious public conflict between Latino groups and African Americans in cities as far-ranging as Miami, Washington, D.C., and Los Angeles. However, the conflict does not always take the same form. While we note a dearth of research on African-American/Latino relations, the studies we did find show that there are differences in attitudes toward African Americans within the Latino population. These differences are usually based on country of origin, the history of immigration in the particular region of the United States, immigration status, and class. By inference, these same studies also underscore regional differences, with generally higher tensions between the two groups occurring in the more southern regions of the United States.[3]

Meanwhile, there has been a growing political criticism of the black/white paradigm that informs much of the legislative and funding priorities in this country, which are often implicitly aimed at redressing the lingering biases and legacies of slavery. As Latino and other populations increase and become more organized, there is more pressure to amend the paradigm so that it incorporates the institutional injustices and biases these other groups have experienced. African Americans, however, feel some resentment that programs designed to redress slavery are broadened to all minority groups, many of which do not extend support to African-American issues.

In fact, several social sectors need to be considered in any discussion of African-American/Latino community issues. At the intellectual level, for example, the Klor de Alva/West dialogue reflects growing discussion and concern among social scientists and scholars. Moreover, the Ford Foundation's previously mentioned promotion of dialogue and partnership between leading African-American and Latino think tanks also indicates increased activity in the policy development field. At the community leadership level, however, the challenges of intergroup tensions often appear to be on the rise. Further marginalization and increased stress between African-American and Latino leaders is likely unless funders and other critical community institutions exert more initiative and influence.

While the terrain is difficult, our review of activity and literature in the field reveals a small but growing number of promising neighborhood and community initiatives that provide opportunities for Latinos, African Americans, and others to broach 'differences'. They accomplish this by focusing on shared community problem solving—as differentiated from head-on discussions of race and culture. These efforts, still few in number and modest in scale, offer important lessons and opportunities of benefit to funders, scholars, policy and community leaders, and to society at large. A primary challenge and opportunity for funders interested in this work, therefore, is to identify ways to strengthen, sustain, and replicate these projects over time.

For funders, these circumstances pose two important questions: Should private grantmaking institutions play a more aggressive role in bridging racial divides between African Americans and Latinos? Do community-based programs of the sort our review identified provide models for successful philanthropic replication? We answer yes to both questions, although with qualifications that are addressed in the last two sections of this article.

One of our core objectives is to expand awareness among funders and civic groups as to the value and lessons of community-based approaches to African-American/Latino coalition building. A related objective is to help articulate the organizational models and tactics that are most likely to promote success. A third objective is to identify corresponding implications for funding and program strategies.

Methodology

The material and findings contained herein were derived from multiple sources. These include a selective review of community programs that actively involve intergroup dialogue and/or collaboration, interviews with community practitioners, funders, and researchers, and a targeted review of available literature and research on the issues. We include reviews of ten community programs and projects. Most of these efforts operate at the grassroots neighborhood/community level. We focused on programs and projects that are consciously multicultural in makeup and direction, rather than identity-based. While most of the programs and projects reviewed do not exclusively target Latino and African-American constituencies and relations, they all do so substantially.

Extensive interviews were conducted with more than thirty staff, volunteers, foundation grantmakers, researchers, and social activists involved with community, civic, and educational institutions in Miami, Houston, Philadelphia, Boston, New York, Los Angeles, San Francisco, San Antonio, Chicago, New Market (Tennessee), and Hartford. An attached appendix lists and briefly describes the organizations included in this article.

The following is a brief review of contextual considerations that kept recurring in the course of this study. The views expressed are my own.

The Issues

For various reasons, there is "uneasiness" and sometimes conflict between Latinos and African Americans across the U. S. During the 1980s The Ford Foundation's Changing Relations Initiative funded studies of interracial/intercultural relations in U. S. cities with large established African-American populations and expanding Latino immigrant communities. These studies found that spatial and economic tensions (both real and perceived) between established residents and newcomers fuel intra-ethnic as well as inter-ethnic conflicts, but the form these conflicts take depends on the history and recent immigration patterns of the given area.[4]

In fact, much of the research reviewed in the preparation of this article suggests that relationships between African Americans and Latinos are most strained across the Southern United States. This is related to the recent influx of Latino immigrants from the Caribbean, Mexico, and Central America into border states and areas of the Deep South, and the resulting pressures to redefine established Black/White power dynamics and relations. Yet the situation in Miami has its own specificity. Alex Stepick, in a report for The Ford Foundation, *Changing Relations among Newcomers and Established Residents: The Case of Miami*, cites many reasons for tension between Cubans and African Americans in that city, among them the exceptionally quick economic and political success of the Cuban community based on a "unique combination of background characteristics and extraordinary federal government support and aid to them."[5] In an article for the *El Nuevo Herald* in Miami, Max J. Castro notes that early Cuban immigrants to Miami often belonged to the elite and/or property-owning class, were politically conservative, and more likely to consider themselves white, which often put them in conflict with African Americans.[6]

A more typical example of the growing friction between Latinos and African Americans is cited in a 1996 report to the Rockefeller Foundation issued by the Highlander Center (a sixty-year-old social justice nonprofit based in New Market, Tennessee). The recent immigration of Mexican and Central American workers into Tennessee, Georgia, the Carolinas, Alabama, and Northern Florida precipitated tensions between Latino and African-American, as well as white, workers. In many cases, these tensions were based on real concerns about the impact of Latinos, especially more recent immigrants—many of them low-paid, nonunionized workers—on the wages and employment opportunities of black and white workers, whose economic circumstances have already become unstable in the face of globalization and economic restructuring. Latinos are seen as threatening to African-American and other working-class groups because they pose a direct threat to job security and because Latino immigrant demands on public service budgets (to support everything from public health to expanded education needs) are seen to increase local tax burdens.[7]

Serious philosophical issues also come into play. The current, ongoing dialogue between Latino and African-American professionals and intellectuals hinges on a distinction, which may be implicit or explicit, between race on the one hand and culture/ethnicity on the other. Aspects of this dialogue or argument are documented in the earlier-referenced *Harper's* discussion between scholars Cornel West and Jorge Klor de Alva. While West calls for African Americans and Latinos to form alliances to deal with environmental racism and other issues they have in common, Klor de Alva proposes developing categories that go beyond culture/ethnicity and race, basing alliances on "common suffering" rather than on "the very tenuous alliances between groups that identify themselves by race or culture."[8] In other words, West would maintain ethnic or racial identity, but suspend it to form tactical alliances in dealing with significant, common issues. Klor de Alva, on the other hand, would define new categories based on common human needs. It should be noted that these perspectives could represent short- and long-term strategies, respectively.

More generally, Latinos fairly consistently argue that the Black/White paradigm precludes ethnicity as a criterion, effectively blocking Latinos from access to their fair share of funding, jobs, and power. Latinos, citizens as well as noncitizens, feel the hostility reflected in the public domain by measures like California's recently passed Proposition 187 which, with substantial White, African-American, and Asian support, effectively cut off state services to noncitizens.[9] African Americans, in turn, feel that Hispanics[10] don't adequately comprehend or respect 'race,' particularly as it has developed in the United States. They feel that Latinos use affirmative action gains to their own advantage, yet pass as white when it is expedient for them to do so. Latinos counter that African Americans, having secured a portion of jobs and political power—particularly in civil service and government jobs—do not want to share social justice gains with other needy groups. As Jorge Klor de Alva argues in the *Harper's* article, "The net effect [of affirmative action] has been to create a layer, essentially of African Americans, within the public sphere that has been very difficult for Latinos to penetrate . . ." African Americans question why they should share or give up hard-won equity gains to benefit Latinos who are unlikely to evolve any differently than earlier "borderline white" ethnic groups that have "made it" in America. From this Black perspective, other ethnic groups have gone on to be integrated, i.e., to become "white," while African Americans have/can not.[11] Latinos respond that the history of racism—some Latinos are of African ancestry—and discrimination against many Hispanic groups is as long and as painful as that experienced by African Americans. The claims and counterclaims tend to reinforce a scenario of unresolvable conflict among different groups of victims.

This leaves us with a number of questions: to what extent are racial or ethnic/cultural identities ingrained in people? Can/should they be supplanted? And what role, if any, can/should foundations and other civic institutions play in helping to resolve such issues, particularly as they apply to African-American and Latino relations?

Race, Ethnicity, and Culture as Constructs

It is well established that race is not a scientific category. It has no basis in biology.[12] Nonetheless race, like ethnicity and culture, is a powerful social and historical reality. Experienced from within, a racial or ethnic identity promotes a sense of belonging or community. But if we move outside that particular identity, we see that race and ethnicity are social constructs based on difference rather than commonality or similarity, i.e., without *them* there is no *us*. That inherent divisiveness, a product of our political and economic context, is the key to tensions between Latinos and African Americans, not to mention other groups.

The most recent attempt at a solution has been to promote multiculturalism as a desirable alternative to traditional racial and ethnic hierarchies. The reason for this is obvious: race is considered a relatively immutable category; culture is more fluid and permeable—a kind of halfway house to no category at all. But thus far, multiculturalism has not developed a successful strategy for cross-group sharing of struggles and possible victories. One major reason for this is that multiculturalism in theory often breaks down into uniculturalism in practice. Or, in the words of Eric Hobsbawm, having to answer to a specific culture or identity prevents us from having the multiple combined identities which are normal to most of us.[13]

Multiculturalism, particularly when it becomes politicized, reproduces the division and contention it was meant to overcome. It has the tendency to turn ethnicity and culture back into something very much like race by presenting them as clearly demarcated, static categories. But cultures are not static. They wash back and forth, into and through each other. Jo Anne Schneider, in an article for the *National Society for Experimental Education*, states that: "A person's 'culture' is often portrayed as the unchanging roots which ground the way that person approaches daily life. [However] each culture is [not only] based in its history, but constantly changes as people develop new products, concepts, or ways of interacting with each other. No culture is formed in isolation."[14]

In fact, despite the growing specter of division between Latinos and African Americans, there is much that both groups share—between them and with other groups—when viewed in relation to economic, social, and political standing and experiences. It is precisely this basis of common disadvantage that creates space to bridge emerging tensions, a fact not lost on the programs and communities examined in this article.

Toward a Solution

In analyzing the complexities of social reality, terms like 'Latino' and 'African American' are at best provisional designations. Neither term defines a monolithic social entity; each is subject to slippage and internal contradiction. Class, for example, or one's economic and employment-related status, may be as important an indicator of 'cultural difference' as either race or ethnicity, a factor sometimes overlooked when analyzing barriers to group interaction. Indeed, more than one expert interviewed for this article noted that within any given racial or ethnic group, class differences may be at least as potentially divisive as social differences with other races and cultures.

We also know that conflict arises within racial and ethnic groups—around such issues, for instance, as native or immigrant status. We observed Latino high school students in San Francisco who were less concerned with inter-racial tensions than with volatile relations between Latino newcomers, who tend to be Central American, and established Latino residents, who are usually Mexican. The same is true for Asian students we observed, for whom deeper conflicts are typically between immigrant- and U.S.-born Asians. In Miami, recent social research informs us that relationships can be hostile between African Americans and recently arrived Haitians. ("Changing Relations Among Newcomers and Established Residents: The Case of Miami." Report to the Ford Foundation, February 1990. Alex Stepick et al.)

As we have noted, "African American" and "Latino" are not homogenous categories. Yet even when our efforts to categorize different communities do describe a particular population, they produce a contradictory dynamic: internally, they promote bonding and accommodation; externally, with regard to "others," they tend to encourage difference, which fosters social atomization and thus competition and, ultimately, conflict over "scarce" resources. Given these considerations, one prerequisite for resolving emerging tensions between Latino and African-American groups is to move through constructs of race, ethnicity, and culture, treating them only as beginnings, not as ends in and of themselves.

In theory, the situation sounds impossible. In practice, however, resolutions do occur. Anecdotal evidence suggests there are programs that successfully apply this principal in their practical undertakings. They do it by focusing efforts at the basic levels of social organization and social need—precisely where there is the most fluidity across race, ethnicity, and culture. In fact, solutions to intergroup community conflicts seem to emerge most readily, and typically without great fanfare, from the purported source of the problem: communities themselves.

Most of the people interviewed for this article differentiate between the grassroots and the "political" communities, expressing the view that there is less divisiveness—which makes it easier to work—at the grassroots level.[15] Several community practitioners commented that in their initial organizing they bypassed the usual political and social agencies and leaders, going instead to grassroots neighborhood and block associations, youth clubs, and churches to gain support. In the case of the Bus Riders' Union in Los Angeles, which has effectively partnered Latinos and African Americans in efforts to improve local public transportation services, organizers went directly to residents and consumers to develop a base of public support. In many communities, we learned that more formalized and established community leadership and institutions, including political leadership in particular, often tend to exacerbate rather than alleviate racial divides. Richard Pérez, a long-time social activist from New York, noted that in the neighborhoods where he grew up, there existed for many years a fairly stable mix of Latinos and African Americans whose interests were largely shared and mutually respected—until the early 1980s when intense and very public rivalries between Black and Hispanic elected officials created conflicts within the community.[16]

These observations suggest that as people or groups move up the ladder of community power and position and become more invested in their respective identities along the way, they become more entrenched in seeking access to funds and power for their particular group, typically at the expense of others; conversely, when people focus on common issues and concerns at the grassroots level, intergroup collaborations are not only possible but are also powerful engines for civic engagement and organization.

A critical discovery in this investigation is that when a grassroots community has the means and leadership, divisions based on race and ethnicity tend to fade. They cease to be issues in part because there is a forum, a common ground on which to take on potentially hot topics. For example, the Los Angeles-based Bus Riders' Union, composed primarily of African Americans, Latinos, and Whites, actively opposed Proposition 187. This coalition is somewhat unique when we consider that a majority of Whites and African Americans in the state voted in support of the proposition.

Communities can and do breech racial, cultural, and ethnic lines when they focus on solutions to basic concerns, which in any given community—no matter how diverse—will frequently converge around public health and safety, youth, housing, and education. In the process, they redistribute the relative weight and impact of ethnicity, race, and culture. By devising strategies that focus tactically on shared community needs and aspirations, notions of community are inherently expanded to become more inclusive and multicultural. Commonality of interest seems to offer the firmest ground upon which to begin building community. What's more, it offers a good working definition of 'community.'

Successful Practices and Their Implications for Foundations

Each of the ten organizations and programs we reviewed for this article, whether in neighborhoods or schools, developed in response to community needs inspired, regrettably, by racist and class-based public policy. Systematic withdrawal of public and private financial support during recent years has left them without adequate resources to sustain a healthy community environment.[17] With the development of multicultural leadership and with outside technical assistance, these groups have responded by mobilizing their most basic resource: the communities in which they live.

The programs we examined all address the question of diversity within community. Each is trying with some success to redefine the way(s) they interact as a community, particularly as a community composed of different cultures and races. Three are neighborhood organizations or initiatives. Two extend beyond neighborhood to encompass regional issues. Two use the arts as a means to build bridges between communities, and three are programs focused on youth and families that operate during and/or after school.

The organizations included in our survey are:

Blocks Together, Chicago
The Bus Riders' Union, Los Angeles.
Cornerstone Theater, Los Angeles
The Dudley Street Neighborhood Initiative (DSNI), Boston
The Highlander Center's Rural Organizing Project, New Market, Tennessee
People Respecting Other Peoples (PROPS), San Francisco
Positive After School Children's Athletic Leadership (PASCAL), Hartford, Connecticut
Project R.I.G.H.T (PRI), Boston
The San Francisco Mime Troupe, San Francisco
Woodrock Youth Program, Philadelphia

Following are some core lessons and imperatives revealed by our review of these efforts relative to what works for grassroots groups engaged in efforts targeted to African Americans and Latinos. In reviewing this list, however, readers should also recognize that the contents pertain more generally to coalition building efforts involving particular constellations of diverse groups.

1. **Emphasize common needs.** Subsume issues of racial and cultural identity into what's good for the entire community, i.e., work out issues between groups while working on issues that affect each. All the programs reviewed in this report incorporate an upfront message of unity, e.g., Unite or Never Rise, the slogan from the Nonpartisan Voter Participation Project/People United in New York during the 1980s.[18]

2. **Promote diversity and inclusiveness in staff and governance appointments.** This is usually essential to incorporate in bylaws or governing policy. However it is achieved, though, board and staff must represent the spectrum of races, ethnicities, and income levels that make up the larger community's constituents. Project R.I.G.H.T. in Boston, for example, actively recruited a Latino director, and has multiracial staff, even though African Americans make up a majority of the neighborhood population. This reflects a conscious tactic to reach out to all neighborhood constituents.

3. **Involve, and build on, a broad base of grassroots organizations that are respected by and represent the community in its diversity from the beginning, instead of starting with established groups or agencies that have a stake in the status quo.** The main point here is to set up an organization that represents a broad base of current community residents who are committed to shared community needs, and to structure organizational priorities around those needs. People we interviewed know that established social and political agencies must be included in the dialogue as an important segment of the community; but they generally believe these agencies become more helpful participants once the community is organized to the extent that it can articulate its own priorities and advocate for itself. Virtually every program we reviewed followed this formula at its inception.

4. **Institute and practice a strong commitment to inclusive democratic process.** It is crucial to put the democratic process, no matter how long it takes, above getting through any particular meeting agenda. This inclusive process provides a forum for airing differing points of view, familiarizing people with one another's perspectives, and working through a consensus-based plan of action. Each of the groups included in this article pays special attention to ensure that all sectors of the community participate fully in substantive and strategic decisions.

5. **Provide language translation services at each meeting to demonstrate a commitment to democratic procedures, as well as to let people know that all opinions are important.** This is a time capsule provision. As people experience the rewards of inclusiveness—more voices make for a richer, more informed discussion—concerns about 'efficiency' come to seem increasingly abstract. Most of the community groups we interviewed invested in simultaneous translating devices. The

Dudley Street Neighborhood Initiative actually goes farther, training community members to become translators and meeting facilitators.

6. **Develop multicultural leadership that can effectively represent community diversity and interests while also dealing effectively with mainstream institutions.** This point has at least two facets: identifying and nurturing cross-cultural leadership from within the community (including schools as communities) and hiring technical assistance providers from outside, as necessary, to support these leaders' efforts in public advocacy. Community leadership development of this sort is crucial to working effectively with organizations and agencies (public and private) that traditionally have not had good relations with community residents, e.g., police, city hall, developers, etc. Blocks Together in Chicago trains multicultural community organizers to develop neighborhood leadership, as does the Dudley Street Neighborhood Initiative and Project R.I.G.H.T. in Boston. The Dudley Street Neighborhood Initiative (DSNI) has been particularly successful at hiring multiracial staff who have proven very effective working with local and state governments.

7. **Emphasize efforts to work strategically with other groups as much as possible in broader coalitions or collaboratives to expand the initiative's capacity, reach, and impact.** Grassroots initiatives in Latino and African-American communities, often small and underfunded, can benefit from strategic alliances with other groups and organizations. Participation in coalitions and/or collaboratives ordinarily offer these groups advantages by exposing them to a broader range of resources and ideas; but various caveats need to be considered along the way. These include the following:

- Establish clear, shared accountability measures and expectations about roles, responsibilities, and intended outcomes.
- Know prospective partners—their history of collaboration and of community effectiveness.
- Nurture small and/or new grassroots organizations in collaborative efforts so that they do not "get swallowed up in the process."
- Assure that there is ample technical support as well as financial support for infrastructure development and overhead.

- Define from the beginning what needs to be accomplished and how each member of the group is expected to contribute, at least during the initial stages.
- Know the difference between a coalition and a collaboration. The former involves the entities in relatively short-term, fluid activities around a particular project or campaign; the latter typically involves more long-term and structured engagement.[19]

What Foundations Can Do

1. **Help to analyze and clarify challenges and opportunities in the field.** This in part means funding more research and dialogue on Latino/African-American community relations, comparative attitudes on public and community issues, and successful models of collaboration between these two groups and others. Included, as key contributors to the research, should be community-based leaders and residents directly engaged at the grassroots level, as well as established experts.

2. **Make reports and studies more widely accessible to community groups and organizations that might benefit from them.** Develop ways of communicating that are more suited to community groups, perhaps by helping create learning communities. Funders can and should address this recommendation by supporting inclusive community-level discussions and briefings highlighting the findings of foundation-commissioned reports and studies. It appears that much of the research commissioned by foundations only trickles into the nonprofit world. A useful model for broadening the audience for reports involving the community recently developed in Houston. Researchers from the University of Houston, collaborating with other colleges and universities, organized a series of meetings with area community groups and organizations to share information on studies of Latino/African-American relationships in Harris County and to discuss opportunities for schools and businesses to do more to bridge real and perceived differences.[20] Plans are underway to convene several more meetings to devise a plan of action for the county and to apply for funds to conduct more research on relationships between the two groups. The University of Colorado at Denver also recently began a collaboration with community agencies.[21]

3. **Target and/or expand funding support to neighborhoods and/or programs that are actively committed to coalition-building and/or collaboration.** Focus especially on capacity-building support that empowers efforts to increase public education and advocacy activities, broaden fundraising capabilities, and access technical assistance necessary for organizational development.

4. **Encourage discussion and interaction, both formal and informal, on issues and opportunities in the field involving Latino and African-American program staff.** As suggested by program officers interviewed for HIP's 1995 Sánchez/Millett study, develop and support internal working groups; experiment with joint and/or cross-programmatic funding initiatives; and support and broadly disseminate model program evaluations to deepen understanding about how to bring African Americans and Latinos together in successful partnerships.

5. **Work with grassroots coalitions of Latino and African-American groups to develop and review evaluation criteria.** It is necessary to develop methodologies that accurately measure success and/or progress in these new and unconventional efforts. The Annie E. Casey Foundation recently funded such an evaluation of the Dudley Street Neighborhood Initiative (DSNI), and the Hyams Foundation completed a similar evaluation of Project R.I.G.H.T. in Boston. Published in February 1998 by the foundation in booklet form as "Safe for Life: The Hyams Foundation's Building Community Initiative," the report made several recommendations, among them involving other funding sources early in the process.

6. **Provide longer-term, multiyear funding.** Coalition-building and collaboration are inherently complex undertakings. This is especially the case when efforts to engage diverse groups of African-American and Latino participants. Consequently, funders need to adjust their normal timelines and expectations when supporting this sort of work. This can be done provisionally, as with the Hartford Foundation for Public Giving originally funding the PASCAL program for two years with an option to renew funding based on performance and impact. The program is now in its fifth year. On the other hand, the Riley Foundation made a multiyear commitment to DSNI from the beginning and, true to its commitment, remains a funder some fifteen years later. The Hyams Foundation's recent report (mentioned above) suggests using matching

grants as a tactic from the onset in order to accustom community groups to the facts of fundraising.

8. **Establish a network of funders and community partners to coordinate information sharing about projects and programs that effectively partner Latino and African-American (as well as other) groups.** Widely disseminate data and lessons of value to other communities and groups, using new technologies like the Internet to identify key lessons, impacts, contacts, and community resources that can help to extend the positive reach and impact of this work.

9. **Before funding a multicultural community/neighborhood initiative, have a clear sense that the problem(s) to be addressed and the strategies proposed to address them are compatible with the foundation's capacities and interests.** Evidence indicates that as problems and response strategies are viewed from the community perspective upwards, issues of common interest supersede race, ethnicity, and other differences. Taking this view generally expands community needs and expectations, however, regarding the level and kind of funding assistance that is required and/or acceptable. Funders need as early as possible to understand and develop comfort with these dynamics, and ensure that they have the necessary capacity and will to meet reasonable community partnership criteria.

Conclusion

Growing tensions within and among increasingly diverse U.S. cultures and "races"—and especially between Latinos and African Americans, the nation's two largest minority groups—suggest that we need to be wary of taking cultural and racial distinctions too far. Clearly, racial and cultural categorizations take on immense historical and social relevance, and convey powerful—and mainly very positive—meaning to all groups. However, we must also recognize that it is necessary to keep redefining and expanding these racial and ethnic constructs, not allowing ourselves to be locked inside them to the point where they pit one group against the other. Our research bottom line is that, while accepting that we live with many varieties of difference, the strategic achievement of larger community improvements and progress depends on recognizing our common needs: safe and sanitary communities, decent housing, meaningful contribution to community changes, gainful employment, education and training.

At the base of each of the programs, projects, and initiatives we reviewed here is a baseline respect for the absolute necessity of expanded dialogue among all the players: in this case Latino and African-American intellectuals, professionals, foundation representatives, and community members. But of even greater importance is the need for these groups and their respective institutions to support the work and aspirations of grassroots community leaders and residents who are actively engaged in coalition-building and partnership efforts. Institutional change, if it is to be effective, comes through the people who experience the problem most directly and who are consequently most affected by the actions taken.[22]

Appendix

The following are programs that volunteered time and staff for interviews. A synopsis of each is accompanied by a brief list of relevant success factors.

The Dudley Street Neighborhood Initiative (DSNI)

The Dudley Street Neighborhood Initiative (DSNI) is located in a neighborhood of primarily African-American and Latino residents in an area that overlaps Roxbury and Dorchester neighborhoods of Boston. A membership organization that claims 10 percent of the neighborhood as members, DSNI was created in 1985 through the joint efforts of neighborhood organizations, the Riley Foundation, and residents. In the years prior to DSNI's development, withdrawal of public resources had turned sections of Roxbury and Dorchester into an area open to illegal dumping and drug-related gang activity. DSNI's success has gained sufficient acclaim to warrant an article written by Jay Walljasper in *The Nation* (March 3, 1997): "When Activists Win: The Renaissance of Dudley Street," pgs. 11-17.

Specific Success Factors

- From its inception, DSNI conceived of the neighborhood as a "political force." Many residents were already politicized, having been previously relocated as a result of various 'community renewal' efforts.
- The Riley Foundation committed from the beginning to work with residents and grassroots organizations as equal partners in revitalizing the neighborhood. It also made a commitment at the outset to multiyear funding in support of community-driven renewal priorities.
- DSNI is guided by a visioning process that involves residents, many of them local homeowners, in deciding how their neighborhood should participate and benefit from community and economic development processes and initiatives.
- Even though there are ethnic/racial groups that have a denser population in the neighborhood, DSNI elects board members in equal numbers from each ethnic group, giving none a plurality.
- DSNI recently voted to give community youth fifteen years old and up the right to vote and to be elected to its governing board.

- A successful campaign to recover and redevelop blighted neighborhood properties allowed DSNI to set up a community land trust. The campaign initially convinced the city of Boston to deed back to the community land that had reverted to the city by tax default. Next, using the right of eminent domain, DSNI won the legal right to buy and develop adjacent land held by private real estate interests.
- DSNI programs undergo periodic strategic, and not merely operational, evaluations. A baseline resident survey recently conducted will help set long-term goals and priorities. On the other hand, a program evaluation funded by the Annie E. Casey Foundation will soon be completed as part of a national survey of successful community-building initiatives focused on youth and family issues.

Project R.I.G.H.T.

Project R.I.G.H.T. is a six-year-old collaborative comprised of grassroots organizations, primarily Latino and African American, and local businesses in a neighborhood that abuts the above-referenced DSNI. The neighborhood is primarily African-American but has a growing Latino population. Organized initially to reduce youth violence, Project R.I.G.H.T. has recently added housing and job development components.

Specific Success Factors

- Project R.I.G.H.T. was one of four projects underwritten by the Hyams Foundation in 1991 as part of a city-wide initiative to make at-risk neighborhoods safer. The Foundation studied the neighborhood for two years prior to program implementation. Project R.I.G.H.T.'s early core support from Hyams was integral to its subsequent success.
- The Hyams Foundation's original plan promised funding for four years and required the participation of eight neighborhood organizations, including churches, youth multiservice agencies, and grassroots organizations. Six years later, Project R.I.G.H.T. is a coalition of thirty-six member organizations with diverse funding sources; it also participates in formal alliances with a state senator and with Alianza Hispana-Americana, a leading social service agency in the area.
- Although targeting a primarily African-American neighborhood, Hyams' hired a Latino as Executive Director for the project.

- Hyams recognized early on that the process of community-building takes time and is not easily measured. Consequently, it has funded an evaluation of the initiative's first five years, as much for internal review as for outside consumption.
- Project R.I.G.H.T. is creating an infrastructure within the community by providing space for group meetings, dialogues, and cross-cultural leadership development for the mainly African-American, but increasingly Latino, neighborhood.

Blocks Together

Blocks Together is a membership organization that operates in an area of Chicago that is 60 percent Latino with an increasing African-American presence. The area has traditionally been a neighborhood of ethnic/racial mixes. And, like DSNI, it includes a good percentage of local homeowners. Blocks Together grew out of a neighborhood association formed in the early '90s to combat drug and gang activity in the West Humboldt Park area of the city. In 1993 the group expanded to include other neighborhoods, organizing them around demands for improved city services. Frustrated by their initial ineffectiveness, this embryonic group retained a community organizer to assist its organizational development through the Chicago-based National Training and Information Center (NTIC). In 1996 Blocks Together incorporated as a nonprofit organization and hired its first director and staff. Originally dedicated to issues of crime and public safety, the organization currently supports various housing, jobs, and youth programs.

Specific Success Factors

- Blocks Together has developed a flexible program of organizing neighborhoods block by block, in an ever widening area. The organization establishes grassroots leadership and programs in one neighborhood, then moves on to organize another. This process allows each neighborhood to respond to its own specific problems while simultaneously setting the stage for Blocks Together to coordinate support for more broad-based actions.
- A study of housing stock in Chicago by a coalition of social service agencies and the University of Chicago discovered that, often, the city redevelopment office issued demolition orders for houses that did not

really need to be torn down. The houses were targeted largely because of their location in low income neighborhoods. Through intervention, Blocks Together presently collaborates with a nonprofit organization to save and rehabilitate many of the houses that in the past would have been demolished. The nonprofit organization then provides counseling and financial information to potential low income buyers in the neighborhoods where Blocks Together works to assist and encourage their qualification for home ownership loans that would enable them to purchase the renovated properties.

The Bus Riders' Union

The Bus Riders' Union (BRU) in Los Angeles has a membership of more than 1,000 comprised mostly of African Americans and Latinos who are bus riders. It has organized successful efforts to improve the quality and quantity of buses available to the city's low income residents, preponderantly people of color, who depend most on public bus transportation. BRU activities revolve primarily around cross-cultural community organizing and public information efforts, as well as periodic legal actions designed to provoke expanded institutional accountability to bus riders' interests and needs.

Specific Success Factors

- In 1996 BRU won a class action civil rights case against the Metropolitan Transit Authority in Los Angeles on the grounds that it discriminates against bus riders through its practice of allotting considerably less money to the bus system than it does to the commuter transit rail system. An overwhelming majority of bus riders in L.A. are Latinos and African Americans who live in the urban centers, whereas the transit rail system caters to suburban traffic that is primarily white and affluent.
- Essential to winning BRU's lawsuit were strategic analyses and extensive research that built on regular attendance at Transit Authority meetings, assistance from employee allies within the Transit Authority, and bus rider testimonials.
- BRU often uses public theater as part of its membership recruitment and education campaigns, as well as at social events. It presently collaborates with Cornerstone Theater (see below) on a series of 'bus plays' that are staged at various times and places throughout the city.

Cornerstone Theater

Cornerstone Theater, an artists' collective, arrived in L.A. in 1992 having traversed much of the U.S. The group began producing Community Bridge shows in early 1994, as a conscious effort to bring various ethnic/racial groups together. In 1994 - 1996 over a fifteen-month period, Cornerstone developed a series of four plays, presented at different venues in the Watts neighborhood. The productions consciously drew on resources from both the Latino and African-American communities in the neighborhood and eventually brought them together as participants and audience members.

Specific Success Factors

- Cornerstone Theater's first two performances succeeded in involving and playing to primarily African-American and Latino audiences, respectively. Members of the Cornerstone collective were surprised at how segregated these first two performances were, given that the neighborhood is so mixed: about 50 percent African-American and 50 percent Latino.

- A third performance, held at an African-American church, invited Latinos involved in the previous production (as participants and audience) to attend; while Latino audience members increased, their attendance was still relatively low.

- A final performance targeted people who attended the first three performances and was advertised widely throughout the neighborhood. It was held at a neutral site, not associated with either the Latino or African-American communities, and it attracted a large multiracial crowd.

- From this experience the Watts Theater Company formed as a separate entity with technical and some financial assistance from Cornerstone. A multiracial group composed of Latinos and African Americans, it recently staged a successful reading and a well-attended Juneteenth celebration.

- Cornerstone donates a percentage of its regular production proceeds to help the groups it spins off, such as the Watts Theater Company.

The San Francisco Mime Troupe

The San Francisco Mime Troupe is a multiracial collective with a thirty-year-old history of producing popular theater. A new project that focuses specifically on African-American, Latino, and Asian Pacific American youth groups, recently completed its second year with funding from the Rockefeller Foundation, among others. The Mime Troupe, which plans to make this project a part of its permanent programming, brings high school students from racially-mixed youth organizations together to 'discover their common ground' through theater.

Specific Success Factors

- Guided by professionals and semiprofessionals—Mime Troupers and San Francisco State University (SFSU) students (who receive credit)— participating teenagers write and perform their own half-hour shows, which are presented midway through the school year at a local theater.
- Working with groups of the most interested student participants, the Troupe goes on to condense each of the student-produced one act plays into one fifty-minute production, which is then performed by Troupe members and SFSU student interns at school assemblies throughout the city.
- The Mime Troupe set wide parameters within which youth participants develop their works. In introductory exercises, for example, students were asked to build stories around "what creates tension in your neighborhood or school."
- In an "atmosphere that is already highly racialized" Mime Troupe staff thinks the process of each group developing separately, then putting their work together, helps them see the similarities in their experiences and outlooks. The similarity of themes and issues among the different ethnic/racial groups became increasingly evident as the project progressed.[23]

Woodrock

Woodrock is a Philadelphia-based nonprofit with a long history of promoting interracial activity. In 1970 it began working in public schools in the Fishtown/Kensington area of Philadelphia. Tensions between the white neighborhood of Fishtown and the Kensington neighborhood, which at that time was primarily mixed African-American/Latino, exploded with the drowning of a Latino youth. This incident spurred a coalition of parents in the school district to press for expanded after-school programs and other interventions. The Woodrock Youth Program resulted.

Specific Success Factors

- The Woodrock Youth Development Program offers a number of in-school and after-school projects for elementary and middle school students. The program helps children 'resist the negative cultures of drugs and violence, develop resiliency skills, and build positive support systems which transcend ethnic and racial boundaries.'
- The program employs five Advocates who teach human relations and life-skills classes based on a curriculum developed by Woodrock and the Philadelphia Commission on Human Relations. The curriculum is constantly reviewed and updated.
- Advocates, who help students to set goals, monitor student progress on a monthly basis. This process involves teachers. The Advocates also provide a link between parents and the schools, often referring parents to community services.
- Woodrock offers parenting classes—twice a month in English, and once a month in Spanish.
- Peer mentors from local high schools are paid to help younger students with homework.
- Mentors, along with Advocates, join students in after-school activities that include clubs, sports activities, and weekend trips.
- Woodrock is primarily supported by the local United Way and school district funds.

The Positive After School Children's Athletic Leadership

The Positive After School Children's Athletic Leadership (PASCAL) program is subtitled: *A Comprehensive Life Skills and Violence Prevention Program.* It receives primary support from the Hartford Foundation for Public Giving which initiated the program three years ago, guaranteeing funds for three to five years. PASCAL is unique to this study in that it involves two virtually segregated elementary schools, one primarily African-American and the other primarily Puerto Rican.

Specific Success Factors

- The program was created, and is directed by, school social workers.
- While most of the programming takes place in the individual schools, i.e., separately, there are two groups that meet monthly: a dance club that studies Latin, African, and ballroom dance, and a leadership club that plans joint school recreational and community service programs.
- This past summer marked the program's first summer school project involving students from both schools. The project incorporates academic support courses with recreation and conflict resolution classes.
- An interesting aspect to this program resulted from a study, completed by one of the school counselors, of inner city children's thoughts about their neighborhoods. The study underscored the children's shared fear of older youth. To help offset that fear, the PASCAL program employs high school students as mentors.
- Mentors receive training from a local violence prevention agency in order to facilitate conflict resolution workshops.
- They also help with after-school recreational activities staffed by volunteers from the community and local academic institutions. PASCAL hopes to enrich the neighborhood, creating a sense of mutual responsibility and participation on the part of Latino and African-American parents and children, as well as school staff.

The last two projects discussed, People Respecting Other Peoples (PROPS) at Mission High School in San Francisco and the Rural Organizing Project sponsored by the Highlander Center in Tennessee, have operated for less than two years, but they tackle issues of race and ethnicity in provocative ways.

People Respecting Other Peoples

People Respecting Other Peoples (PROPS), the brainchild of a University of California at San Francisco sociology professor and a Mission High School counselor, is primarily funded by the Carnegie Corporation of New York. With the help of a core group of fifteen students, the entire Mission High School student population of 1200 participates in a two-year study and discussion of its attitudes about race and ethnicity.

Specific Success Factors

- The project is based on the premise that the crucial arena for change is the neighborhood (or school as neighborhood), not the individual or the community leader, per se.
- Rather than develop a curriculum, the project seeks to develop a process that helps people understand the dynamics of their responses to race and culture issues, and find ways to direct these responses to positive ends.
- The core group consciously includes gang members and others who are traditionally marginalized from school activities of this sort.
- This core group works closely with the two project coordinators. During the two-year period, they develop, administer, and evaluate question-naires that are given to the entire student body. Using the questionnaire results, they interview representatives from the spectrum of student cliques, videotaping the interviews. With supervision, again from the coordinators, the videotapes are edited to a forty-minute version and used in classrooms as a basis for discussion, training, and related problem solving.
- The core group of fifteen students receives a modest stipend for participating.

Global Education and Cross Cultural Labor Initiative

The Highlander Center Global Education and Cross Cultural Labor Initiative (GECCLI) is a response to increasing tension in the Southeast, both in rural and urban areas, resulting from the recent influx of Mexican and Central American workers. Many of the workers are 'imported' by factories into areas where the turf battles have been traditionally between black and white workers. GECCLI attempts to create structures that will help bridge differences between more established African-American and White residents and the Latino newcomers.

Specific Success Factors

- The Initiative is designed to promote dialogue through social events that use theater and crafts to help people address their similarities as well as differences.

- Workshops treat the changing nature of work in the global economy, providing a current, rather than outmoded framework, for participants to share ideas about their situation as workers, whatever their particular racial/ethnic background.
- The Initiative is a coalition of Appalachian and Southeast organizations that work with Latinos, African-Americans, and Anglos. The constituent organizations recommend participants and help structure the workshops.

Notes

[1] From "Blacks and Latinos: Understanding and Resolving Racial Conflict," in *CAHRO News*, California Association of Human Relations Organizations, San Francisco, February/March 1998. pp. 1, 4. The author is indebted to Debbie Greiff, Principal at Debbie Greiff Consulting; Ricardo Millett, Director of Evaluation at the W. K. Kellogg Foundation; Diane Sanchez, Principal at Sunset Associates, Wayne Winborne, Director of Program and Policy Research at the National Conference; and especially Henry A. J. Ramos, Project Editor, for their helpful comments and suggestions. Special thanks also to Susan T. Vandiver, Vice President of Grant Programs at the S. H. Cowell Foundation, for her encouragement and interest in this project.

[2] People interviewed whose programs are represented in this article include Joe Dagrosa and Margaret Penn, social workers, PASCAL, Hartford, CT; Roz Everdell, community organizer, Dudley Street Neighborhood Initiative, Boston; Bonnie Friedman, project director and Patrick Osbone, development director, San Francisco Mime Troupe; Martín Hernández, community organizer and Norma Henry, BRU, Los Angeles; Alden Lanphear, executive director, Woodrock, Philadelphia; Ekem Larston, project director, Highlander Center, New Market, TN; Jorge Martínez, director, Project R.I.G.H.T., Boston; Howard Pinderhughes, University of California at San Francisco; Charles Perry, and PROPS students at Mission High School in San Francisco, CA; Hugo Rojas, director, Blocks Together, Chicago, IL; and Leslie Tamaribuchi, managing director, Cornerstone Theater, Los Angeles, CA. The following people provided information used in the text: Sharvell Becton, program officer, Community Foundation of Palm Beach & Martin Counties, Florida; Tatcho Mindiola, University of Houston; Alex Stepick, Florida International University; Max Castro, University of Miami, North South Center, Coral Gables; Jo Anne Schneider, Temple University; Raúl Martínez, ASPIRA, Miami; Maurice Wallace, Family Christian Association of America, Miami; Guarioné Díaz, Cuban-American National Council, Miami; Ari Sosa, Dade Community Relations Board, Miami; Karen Helmerson, Educational Video Center, New York City; Richard Pérez, Hunter College, NY; Beverly Watts Davis, executive director, Fighting Back, San Antonio; Steve Perkins, associate director, Center for Neighborhood Technologies, Chicago; Diana Duby, director of Students Talk About Race (STAR), a project of People for the American Way, Washington, D.C.
    The following people provided information and referrals. Anthony Jackson, the Carnegie Corporation of New York; Stephen Viederman, the Jessie Smith Noyes Foundation; Adriana Falcón, the Hartford Foundation for Public Giving;

Jean Entine, the Boston Women's Fund; Joan Shigakawa, Carol Atlas, and Tomás Ybarra Frausto, at the Rockefeller Foundation; Antonio Romero and Michael Seltzer of The Ford Foundation; Charisse Grant, Dade Community Foundation; Hugh Burroughs and Gwen Foster of the David and Lucile Packard Foundation, Hahn Cao Yu, Social Policy Research Association, California; Helen Safa, University of Florida at Gainsville; Alfred McAlister, Interethnic Forum, University of Texas at Houston; Margaret Simms, Joint Center for Political & Economic Studies, Washington, D.C.; Rodolfo de la Garza, University of Texas at Austin and the Tomás Rivera Center, Texas; and Frieda Garcia, director of United South End Settlements in Boston.

[3] Besides the well publicized tensions in Los Angeles, this was corroborated by our inability to locate sustained programs involving Latinos and African Americans in the Miami area. Studies cited in this report include a 1996 report to the Rockefeller Foundation's Partnerships Affirming Community Transformation (PACT) program from the Highlander Center's Cross Cultural Labor Initiative, which discusses tensions in Southern states, including Alabama, Florida, the Carolinas, Georgia, and Tennessee among African Americans, Latinos, and Whites; "Changing Relations Among Newcomers and Established Residents: The Case of Miami," a final report to The Ford Foundation, February 1990; research completed in 1996 by professors Tatcho Mindiola and Nestor Rodríguez at the University of Houston's Center for Mexican-American Studies in collaboration with the University's African-American Studies program. All are cited later in the paper.

[4] Youth participating in The San Francisco Mime Troupe's after-school project exhibited as much preoccupation with intra-ethnic tension as friction between ethnicities (tensions based on newcomer versus established residents). See also Alex Stepick, et. al, "Changing Relations Among Newcomers and Established Residents: The Case of Miami" regarding African Americans and Haitians. Chapter 6, pp. 67-82.

[5] "Changing Relations Among Newcomers and Established Residents: The Case of Miami." Final report to The Ford Foundation, February 1990. Alex Stepick, et. al., Introduction, p.1.

[6] From an article titled "En Blanco y Negro" that appeared in *El Nuevo Herald* in Miami, lunes, 10 de Marzo de 1997. Mr. Castro begins the article with a quote from W. E. B. DuBois: "The problem of the 20th century is the problem of the color line . . ." Mr. Castro adds that at the end of the century, it is still the problem.

[7] See, for example, McCarthy, K. and Verrez, G., "Immigration in a Changing Economy..." Rand Corporation, Santa Monica, CA, 1997.

[8] *Harper's* Magazine, "Our Next Race Question: The Uneasiness between Blacks and Latinos," a dialogue between Jorge Klor de Alva and Cornel West. April 1996.

[9] The actual percentages in favor of Proposition 187 were 61% of whites, 47% of African Americans and Asians, and 23% of Latino voters. The *Los Angeles Times,* cited in *Reweaving Our Social Fabric: Challenges to the Grantmaking Community after Proposition 187*, published by Hispanics in Philanthropy with Grantmakers Concerned with Immigrants & Refugees and Asian Americans and Pacific Islanders in Philanthropy (AAPIP), 1995.

[10] In this article, Hispanics and Latinos are used interchangeably.

[11] There appears to be some data to back up this assessment, at least in Los Angeles. Gregory Rodríguez, a research fellow at Pepperdine University presents evidence, based on 1980 and 1990 census data, that established Latinos, i.e., not recently immigrated, in Greater L.A. are moving into the middle class "faster than Blacks and Asians combined." *The Economist*, December 1996. "Latinos in California, The Next Italians."

[12] See Kenan Malik, *The Meaning of Race,* Chapter 6, "From Biological Hierarchy to Cultural Diversity," page 150, for a discussion of race as arising from "the naturalization of social differences. Regarding cultural diversity in natural terms can only ensure that culture acquires an immutable character, and hence becomes a homologue for race." An interesting historical note on this subject: Naturalization papers dated 1943 identify the holder's 'race' as Irish (nationality British).

[13] Eric Hobsbawm, "Identity Politics and the Left," *New Left Review* 217, May/June 1996, p. 39.

[14] National Society for Experimental Education, "Intergroup Relations in the United States: Some Basic Concepts," Jo Anne Schneider, fall 1996.

[15] The distinction here between *grassroots* and *political* seems to hinge on the latter being seen as providing services to the grassroots, but in a more narrowly self-interested way and not necessarily with broad-based community input or support.

[16] Interview with Mr. Pérez, who presently works at Hunter College in New York City developing a Comprehensive Community Initiative in Bedford Stuyvesant. Jorge Klor de Alva makes a similar observation in the *Harper's* article "Our Next Race Question": "At the level of the working class, we're seeing a great deal of cooperation, but as you move up the economic scale you have progressively more turf wars."

[17] A Project R.I.G.H.T. publication puts it succinctly: "The collaborating organizations believe that violence is a symptom of economic and social distress . . . perpetuated in part through the development of public policies that fail to allocate resources proportionally . . . and do not take into account our immediate and longer-term needs."

[18] This organization is now defunct, but spawned other community organizations in Brooklyn and the South Bronx that function today, according to Richard Pérez, former People United director, during interview with the author.

[19] For a good discussion of coalitions and collaboratives, see "Building Collaborative Communities," *Pew Partnership for Civic Change*, 1996, Suzanne W. Morse.

[20] At a public meeting in 1996, two sociology professors at the University of Houston, Tatcho Mindiola and Nestor Rodríguez, presented the results of their survey of 600 African Americans and 600 Latinos in the Houston area. Findings show, for example, that the Black community is split on issues of English Only and Latino immigration as a threat to jobs—a hopeful sign, according to Mindiola because, by not being lopsided, it encourages discussion. He is director of the Center for Mexican American Studies; Rodríguez directs the Center for Immigration Studies. They are part of a coalition of African-American and Latino college professors that formed to research relationships between African Americans and Hispanics in the Houston area.

[21] Michael Cortés codirects the University of Colorado Latino Research and Policy Center that recently began a project developing reciprocity between community needs and university-sponsored research.

[22] One of the Highlander Center's principals.

[23] A recent Mime Troupe project report points out that urban youth culture "transcends racial, ethnic and class divisions" and that a "common culture [is] evident in the language, characters and themes of our workshop plays."

Bibliography

Ahmad, Aijaz, "Issues of Class and Culture: An Interview with Aijaz Ahmad" by Ellen Meiksins Wood, *Monthly Review*, Vol. 48, No. 5, (October 1996): pp. 10-29.

Goode, Judith & Schneider, Jo Anne, *Reshaping Ethnic and Racial Relations in Philadelphia: Immigrants in a Divided City*. Philadelphia: Temple University Press, 1994.

Hartman, Chester (ed.), *Double Exposure: Poverty and Race in America*. Armonk, New York: M.E. Sharpe, 1997.

"Latinos in California, The Next Italians." A review of Gregory Rodriguez' study of Latinos in Los Angeles, *The Emerging Latino Middle Class*. *The Economist* (December 14, 1996): pp. 28-30.

Malick, Kenan, *The Meaning of Race: Race, History and Culture in Western Society*. New York University Press, 1996.

Morse, Suzanne W. *Building Collaborative Communities*, Leadership Collaboration Series. Tonya M. Yoder (ed.). Charlottesville, Virginia: Pew Partnership for Civic Change, 1996.

Omi, Michael and Winant, Howard, *Racial Formation in the United States from the 1960s to the 1990s*, 2nd edition. New York: Routledge, 1994.

Schneider, Jo Anne, "Intergroup Relations in the United States: Some Basic Concepts," *National Society for Experimental Education Quarterly* (Winter 1996): p. 4.

Stepick, Alex, et. al. *"Changing Relations Among Newcomers and Established Residents: The Case of Miami."* Final report to The Ford Foundation. New York: Ford Foundation, 1990.

West, Cornel, and Klor de Alva, Jorge, "Our Next Race Question: The Uneasiness between Blacks and Latinos," New York: *Harper's*, April 1996: pp. 55-63.

Part II

Expanding Latino Participation in U. S. Organized Philanthropy: Best Practices and Evolving Models

New Pools of Latino Wealth:
A Case Study of Donors and Potential Donors
in U. S. Hispanic/Latino Communities

Ana Gloria Rivas-Vázquez[1]

Introduction

The numbers of Hispanics in the United States have increased dramatically in recent years. Presently, Hispanics (or Latinos)[2], the fastest growing diverse group[3] in the country, are far outpacing the rest of the nation's population growth.[4] In fact, Hispanics are soon expected to become the largest diverse group in the U. S. It is estimated that by the year 2050, nearly one in every four Americans may be Hispanic.[5] While most Latinos are poor, many have experienced real business and economic success in America, leading to expanded wealth and potential new contributions to organized philanthropy. This combination of rapid Latino population growth and emerging wealth has presented important new issues and questions in the philanthropic arena, ranging from how best to expand Latino representation, participation, and services in the independent sector to how more effectively to tap Latinos as philanthropists and sources of philanthropic capital.

It is too frequently said that "Hispanics don't give" as a summary dismissal for why many nonprofit organizations in the United States have not been as successful as they would like in raising funds from this increasingly expanding and affluent group. However, this myth ignores a cultural framework where giving has different meaning and expression than it does in Anglo culture, and belies the fact that few nonprofits have developed effective strategies designed to reach Latino donors.

A significant amount of the giving that occurs in Latino culture takes place within networks of family and friends, and is never formally counted or reported. It is giving that does not qualify for the charitable tax deduction. Although it is sometimes described as informal, this giving often provides on a systematic basis for family, extended family, friends, and employees, and is relied upon by recipients much in the same way that others in this country rely on the social services safety net. In fact, Hispanics do give—and quite generously—only not always in ways that fit neatly within traditional U. S. models of philanthropy.[6] In addition, while the for-profit sector has aggressively targeted marketing efforts to Hispanics, who represent $228 billion in annual domestic purchasing power,[7] the nonprofit sector has been slow to craft approaches designed to attract Latino donors.

Given the rapidly changing demographics of the United States and the resulting shifts in economic power they are beginning to produce, the nonprofit sector will be increasingly challenged in the years to come to reach out to Latino and other diverse donors in order to sustain and build philanthropic activity in this country. This article, which began as a smaller case study of donors and potential donors in Miami,[8] focuses on elements of Hispanic culture that influence charitable giving, characteristics of Hispanic giving, and the preferences and customs of Latino donors nationally. It is intended to assist nonprofits and others in the philanthropic community to develop more effective approaches designed to expand charitable giving and activity among Hispanic donors and potential donors.

Methodology

The research for this article consisted of structured interviews with sixty Latino donors in the five states with the largest Hispanic populations: California, Florida, Illinois, New York, and Texas. Seventy-five percent of the U. S. Latino population lives in these five states. The largest Latino populations in the United States are from Mexico (64 percent, 14.6 million), Puerto Rico (11 percent, 2.4 million) and Cuba (5 percent, 1.1 million). The remainder of the Latino population is comprised of Central and South Americans (13 percent, 3.1 million) and other Hispanics (7 percent, 1.6 million).[9] Accordingly, individuals from Mexican, Puerto Rican, and Cuban origins represent the majority of those interviewed. Of the sixty persons in the sample on which these findings are based, twenty-five are of Cuban origin, nineteen are of Mexican origin, eight are of Puerto Rican origin and another eight represent other Latino subgroups.

The interviews were conducted using a schedule of questions developed in conjunction with academics as well as professionals in the field of philanthropy. Interviews typically lasted between thirty minutes and one hour. About half of the interviews were done in person while the other half were conducted over the telephone. All interviews were conducted by the author.

The individuals interviewed are all persons of relative means who have made charitable gifts of at least $1,000 or who, in this researcher's estimation, could make a charitable gift of at least $1,000 on an annual basis. Of those interviewed, at least four have made gifts of $1 million or more. At least one has made a gift of $100,000 and many have given more than $10,000. The author also interviewed one individual listed on *Hispanic Business* magazine's roster of the eighty wealthiest Hispanics in the country.[10] The respondents range from working professionals to millionaires, and include individuals who work in both the private and nonprofit sectors.

The ages of the respondents range from 31 to 72 years. Thirty-five of the respondents are male while twenty-five are female. All except three (95 percent) of the sixty respondents have attended or graduated from college. The majority hold professional, doctorate, or other postgraduate degrees. Almost all of the degrees were awarded at U. S. institutions. These educational characteristics are important because to a certain degree they illustrate the Americanization of the respondents.

Several questions were set out in the initial research project description:

- Is there a preference among Hispanics for cause-related giving versus institution-based giving?
- Do Hispanics/Latinos tend to avoid large institutions and endowments? Why?
- What key values related to Hispanic culture influence philanthropic giving?

- Are there causes related to the immigrant history of Latinos (such as emphasis on education as the road to success) that affect giving decisions?
- What are the characteristics of organizations preferred by Hispanic donors?

In addition, in a 1989 paper titled "Latino Philanthropy: Some Unanswered Questions,"[11] Michael Cortés raised several key questions that informed aspects of the research and interviews conducted for this article, including:

- What community traditions predispose Latinos to charitable giving?
- What impediments discourage Latinos from other forms of charitable giving and philanthropy?
- What sorts of organizational arrangements are most likely to facilitate Latino philanthropy?[12]

Dr. Cortés' questions provide an important backdrop against which to analyze the data produced by this research and a critical framework for discussion of Hispanic philanthropic traditions, current giving patterns, motivations for giving, and giving preferences. And, as Dr. Cortés so correctly notes: "The goal should not simply be to enable wealthy Latinos to become philanthropists. The higher goal, as always, should be to direct additional resources where they are needed the most."[13]

In order to increase this country's philanthropic resources, it is important to elevate mainstream institutions' comprehension of the philanthropic culture of Latinos, what motivates them as donors and what preferences they have as givers. Bridging the gap between where this important group of donors is conceptually and mainstream philanthropy is a core challenge facing nonprofits and the philanthropic sector in more and more communities across the United States. As the findings of this research indicate, the key to accessing Latino giving is to develop a clear understanding of the culture, and to identify culturally relevant methods of cultivating and soliciting Latino donors.

Key Findings

While the information contained in this article cannot be considered conclusive given the relatively small size of our survey and the highly qualitative nature of the research, it is the author's hope that it can contribute to more effective approaches to Latino donors and nonprofit/community constituencies.

Following are the key findings derived from interviews and research undertaken to produce this article.

Ethnic identity is a subjective determination that reflects strong ties to family culture and countries of origin.

One of the most interesting responses of those interviewed relates to how they identified themselves ethnically. This self-identification at times depends on context, and nearly all of the respondents hesitated before answering and frequently felt the need to give supporting explanations for their replies.

The responses indicated a preference for preservation of heritage rather than assimilation (or at least a strong identification with heritage and country of origin), and illustrated the subjectivity of ethnic or national identity. These issues are significant in the context of this research because strong identification with one's heritage may impact charitable giving behavior as it translates into:

- a desire to preserve traditions;
- a sense of responsibility for family members and friends that results in direct giving to individuals, rather than nonprofit organizations;
- remittances to countries of origin; and
- an openness for giving to nonprofit organizations that assist members of one's own ethnic or national community.

None of the respondents, except one woman, described herself or himself as simply (or only) American absent elaboration. One young woman who was born in Cuba and has lived nearly her entire life in Miami said: "If a Latin asks me here, I say I'm Cuban. If I'm abroad, I'm American." One man who was born in Puerto Rico responded: "Hispanic because I was born in Puerto Rico. [But] I hate ethnic classifications. I think we are all Americans." Some respondents answered that how they label themselves ethnically or nationally "depends" on the context, and sometimes complicated or multifaceted informing influences. For example:

- A male respondent in his 40s, who was born in Buenos Aires of Cuban parents and lived most of his life in Florida, considers himself Cuban American.
- A woman in her 30s who was born in Puerto Rico of Cuban parents and has lived nearly all her life in Florida labels herself Cuban/Puerto Rican.
- Two women in their early 40s, who were born in Cuba, but have lived in the United States for more than 35 years (in states outside Florida), call themselves Cuban.
- A young man in his 30s who was born in California and has lived his entire life in the United States self-identifies as Mexican.
- A woman in her 50s who was born in New York of Puerto Rican parents identifies herself as Puerto Rican.
- A woman in her 50s who was born in the United States of Latin American parents self-identifies as Latin American.

Although not too surprising, these responses indicate how strongly respondents identify with their parents and their countries or cultures of origin. Two other interesting issues surfaced in these responses: One involves the various terms with which respondents of Mexican origin self-identify and the other relates to the way that respondents of Cuban origin see themselves.

Respondents of Mexican origin identified themselves with a variety of labels, including: Chicana or Chicano, Hispanic, Latina or Latino, Mexican and Mexican American. The term Chicana or Chicano was used by respondents in their late 40s and 50s, and not by younger respondents. One respondent in his 40s said that he used to call himself Chicano, but does not use that term anymore. Instead, he uses Hispanic or Latino, but not Mexican American. The use of Chicano "is generational," he said. Another self-described Chicano in his 50s said that it "is a California term. I consider Chicano someone who is Mexican in their heart, but born on this side. I feel more Mexican than I do American."[14] A woman in her 60s of Mexican heritage in Texas calls herself Mexican American and added that she "hates" the term Chicano.

Responses to the self-identification question were different for Cubans in one regard. None of the twenty-five respondents of Cuban origin identified herself or himself as Hispanic or Latina/o except for one who lives outside of the strongly Cuban enclave in Miami, who said that he is Hispanic or Cuban American, but "typically, I refer to myself as Hispanic first." In fact, some Cubans emphatically said that they are not

Hispanic or Latino. There may be several reasons for Cubans' not identifying with a larger, national Hispanic community, including the relative youth of Cuban immigration (the bulk of it has occurred within the last 40 years), the fact that most Cubans consider themselves exiles or political refugees as opposed to immigrants,[15] the strength of the Cuban enclave in South Florida,[16] and other unique characteristics of the Cuban population (such as relatively high levels of education and wealth).[17] Being born in Cuba is not a prerequisite for feeling Cuban or Cuban American; and the fact that individuals have lived most of their lives in the United States does not mean that they feel any less Cuban, although for some who could have called themselves Cuban, the fact of having lived half or most of their lives in the United States translates into the hyphenated Cuban-American.[18] If Cubans do not identify with a larger Hispanic or Latino population, this could disproportionately impact national strategies to influence Latino philanthropy as Cuban Americans are the third largest U.S. Hispanic subgroup and top the country's list of wealthiest Hispanics.[19]

One of the most important characteristics of Hispanic philanthropy is the personal nature of giving. Whether it relates to who is asking, who is receiving, or who is involved in the organization that is soliciting, people matter most.

Responses to questions about why individuals give varied somewhat, but several themes emerged that should prove helpful in crafting approaches and philanthropic vehicles targeted to these groups. One of the most important characteristics of Hispanic philanthropy is the personal nature of giving. As one respondent aptly said about his giving, "Primarily, it's people related."

"When I'm asked for money, there are some people you just can't say no to," said one young Cuban American. "Maybe it's because they've supported my causes in the past, maybe it's because they play a prominent role in my life—my physician or my client."

Supporting specific people in their fundraising efforts was cited by several respondents as one of the reasons they give to certain charitable organizations. One Mexican-American woman in her 50s in Texas said she follows the example of a "friend and mentor." One young Hispanic professional in Texas said that one of his reasons for giving is "to support my friends and families with their activities in charitable organizations." A wealthy Latin-American woman in New York said: "You also do it to be supportive of your friends, that's very important. I also think it's because I live a certain type of life and you support your friends."

Another respondent, an older Hispanic corporate executive who has had significant success in raising funds for several projects, said: "When I ask Anglos for donations, the first question is, *Is that a 501(c)(3)?* When you ask Hispanics for a donation, the questions are about who is involved."

A self-described Chicana in California said: "In the Hispanic community, people give to people they know and the cause kind of slides in."

In addition to considering the people who make the solicitations, respondents also take into account the people running the organizations that are asking for funds. One respondent, for example, gave as one of the three most compelling reasons he gives to particular organizations that "the people heading the organizations are very dedicated people . . . It inspires me to give." Conversely, a young Mexican man in California said: "Many times when I get solicited to certain causes, I am aware of the people who are running the organizations and that hampers my decision to give."

Many interviewee responses reflected a predisposition to focus on institutional and/or administrative considerations; others focused on more cause-related considerations. Some responses, moreover, expressed a tendency to trust grantee managers implicitly in their use of funds; others were more skeptical of grantee management practices.

- "I choose the institution," said a Hispanic businessman in Texas, for example. "It's a given that the institution that I give to is well managed. With that given, I elect to give flexibility to the management of the organization to use the funds in the manner they see fit."
- "I start with a cause and follow with the institution," said a Puerto Rican respondent in what may represent a more typical response. "There's another thing that I consider: How are the funds utilized, how much goes to administration, and how much to the recipient."
- Importantly, many respondents mentioned their dislike of "large, generic organizations" and echoed the last respondent's concern about funds supporting nonprogram purposes.
- One older Cuban-American man, for example, said that one of three reasons he gives to certain organizations is because very little money goes to administration: "Every dollar goes for actual benefits with min-

imal expenses. I hate to give a buck to a nonprofit where the [CEO] goes on a private jet."

- A young Cuban-American woman with experience working at a nonprofit organization she now supports went even further to reflect her concern about nonprofit sector management practices, saying she does not believe that money (even in the organization where she worked) goes for the intended purpose: "I don't believe that when you give money to an organization, they use it for what they say it's going to."

Not surprisingly, given their cultural traditions, Latino donors are especially interested in causes and organizations related to family (children, youth, and the elderly), education, and religion.

Three program areas of interest emerged as especially significant for Latino donors: education, family (children, youth, and the elderly), and the church (or religion). This is hardly surprising given that for many Latinos (as well as other immigrants), education has been the key to success in the new country,[20] Hispanics are overwhelmingly Catholic and there is a strong tradition of giving to the church,[21] and Latinos are more likely to rely on family members or friends to meet needs than on government or social service agencies.[22]

Of the sixty individuals interviewed in this first sample, forty-one of the respondents (68 percent) said education was one of their areas of interest. Several people said it was number one or the only one.

One businessman in Texas said his three areas of interest are "education, education, and education." He explained: "Because I think that education is the great equalizer in terms of allowing people with varying races, ethnicities, religions, genders, and whatever other differences and diversity . . . to succeed in accordance with their potential."

One woman who worked for more than fifteen years as a fundraiser for a university in Florida said: "A lot of our charities are tied to education. And education is a great equalizer. As immigrants, you have your faith, your love, and an education. By enhancing the area of education, you're protecting your children's future."

Children and youth or education were mentioned by all but ten (83 percent) of the respondents. Of those ten that did not include education as one of their interest areas, five made gifts to educational institutions.

Although only nine (15 percent) of the sixty respondents listed the church or religious activities as an area of interest, forty-eight (80 percent) of the respondents said that they contribute to the church, religious organizations and/or religious education, that their family contributed to the church, or that they began giving through the church. Some respondents did not include the church in their list of organizations to which they contribute, but mentioned their church giving. This may indicate that for many Hispanics, giving to the church is a given and that it ranks outside, if not above, all other giving. As one woman, who did not list the church among her areas of interest, said: "The largest contribution that we give is to the church. I put it in a separate category. In our minds, we don't even question that." Examples of other responses included:

- A Mexican-American woman in Texas said: "I make it a point of giving [to my church] a percentage of how good life is."
- A Cuban-American man in Texas said: "Our tradition of giving was basically to the church."
- A Cuban-American woman in Florida said: "I personally began giving in grammar school to feed the children in India, then to maintain a child in Guatemala and to the International Red Cross during the war in Vietnam. But basically [it was] Catholic schools that instilled that responsibility of charitable giving to help others who were less fortunate."
- Another Mexican-American woman in Texas said: "It started with going to church and we had to give. It was something that my father and mother instilled in us. And we also went to Catholic schools . . . We grew up knowing that we had to participate, that we had to give to religion and education."
- A Colombian-American woman in New York said: "In Latin America, giving to the church is very standard. It's something you do."
- A Puerto Rican man in New York said: "It was always through the church. We were very Catholic . . . in the collections in the church, when there were major drives. They gave in very limited amounts. My father never made more than $10,000."
- A Mexican-American woman in Chicago said: "We didn't have money to give except to the church. That I know of, I don't think my parents ever gave money to nonprofit organizations. They might give money to a family that needed help or friends . . . but not to organizations."

Although sometimes not stated or recognized by Latino donors themselves, Hispanics generally feel a special connection to causes or organizations that provide for their own ethnic communities.

Interestingly, only nine (15 percent) of these sixty respondents said that issues relating to Latinos or their specific subgroups is one of their areas of interest for giving. However, more than forty respondents (68 percent) contribute to Latino nonprofits. (This percentage is probably larger given that some organizations without obvious Latino affiliation serve primarily Hispanics.) Thus, despite not expressing an interest in Latino causes, a strong majority of the respondents do support Hispanic organizations.

- A Mexican-American woman in her 60s in Texas said that she does not always contribute to organizations because they focus on Hispanics or Mexican Americans, "but [they are] the major ones where I give money, . . . because they are Hispanic and there is a big gap in the delivery of services—health, education, arts—to those people and [so] I am more prone to help them. They are the underdogs right now."
- An attorney of Mexican origin in his 40s in California said that Latino-targeted giving is "sometimes" a factor, "only because I recognize that the Hispanic community doesn't get as much in terms of charitable contributions as it should."
- A Hispanic businessman in his early 60s in Texas said: "It is a very prominent factor. I get a lot of calls for a lot of donations and I tell them that I have just so much money and I like to direct the money I have to Hispanics. I feel that we have to take care of our own. It's very important for our people to be taken care of."
- "I'm not going to solve the problems of the world," one Cuban American said. "But the little I can help, I want to help my own."
- A young professional in Florida who described herself as Cuban/Puerto Rican stated: "If I'm going to support anyone, it's going to be first Hispanics. If I have a budget, I'm going to spend it on Hispanics first and then on everyone else. If you don't help your people, who is going to help them? If you don't take care of your house, your neighbor isn't going to come over and clean it."
- A Cuban-American banking executive said: "I believe that it is important to support your heritage, your culture, where you came from and it is important that identity is not lost. And in a world where you are encouraged to blend, it's important to preserve your cultural identity."

• A Mexican-American businesswoman said: "I don't think enough of us Hispanics do charitable giving to our organizations and I think they need support from people within our own communities."

In addition, there seems to be a disconnect between what some people said about the impact of an organization's service to Latinos generally (or members of a particular subgroup) on the decision to contribute and their actual behavior. Twenty-three respondents (38 percent) answered "no" or "not really" when asked whether the fact that an organization focuses on their ethnic group impacts their giving. Of these twenty-three, twelve contribute to Hispanic organizations, which leaves only eleven respondents (18 percent) having little or no articulated interest in organizations that primarily serve Latinos.

This gap between some donors' perceptions of their preferences and their behavior is further illustrated by one respondent: He indicated that merely because an organization focuses on his subgroup does not compel his giving, but he listed issues relating to his ethnic subgroup as one of his three areas of giving interest. Another who replied with an unqualified "no" to the same question consistently contributes to a charity in Latin America as well as to an organization whose name is in Spanish and serves primarily Hispanics. Another respondent's answers also are worth noting: He answered "not really" and then added "but it's a factor"; in fact, his local giving is exclusively targeted to Hispanic religious organizations.

This contradiction between what Latinos say influences their giving and their behavior is important because it suggests that despite some respondents' indications, causes that serve their own communities are especially likely to win their support. This suggestion of Latino responsiveness to culturally-oriented emotional tugs at the heartstrings—and ultimately at the purse strings—is in keeping with interviewee responses to other questions, particularly those relating to the importance of self-identification with Latino ethnic or national subgroups and those reflecting the significance of personal relationships. By recognizing their ethnic and national heritage in labels they apply to themselves, Latinos acknowledge their cultures' significance in their lives and in their charitable giving. Another possibility is that Latinos support their own causes and programs because those are the ones for which they are most typically asked to contribute through their established networks and personal relationships rather than because of any inherent predisposition against more externalized giving.

Much Latino giving is never measured or recorded because it occurs outside organized philanthropy as it is defined in the United States.

Contrary to the myth that "Hispanics don't give," Latinos give significant amounts of time and money each year that are never counted or recorded, and that are not deductible for tax purposes. These resources are given in various ways, including: remittances sent to countries of origin; money given to assist family and friends; and noncash donations contributed to family, friends, and others.

In effect, the tax deduction does not figure prominently in Latinos' decision to give. Of those interviewed, only one respondent answered an unqualified yes to the question about whether the tax deduction was an incentive for her giving. She then said: "You either send it to the IRS or you have control over what you do." Another Hispanic businessman said: "It's an incentive because if I don't give it, I have to [give it to the government]. This way the government gives to my charity." A young Cuban-American professional in New York said: "[The deduction] is nice, but if it's driven by that, that defeats the purpose."

There are historical reasons for this lack of emphasis on the deduction. The U. S. philanthropic system is connected to the tax exemption, which has its roots in early seventeenth century English law. Exemption is based on the theory that government foregoes tax in return for services it would otherwise have to provide or for the benefits resulting from the promotion of the general welfare. In contrast to the English law-based system of the United States, Latin American systems are rooted in the Napoleonic Code, French civil law enacted in the early nineteenth century. In many Latin American countries, there is no deduction for charitable giving. And, in the countries where it does exist, according to U. S.-based lawyers who either practiced in Latin America or have Latin American clients, it is either so negligible so as to be unimportant or income is so underreported that a deduction is insignificant.

The Latino system of giving is based on a fundamental belief in taking care of your own (which is broadly defined) and sharing with those who are less fortunate: *Es mejor dar que recibir.* [23]

As one Mexican-American woman in Texas said: "Latinos have been very generous with the church and with their time with their family members and extended family network . . . You don't turn to an outside group or agency . . . The biggest distinction is the lack of involvement in the Anglo traditional social service organizations. The safety net for Hispanics has often been their extended families and not the social service organizations."

"I give to my grandmother and my mother-in-law sizable amounts of money," said a Cuban-American executive in Florida. "A lot of charity goes to my family. If I can give $100 to my grandmother, I'm going to give it to her over a charity. Same thing with my mother-in-law. Technically, we don't consider that charitable giving. But that's money I don't see and don't get a deduction for."

A Mexican woman in Illinois who contributes to many nonprofit organizations said that the tax deduction "helps," but that many of the contributions she makes to organizations, including those in Mexico, are not deductible. "But that doesn't matter if I know they need it," she said.

An Uruguayan woman in Florida said: "I send money to my family in Uruguay, my aunt who is sick. If I have to choose, our family comes first. In Uruguay, when someone in the family didn't have a place to live, they would come to our house. Before I came to this country, I worked to support my mother, who was divorced, and my aunt. I never thought of it as giving. It's just what you did. What good is it to give to a charity if your family doesn't have what it needs?"

A Cuban real estate executive in Florida said: "One of the big differences is that Hispanic donations—and mine certainly—are much more direct. There are a whole bunch of people that you give to [for reasons that have] nothing to do with organized charity. Like last year, I paid probably $2,000 in medical bills for a family member. It would never occur to me to call the Salvation Army to pick up furniture at my house because [I'll give it to] the maid. It's charity as we know it in Latin America: Individuals step in where the government doesn't provide. It's a less structured mentality. You feel more accountable for the people around you." She explained that she often has to dispose of belongings left in apartments and will call the former owners to ask whether she can give what is left behind to a needy family instead of to an organized charity, such as the Salvation Army. "[Anglos] said 'No, no, I need the tax credit.' Americans are much more in tune with giving through charity rather than giving directly because they see direct giving as a handout. The charity cushions the gift."

A very successful Mexican-American businesswoman in Texas said that when she was growing up, her parents were at the center of many efforts to meet the community's needs: "When we had floods, my mother would pass out clothes. She was the central focus . . . There was not an organization that would give to Hispanics, so my parents did. My mother still runs an underground railroad. She gives away everything. Sometimes she goes overboard. Whatever we give her, she gives away. Sometimes she gives the shoes I've given her. She says, 'I'll take the shirt off my back if they need it.' She's 80 now."

Predictably, given their predilection to contribute when there is a need, most Latinos in the survey said that they do not plan their charitable giving. Of the sixty respondents, only twelve (20 percent) said that they plan their giving to some extent. The most-often repeated answer to the question was: "No, it just happens."

A Puerto Rican professional in Florida said: "It's more spontaneous. I approach a situation, I check my bank account and I check my spirit." The response of a female business owner of Spanish origin in Florida is typical of those who do plan their giving: "We do plan it. But after a year, it's always more. It's people you know—you can't say no." A young Cuban woman in California said that she does not plan her giving because she is "not that organized." In describing her family's tradition of giving, she said: "It wasn't organized. It was on a case-by-case basis. If someone who couldn't pay for a funeral died, my family paid for it. An organization is too cold for them. You have to have a face tied to the giving. They're not used to giving just to a building or something cold. It's part of the Latin temperament. They don't allocate money. They don't have anything organized. A friend needs something and you just do it."

Interestingly enough, none of the four $1-million donors interviewed for this article plans her or his giving.

Hispanics are not comfortable with many concepts that are intrinsic to institutionalized philanthropy in the United States, including large organizations, endowments, foundations and planned giving.

As stated earlier, Latinos are not particularly trusting of organizations or large institutions and instead focus on the personal factor. Given their inclination to focus on individuals, Hispanics have difficulty with various areas associated with traditional U. S. models of philanthropy, including endowments, foundations, and planned giving.

Twenty-three (38 percent) of the respondents said that they had contributed to endowments. However, it was clear that some who thought they had, had not and some who had given to endowments did not initially or fully understand the concept of a permanent pool of money from which earnings (or in most cases, a portion of the fund's assets) are distributed. Nearly all the individuals who contributed to endowments gave to endowments for educational purposes. The reasons why they gave reflect findings described earlier related to who solicits them and to their interest in education. One Puerto Rican business executive said he made a gift to a college's endowment "mostly because of the people involved with it . . . It's mainly that I like the people."

One respondent who made a major gift to establish an endowment fund said she did so without being aware of the fund's permanence and subsequently did not like the fact that she had "no control" over contributions from the endowment. She said she did not like "not being able to give to whatever organization I want." Although it was a substantial gift with significant tax implications, this respondent said she would have preferred not receiving a charitable deduction and instead retaining the ability to earmark the money for an individual, a family, or wherever else she decided it should go.

Respondents gave several reasons for not contributing to endowments. Most often, they said that endowments were for people with more money; this perception was verbalized by respondents who have given thousands of dollars to charitable organizations. Respondents also gave as reasons the fact that they had not been approached to donate to an endowment and that they have other responsibilities (such as family). A Hispanic banker in Texas said: "The only endowment I have is my two daughters."

Two of the sixty respondents have established foundations. One business owner in New York has recently established a family foundation. The other respondent is a business owner in Florida who established an endowed college scholarship fund for relatives of employees.

As might be expected, planned giving is an area with which many Latinos are either not familiar or not comfortable. Only about half of the respondents said that they knew about planned giving or were familiar with the term. In fact, several attorneys said they were not familiar with the concept. Only nine respondents (15 percent) said they had made a planned gift.

One Cuban-American former business executive said he told his attorney he wanted to provide for an organization in his will because he was familiar with the concept from years of fundraising for organizations. His gift is interesting in that it illustrates an attitude that was reflected in several responses. This respondent has made a bequest to a university; however, he plans to give the organization the amount he has bequeathed during his life and then take the organization out of his will. He said he structured the gift in this manner to ensure that the university receives the amount he wishes to contribute even if he dies before he has finished making the total gift.

Several respondents stated that they want to contribute only during life. One young Cuban real estate executive said: " I'm not sure you can reach out of the grave . . . The needs of the world change. The people who stay behind me can make those choices. It's a very American concept. Maybe my great-grandchildren will do it." Asked if she wanted to learn more about it, she answered: "No. Conceptually, I have a problem with it. You are abdicating the ability of your children to make choices."

Replies to the questions about planned giving also illustrate the importance placed by the Hispanic culture on providing for family. Parents' sense of loyalty and responsibility for their children seems to prevent them from considering planned giving to charitable organizations as an alternative or in addition to leaving their wealth to their families.[24] Many said that they were not at a point in their lives where they could consider planned giving.

One attorney, whose practice consists of tax planning for wealthy clients in Florida, recounted an experience that echoed other respondents' dislike for relinquishing "control" as a reason for not contributing to endowments. "It's hard to sell planned giving with Latins," he said. "I tried once with a major client. We worked out the numbers . . . We spent a lot of money doing it. He didn't do it. The thought of putting away $1 million and losing control of it and waiting ten years didn't appeal to him."

Respondents offered reasons similar to those they gave related to endowments for why they had not made planned gifts: They have not been approached; planned gifts are for wealthier individuals; and they have other financial responsibilities, namely family.

Although several respondents expressed a dislike for United Way, at least one third of the Latinos interviewed contribute through United Way.

While their comments about United Way are interesting and should be noted as reflective of cultural idiosyncrasies, United Way has played an important role in getting many individuals started with giving in a consistent, institutionalized manner.

One Cuban-American respondent said that when he agreed to let United Way conduct a giving drive in his company, he told those who had approached him: "Ninety-nine percent of my employees will think I am getting a cut." He echoed other comments about Latino perceptions: Hispanics are very "distrusting of what is organized."

The same respondent, who spent years in corporate America, said: "I was first forced to give. It was good for my career to give and to be at those places. I never thought I'd give $1,000 to anything. If I had told my father, he would say I was stupid."

He said that when he was a young partner at a professional firm, his partner told him he had to contribute at a certain level to the United Way. The partner told him if he didn't, his bonus would reflect it at the end of the year. So, he said he marched angrily into his office and looked at the list of United Way agencies and chose a Hispanic one. "I rebelled at the Anglo system of philanthropy by giving one hundred percent of my United Way contribution to [the Hispanic organization]," he said. "I wasn't giving to them, I was slapping United Way."

He said that he has since learned the benefits of giving in an Anglo society. "What is the benefit of giving?" he asks. "Having access. It's the network . . . We don't grow up with that. In Cuba, we had our own networks. We had our social networks that had nothing to do with giving . . . Our traditions are centuries old and aren't going to die overnight because we've immigrated."[25]

The United Way has served an important function in promoting institutionalized philanthropy among Hispanics. In addition to giving at church and through religious programs, many respondents said they began giving in the workplace through United Way. Although several respondents said they had negative feelings about United Way based on their perception that they had to give, United Way played a key role in their becoming philanthropists.

Conclusions

This paper reflects preliminary findings based on interviews with an initial group of sixty respondents. The author has continued to expand the respondent pool and anticipates interviewing a total of 100 individuals. Several important points can be drawn even from this early research, however, to craft more effective approaches to Hispanic donors and prospective donors who represent financial resources that can significantly increase the pool of philanthropic dollars in the United States. An increase in philanthropy from the expanding Latino population in this country will benefit both Latino and other U. S. nonprofits.

Specific approaches need to be developed for prospective Hispanic donors. Fundraisers need to approach prospective donors in Hispanic communities in a manner very different from how they approach Anglo or other donors who are not only familiar with traditional U.S. models of philanthropy, but also culturally comfortable with them. Development professionals and key solicitors, such as the executive directors of nonprofit organizations and board members, need to learn, understand, and accept the elements of Hispanic culture that influence behavior related to charitable giving. This includes acknowledging Latinos' strong identification with national origin and culture, understanding their desire for maintaining connections with family as well as with culture and country of origin, and learning about their interests and preferences. In addition, solicitors must develop an understanding and an acceptance of what giving means in those communities and that individuals may already be giving in ways that are not counted or tax deductible.

The personal connection is crucial to Latino donors. Nonprofit organizations need to keep in mind the significance of the personal connection in Latino decisions related to charitable giving when putting together boards, and hiring staff. The identities and personal relationships of those on the development team, the board and the organization will be significant as Latino donors are typically more concerned about who is soliciting them than about some of the other benefits usually touted by development professionals. It is critical that the boards, staffs, and constituencies of organizations soliciting Hispanics include Hispanics.

Connection to the gift is important for Hispanic donors. In light of the preference among Latino donors for a connection with the gift, nonprofits approaching Latinos for financial support should attempt to create a personal relationship between the donor and the organization or recipient. Although very time-consuming, this effort could over time contribute to a comfort level resulting in larger gifts. This preference for a connection with the gift coupled with Latinos' universally strong focus on education makes scholarship funds especially attractive to Hispanic donors. This cause is one to which they especially relate; the recipient provides a personal connection and gratification is immediate. Efforts that combine the personal factor and priority areas of interest in the Hispanic community (education, family, and religion) are most likely to have appeal for Latino donors.

Latino donors are interested in organizations that serve Latinos. Despite some statements that ethnic connection to the organization is not important, programs that both operate in Hispanics' stated areas of interest and that serve Hispanics or their particular subgroups have added appeal for Latinos. One respondent made an illustrative comment: She said that she donated to a scholarship program that benefits Hispanic students not because the students are Hispanic, but because "the kids have first and last names" (they become real to her). The personal connection again plays a critical role.

Fundraisers need to understand and accept that cultivation of Hispanic donors takes more time. Fundraising in Latino communities—just like doing any kind of business with Hispanics—takes a larger investment of time than fundraising in other communities where there is an established comfort level and greater experience with institutionalized philanthropy, large organizations, endowments, foundations, and planned giving. As one Cuban-American woman who has twenty years' experience in fundraising said: "You need to cultivate the Hispanic donor more than the Anglo donor because they tend to give to people first and causes second. The tradition of philanthropy, the tax incentive is not there for them . . . In soliciting Hispanic donors, I have tried to get to know them intimately and then get them involved in the program. With Anglos, if they have a passing interest, they give. It becomes a business transaction more than a gift."

Presently, planned giving does not hold great appeal for Latinos.
Despite the popularity of planned giving among development officers
and nonprofit organizations, this is not an item that is received with great
enthusiasm by Latinos. Development professionals need to be cautious to
meet donors where they are conceptually and not try to sell them something that is not appealing or culturally relevant. Planned gifts and
endowments are not going to be immediate bestsellers with prospective
Latino donors.

The Hispanic market needs to be segmented (or *habichuelas* v. *frijoles*).
Development professionals, board members of organizations, and others
interested in promoting institutionalized philanthropy among Latino
groups need to approach this market in the way that for-profit corporations do for marketing and advertising. They need to segment the
Hispanic market and understand that what may work with Mexican
Americans in California may not work with Cuban Americans in Miami
or with Puerto Ricans in New York. (As companies like Goya Foods
know, you will be more successful selling black beans if you market them
as *habichuelas* to Puerto Ricans in New York and as *frijoles negros* to Cubans
in Miami.)[26]

The charitable giving preferences of Latinos will evolve as they
remain in the U. S. longer, as they become more a part of corporate
America and recognize the benefits of networking through community
involvement and giving, and as their professional advisors tout the benefits of charitable deductions. However, the process will take some time.
Given the increase in the Latino population and their growing financial
resources, both Latino and other U. S. nonprofits (as well as the larger
philanthropic community) need to pay attention to these current and
prospective donors. Based on this research as well as the author's experiences in raising funds from Hispanics, three elements are critical to
success with these communities: knowledge and understanding of the
donors' cultural background and giving behavior; acceptance and respect
of donors' traditions, motivations, and preferences; and approaches that
specifically respond to Latino experiences, interests, and needs. These elements coupled with the patience to develop personal relationships over
time will be key to cultivating Latino donors.

Notes

[1] Ms. Rivas-Vázquez is Vice President for Development and External Relations at St. Thomas University in Miami, Florida. She received her bachelor's and master's degrees from Georgetown University in Washington, D.C. and her juris doctor *cum laude* from the University of Miami School of Law in Miami, Florida. Ms. Rivas-Vázquez serves on the national boards of Hispanics in Philanthropy and the Esquel Group Foundation. In Miami, she serves on the boards of the Planned Giving Council of Miami-Dade County and the YWCA, as well as on the Leave A Legacy Steering Committee and the Carrollton School of the Sacred Heart Alumnae Council. Previously with Dade Community Foundation, Ms. Rivas-Vázquez has been researching the philanthropic and giving traditions of Hispanics for more than three years. In addition to her fundraising work in the United States, Ms. Rivas-Vázquez has trained board and staff members of non-profits in Central America.

[2] The terms Hispanic and Latino are used interchangeably in this paper. The author acknowledges that most individuals of Hispanic, Latino, or Latin-American origin have specific preferences for one or even none of these terms.

[3] The author uses "diverse" group, population, or background rather than "minority" because she feels that the term "minority" was developed by those in authority (or the majority) to say that a group was "less than." In addition, the term is not accurate with respect to Latinos in many communities where they now comprise more than 50 percent of the population.

[4] Bureau of the Census, Statistical Brief, September 1995.

[5] *Ibid.*

[6] Giving as measured and reported in this country also is increasing among Hispanics. See Marina Dundjerski, "Tapping the Wealth of Hispanics," *The Chronicle of Philanthropy,* October 31, 1996, 33 ("The average amount donated by contributing Hispanic households rose 22 percent from 1993 to 1995 after accounting for inflation . . .").

[7] *Ibid.*, 34.

[8] See Ana Gloria Rivas-Vázquez, "New Pools of Latino Wealth: A Case Study of Donors and Potential Donors Among Miami's Immigrant Communities" (paper

presented to the Second International Conference of Hispanics in Philanthropy, Albuquerque, New Mexico, October 3, 1995).

[9] Harold Hodgkinson and Janice Hamilton Outtz, *Hispanic Americans: A Look Back, A Look Ahead* (Washington, D. C.: Institute for Educational Leadership, Inc./Center for Demographic Policy, 1996), 5-8.

[10] Mimi Whitefield, "Cuban Americans Top List of Rich Hispanics," *The Miami Herald,* March 5, 1997, A1.

[11] Michael Cortés, "Latino Philanthropy: Some Unanswered Questions" (paper presented to the Pluralism in Philanthropy Project of the Council on Foundations, Washington, D. C., June 1, 1989).

[12] *Ibid.*, ii.

[13] *Ibid.*, 21.

[14] See Hodgkinson and Outtz, 4 ("The term 'Hispanic' is used far more often in the Eastern part of the United States. In California, the preferred term is often 'Latino' or 'Chicano.'").

[15] Hodgkinson and Outtz, 7.

[16] For a good discussion of the importance and impact of the "enclave" in the evolution of the Cuban-American community in Dade County, see Lisandro Perez, "Philanthropy Among Cuban Americans: The Demographic, Social and Cultural Factors Relevant to the Development of Organized Philanthropy Among Cuban Americans" (paper presented to the Pluralism in Philanthropy Project of the Council on Foundations, Washington, D. C., June 1, 1989).

[17] See Hodgkinson and Outtz, 10 (The median family income for Cuban Americans, although still lower than the median income for all families in the United States, is higher than that of all the other Hispanic subgroups) and 20 (Cuban Americans have higher levels of high school and college graduation rates than the other Hispanic groups).

[18] See Gustavo Perez Firmat, *Life on the Hyphen: The Cuban-American Way* (Austin: University of Texas Press, 1994).

[19] Whitefield, A1.

[20] For many immigrants, education often is the entry to a desired socioeconomic level. Consequently, Latino philanthropy reflects this value. This differs from established U. S. elites, for whom education is a matter of maintaining status. See Francie Ostrower, *Why the Wealthy Give* (Princeton: Princeton University Press, 1995) ("In cultural and educational philanthropy, we find individuals supporting organizations that have a significance for the maintenance and reproduction of their class."), 87.

[21] Dundjerski, 36 (70 percent of Hispanics are Roman Catholic.).

[22] See Hodgkinson and Outtz, 13 ("Because of the multigenerational quality of Hispanic families and households and other reasons, the Hispanic elderly are much less likely to be institutionalized than non-Hispanic White or African American elderly.").

[23] A frequently used adage, it translates as: It is better to give than to receive.

[24] This is in contrast to Ostrower's findings on the philanthropic giving of the U. S. elite: "The absence of a framework providing for a hereditary or natural right of children to inherit can be seen repeatedly in donors' comments." Ostrower, 101.

[25] See Ostrower on the significance of philanthropic institutions for the U.S. elite ("Nonprofit organizations are an important part of the milieu in which elites live. They provide an organizational basis for social and cultural life . . ."), 98.

[26] Presentation by Joseph F. Unanue, Executive Vice President, Goya Foods, Inc., New Jersey, at the Greater Miami Chamber of Commerce's Hispanic Market Seminar, September 25, 1997, Miami, Florida. Mimi Whitefield, "Goya Targets 'New Hispanics'," *The Miami Herald,* September 26, 1997, C1.

Latinos and Community Funds:
A Comparative Overview and Assessment of Latino Philanthropic Self-Help Initiatives[1]

Henry A. J. Ramos and Gabriel Kasper

What we seek—at every level—is pluralism that achieves some kind of coherence, *wholeness incorporating diversity*. . . . To prevent the wholeness from smothering diversity, there must be a philosophy of pluralism, an open climate for dissent, and an opportunity for sub-communities to retain their identity and share in the setting of larger group goals. To prevent the diversity from destroying the wholeness, there must be institutional arrangements for diminishing polarization, for teaching diverse groups to know one another, for coalition-building, dispute resolution, negotiation and mediation.

John Gardner, *Building Community*[2]

Over the last two decades, American philanthropy has begun to embrace the ideal of communities characterized by a wholeness that incorporates diversity. As the field has looked inward at increasing the representativeness of its institutions, the nation's expanding minority communities have simultaneously begun to develop new mechanisms and institutions to increase their voice in the philanthropic arena. The recent development of minority funds is a manifestation of this trend towards community-based self-help and institution building.

This article examines Latino community funds and their prospects for meaningfully adding value to mainstream philanthropy and Latino communities.[3] It reviews the evolving work of Latino funds and contextualizes assessments of the various philanthropic experiences and activities of African Americans, Asian/Pacific Americans, and women.[4] The article focuses on the strengths and weaknesses of Latino funds as perceived by practitioners and observers in the field, and it contemplates what role, if any, organized philanthropy should play in facilitating the evolution and institutionalization of these funds.

The contents of our review are based on information derived from several sources. First, we consulted relevant literature from highly-regarded scholarly and public information sources in the independent sector, including books, journal and magazine articles, and special reports. Second, we reviewed and assessed selected materials and records of leading Latino and other emerging community funds. Finally, we confidentially interviewed more than forty trustees, executives, and staff of leading private and community foundations and other key institutions in philanthropy—as well as various representatives of Latino funds— across the nation.[5]

While we conclude that Latino funds warrant expanded attention and support by organized philanthropic institutions, we believe several critical questions about the field still need to be addressed and resolved by practitioners in order to maximize the opportunities for philanthropy and Latinos to mutually benefit from this work. We believe that further research would help to resolve these questions, by helping to clarify the impacts and limits of Latino funds, their strengths and weaknesses, and their prospects for refinement and improvement. Finally, we believe that Latino fund principals and representatives of organized philanthropy would benefit from expanded opportunities to interact in order to share information, knowledge, and learning of value to the field.

Overview of the Community Fund Movement

Demographic shifts in the United States have pushed questions of diversity and pluralism to the forefront of public debate. Although today, white Americans constitute nearly 75 percent of the U. S. population, by the year 2000 it is estimated that one out of every three American workers will be nonwhite.[6] According to a recent U. S. Census Bureau count, by 2050 nonwhites will make up 49 percent of the U. S. population.[7] African American, Asian/Pacific American, and Latino communities are growing at such a rapid pace that "minority" populations appear destined to become the American majority.

As these populations grow, many of them face severe and deteriorating socioeconomic conditions. Between 1980 and 1990, for example, the number of African Americans living in concentrated areas of poverty increased nearly 40 percent;[8] and by 1996 the overall poverty rate for African Americans exceeded 28 percent.[9] The poverty rate for Hispanics in the U. S. is now greater than 29 percent,[10] and for the large and growing Asian/Pacific American immigrant communities of New York and Los Angeles, the poverty population was about 25 percent in 1990.[11]

The depth of need within many communities of color poses serious problems and choices for the country as a whole. As minority populations rapidly become the American majority, expanded investment in their health and development will be critical to stem the troubled trajectory of a large proportion of the nation's people.

Over the past twenty years, these circumstances have led philanthropy to expand its attention to the inclusiveness of its organizations and practices relative to growing minority populations. Beginning in the 1970s, mainstream foundations began to address research that illustrated the lack of minority representation in philanthropy and that highlighted the dearth of funds provided to minority constituencies.[12] Foundations began to recognize the need to promote pluralism in order to expand their social responsiveness and impacts. According to a statement by the Council on Foundations in 1973, "Diversified boards and staffs will insure the sensitivity of foundations to the needs of segments of the society who have often been denied adequate voice and representation."[13]

Since that 1973 policy statement, foundations have made inroads towards increasing the diversity of their staffs. For African Americans and women, who respectively make up about 13 percent and 51 percent of the total U. S. population,[14] the percentages of foundation staff representing those constituencies now actually exceed their proportional representation in American society.[15] Other groups, like Hispanics and Asian/Pacific Americans, who respectively make up roughly 11 percent[16] and 4 percent[17] of U. S. society, have a longer way to go, however. According to a 1991 study by Emmett Carson, 78 percent of program staff professionals at 721 foundations reviewed were white, 14 percent were African American, 5 percent were Hispanic, and 2 percent were Asian/Pacific American. Women were especially well represented, making up some 66 percent of program staffs reviewed.[18]

Compared to the gradual diversification of foundation staff in recent years, the composition of philanthropic leadership in CEO positions and on foundation boards has not kept pace with the nation's evolving demography. According to a 1994 Council on Foundations report, only 4 percent of foundation CEO positions were held by people of color.[19] And Carson's 1991 study found that just 20 percent of the members of foundation governing boards were women, and only 14 percent were people of color.[20] Twenty-three of the seventy-five foundations reviewed in a 1990 Women and Foundations/Corporate Philanthropy report, moreover, had no women trustees at all. Almost half had no racial minorities on their boards.[21]

As minority populations and their share of social and economic needs have grown, mainstream philanthropic institutions have been accused by some observers of slowness to sufficiently expand their institutional diversity and hesitancy to change their funding agendas in response to changing realities. Many minority and independent sector leaders acknowledge a significant gap between the growth and needs of minority communities and the support they receive from organized philanthropy.[22] In fact, in 1992, foundation support for specifically Black, Hispanic, and Asian/Pacific American organizations was only about 5 percent of all foundation giving.[23] African-American groups received just over 3 percent of foundation grants; Hispanic nonprofits, less than 2 percent; and Asian/Pacific American agencies just 0.2 percent. Of course, *these statistics do not reflect the reality that many foundation grants to mainstream organizations substantially benefit minority constituents.* They do, however, suggest a disconnect between the largely minority makeup of society's neediest constituencies and organized philanthropy's overwhelmingly mainstream grantee pools.

Foundation Giving to Minority Populations (1992)		
RACE/ETHNICITY	U. S. POPULATION (%)	DOLLARS AWARDED (%)
Hispanics	9.5	1.4
Asian/Pacific Americans	3.2	0.2
African Americans	12.4	3.4

Sources: Bothwell and Priestman, Foundations and Civil Rights, 1995 and U. S. Bureau of the Census, Statistical Abstract, 1995.

Minority community funds have emerged, in large measure, as a response to the sense among many within communities of color that organized philanthropy has not fully or sufficiently reached them. According to community fund leaders and supporters, the funds are logical vehicles for self-help in this context. One fund executive we interviewed explained, "[The mainstream] is not responding, so [we've] got to do it [ourselves]." Community funds aim to increase the amount of corporate, foundation, and individual donations directed to underserved minority populations, to promote leadership and participation by communities of color in the philanthropic process, to expand philanthropic responsiveness to changing community needs, and to serve as intermediaries to convene and advocate for minority nonprofits and constituencies.

Critics of minority funds question whether the establishment of separate, ethnically-concentrated funding institutions advances the interests of a truly inclusive philanthropy. They worry that the creation of a set of specialized funds may ultimately run counter to the goal of pluralizing mainstream philanthropy and they highlight a number of practical, structural, and operational issues that limit the effectiveness of these organizations, including, among other things, their perceived lack of administrative efficiency, program sophistication, and leadership.

Group-specific philanthropic institutions are not unprecedented in American history. In fact, U. S. religious communities of Protestants, Catholics, and Jews have long supported far-reaching philanthropic programs designed to promote education, social investment, and political agendas of particular interest to their members.[24] Late nineteenth and early twentieth century social reformers, such as Jane Addams, were instrumental in developing and soliciting charitable support for benevolent societies, settlement houses, and education and training programs targeted to immigrants in the nation's large northeastern and midwestern cities.[25] And, more recently, women's funds have emerged across the nation to expand philanthropic and charitable attention to the needs of American women and girls.[26]

Drawing on these traditions, supporters of minority funds argue that their efforts are simply a natural extension of established philanthropic models for community building and civic participation in America. They see these funds as efforts to help strengthen organized philanthropy by channeling more capital from a mix of community and mainstream institutional sources into rapidly expanding communities that otherwise lack the experience and/or the resources needed to maximize their potential contributions to the field as donors, grants administrators, and volunteers.

More critical observers argue, on the other hand, that minority funds differ from earlier efforts, such as those targeted to religious and immigrant communities, or more recent efforts targeted to women and girls. Today's minority funds, they say, primarily seek capitalization and public legitimacy from large, mainstream philanthropies that earlier groups first sought and obtained through decidedly community-based fundraising efforts. This tendency to look first to established philanthropic institutions rather than community-based sources of support appears to some to distort the traditional process through which newcomer constituencies have achieved standing and impact in America's independent sector. For many established philanthropic leaders, therefore, the emergence of minority funds has provoked reservations and doubts about their compatibility with mainstream foundation priorities and interests.

Our review seeks to examine these tensions in perspective and evolving practice as they apply to emerging Latino funds. In order to place this work in context, however, our assessment incorporates a broader examination of the *various* institutional models, practices, and constituencies that inform the minority fund field. We also consider—for purposes of comparison and contrast—the work and experiences of women's foundations and funds, which to some observers establish a model of sorts for sustainable philanthropic self-help in Latino and other minority communities.

Types of Community Funds

Community funds typically use various organizational strategies to generate contributions, including organizing benefits, charitable drives, and other events, as well as soliciting funds from individual, corporate, and foundation donors. Based on their structure for obtaining and managing money, most of these funds follow one of three distinct organizational models: the Workplace Giving Fund Model, the Field of Interest Fund Model, or the Independent Fund Model.[27]

The Workplace Giving Fund Model

Funds that follow the workplace giving model generate money primarily from members of their respective ethnic constituencies through annual worksite fundraising drives that channel monies raised back into community-based nonprofits. Some of these funds act as independent grantmakers and technical assistance providers to new and emerging groups in their communities of interest. Others function as formal federations of established minority nonprofits that raise money and conduct technical assistance programs primarily for the benefit of their member agencies.

These funds began largely as an effort to add more choice and reach to the workplace giving campaigns run by the United Way of America. The United Way of America was incorporated in its present form in 1970 to reach charitable contributors at the workplace, and until recently it has maintained a virtual monopoly on worksite and employee payroll deduction campaigns.[28] Its campaigns have raised as much as $2 billion in charitable contributions each year to be distributed at United Way's discretion. But United Way's dominance in workplace giving has increasingly raised criticisms and challenges among minority constituencies and emerging nonprofit groups. According to the National Committee For Responsive Philanthropy (NCRP), new and small agencies, such as those that typically make up the nonprofit sector in many U. S. communities of color, have difficulty getting support from the United Way. Although the United Way helps to support 45,000 agencies, nearly half of the United Way's money goes to affiliates of twelve long-established agencies like the Boy Scouts, the YMCA, and the Red Cross, whose proximity and responsiveness to minority populations are often perceived in communities of color as wanting and insufficient. In addition, fewer than two new organizations are added to the largest United Way campaigns each year. This makes it extremely difficult for even the most innovative and effective emerging minority nonprofits to gain access to workplace campaign funds.

Since 1976, debate over the practices of the United Way has been focused on access to the Combined Federal Campaign (CFC), the federal government's annual workplace giving drive. The eventual opening of the CFC, the largest workplace charitable drive in the country (accounting for more than $200 million in annual donations from federal and military employees), was the result of pressures applied from a variety of sources. In 1980, as a result of Congressional hearings and recommendations that the CFC be opened to more charities, the U. S. Civil Service Commission (now the Office of Personnel Management) opened the CFC to a new category of National Service Agencies and to local unaffiliated agencies. One month later, the National Black United Fund (NBUF) won a four-year lawsuit in U. S. federal court to allow it entry into the CFC. In December of 1987 federal legislation finally completed the opening of the CFC.

This course of events allowed hundreds, and eventually thousands, of new organizations to enter into the CFC, and was followed by the opening of many corporate giving campaigns across the country. According to NCRP, by 1992 nontraditional funds such as the Black United Fund had expanded their contributions in this new environment by more than 22 percent. Meanwhile, the United Way, adjusted to account for inflation, grew just two percent *in toto* in the twenty years from 1971 to 1991. Between 1991 and 1996, total giving to alternative funds grew $64 million (to $310 million in 1997), nearly approaching the United Way's $82 million (to $2.119 billion) in growth, despite the United Way's enormous advantages in size and national name recognition.[29]

These dramatic figures suggest that the United Way's single, general fund model (with limited community reach and accountability) has fallen into increasing disfavor with the donor public during recent years. As this has occurred, a wide variety of local minority funds in places such as Los Angeles have succeeded in workplace campaigns that raise funds from and for their respective ethnic constituencies, in direct competition with United Way affiliates. Some minority funds, such as those in San

Francisco and New York City, have leveraged the field's expansion to broker mutually beneficial partnerships with United Way affiliates.

Notwithstanding these indicators of expanding success, minority workplace giving funds have experienced contemporaneous challenges that have compelled many of them to seek substantial new revenue streams from foundations, corporations, and private individual donors of means. To begin, the very nature of cyclical workplace giving campaigns, and their derivative community grantmaking initiatives, has prohibited the development of endowment resources and unduly subjected fund growth and outputs to the vagaries of each year's highly uncertain fundraising inputs. Second, corporate downsizing resulting from the pressures of expanded international competition, merger activity, and public deregulation has altered the shape of the American workforce.[30] The increasing percentage of U. S. workers employed by small businesses has reduced the size of workforce giving pools, as smaller employers generally have not participated in workplace solicitation campaigns. Finally, the simultaneous impacts of recent economic restructuring and governmental disengagement in minority and disadvantaged communities have dramatically expanded the human problems and needs that minority funds have been established to address;[31] not surprisingly, such problems and needs are radically outstripping the response capacities of even the most successful workplace fundraising institutions.

The Field of Interest Fund Model

Field of interest funds are typically started as specific, targeted funds housed within a community foundation. These special interest funds attempt to build endowments and to make grants from interest earned on their endowment corpus. Final grantmaking authority over the distribution of these funds is usually retained by the sponsoring foundation's board and staff, but with meaningful involvement of boards of local minority leaders. Such funds generally operate, in fact, with substantial assistance and oversight from community volunteers and with limited community foundation staff engagement. Because of their formal affiliation with larger community foundations, however, the administrative, investment, legal, and accounting functions of these funds are managed, and ultimately controlled, by foundation staff.

At the end of 1992, there existed at least 100 community foundation funds throughout the United States that targeted ethnic minorities.[32] About 40 percent of these funds were African American community-focused, some 37 percent were Hispanic funds, and about 10 percent were Asian/Pacific American funds. Asset bases in this cohort of minority funds ranged from $1,000 to $1.1 million.

Community foundation fundraising targeted to minorities and women is expanding as these institutions come to appreciate the nation's rapidly changing demography; and the trend is being accelerated by forward-looking grantmaking and promotional efforts focused on community foundations recently undertaken by influential leaders in philanthropy, such as the Ford Foundation and the Council on Foundations. According to a recent Council on Foundations report, *The Value of Difference: Enhancing Philanthropy Through Inclusiveness in Governance, Staffing and Grantmaking*:

> [D]emographic shifts so apparent on the grantmaking side of philanthropy are also changing the terrain on the fundraising side . . .
>
> Funds within community foundations by and for African Americans, Latinos and women are growing steadily. In Ohio alone, for example, there are two new African American funds, one at the Dayton Foundation, the other at the Community Foundation of Greater Lorain County, where an Hispanic fund and a women's fund has also just been created.[33]

The expanding convergence of community foundation grantmaking interests and activities with those of minorities and women has also recently been evidenced by significant new initiatives in states like Arizona, Minnesota, and Texas. In Arizona, the state's community foundation recently received a $6 million bequest, its largest ever, from Florita Evans, a Puerto Rican woman and long-time resident of Phoenix. The donation will be used to challenge other women and persons of color to expand their charitable contributions through the community foundation. In Minnesota, the Saint Paul Foundation has recently committed $2 million to leverage an equal amount of giving towards the establishment of a Diversity Endowment Fund. The Fund will seek 1:1 match donations from minority donors of Black, Latino, Asian/Pacific American, and Native American ancestry, to establish a grantmaking endowment that will support community nonprofits in each of the target fundraising communities. And in Texas, the El Paso Community Foundation has recently raised more than $8 million in mostly unrestricted funds from some fifty Latino families to support its largely Hispanic-focused grantmaking programs.

Many minority leaders in the philanthropic and community foundations, encouraged by these developments, are quite optimistic about the emergence of wealthy philanthropists within their communities and about the prospects for minorities and women to play an increasing role in the independent sector as it prepares for substantial infusions of new wealth during the coming decades.[34] But even optimistic observers are uncertain about the real, long-term likelihood of community foundations successfully pursuing more diverse donors, absent substantial external support and technical assistance. And many observers express reservations about the potential opportunity costs for minority constituencies, if historically unrepresentative community foundations are encouraged to benefit from increased minority donations without being challenged to expand minority engagement in their governance and staffing. Consequently, some believe that private foundations and corporations committed to diversity and the nonprofit sector should increase their funding support for community foundation initiatives that help simultaneously to expand diversity-focused giving, programming, and representation at these institutions.

The Independent Fund Model

The Independent Fund Model consists of community-driven efforts to develop freestanding, private grantmaking institutions that are neither dependent upon workplace giving campaigns nor affiliated with a local or regional community foundation. These efforts, relatively few in number, substantially mirror the tendencies of established mainstream grantmaking institutions, both with respect to their organizational structures and their focus on servicing the financial and community interests of wealthy donors. What differentiates this work from standard philanthropic norms is its conscious predisposition to promote decidedly group-specific grantmaking and community interests that are typically underrepresented in organized philanthropy.

Independent funds are especially limited in number within the African-American and Latino communities. A 1994 listing of African-

American foundations and funds of all types assembled by the Council on Foundations includes some twenty private, freestanding Black grantmaking institutions. Most of these entities are affiliated with noted African-American entertainment figures, such as Motown records founder Berry Gordy and entertainer Bill Cosby, or sports celebrities, such as Olympic medalist Jackie Joyner-Kersee and baseball star Dave Winfield. For the most part, these grantmaking organizations support activities focused on youth, education, arts, and economic development in the black community.

Latino independent funds appear to be even fewer in number, more celebrity-focused, and more geared to youth educational opportunities than the African-American funds. One recent survey conducted with support from Hispanics in Philanthropy identified three independent Latino funds. Two of these funds were sponsored by entertainers, namely singer/recording artist Vikki Carr and television talk-show host Geraldo Rivera. The third fund was supported by former NFL football player-turned businessman Danny Villanueva. Each of these funds focuses on educational scholarships for Latino high school and college students.

Asian/Pacific American participation in the independent fund field is more difficult to track owing to a scarcity of data on the subject; but a 1990 *Foundation News* report on Chinese-American family foundations estimates the existence of more than 100 such foundations with combined annual giving totaling some $3.5 million.[35] Among the priority areas funded by these family grantmaking institutions are church development campaigns and senior health care and housing programs in largely Chinese-American neighborhoods. A recent, informal Ford Foundation listing of seventy minority foundations, however, includes only three Asian/Pacific American foundations, two of which are focused on Chinese Americans.[36]

Women are both well represented and well organized in the independent fund sector, with some sixty-five foundations, federations, and funds operating under the umbrella of the Women's Funding Network, including such reputable groups as the Ms. Foundation and the Global Fund for Women.[37] During recent years especially, independent women's foundations have been particularly effective fundraisers. A 1993 assessment of the field places the assets raised by forty leading women's funds during 1985-1992 at more than $80 million.[38]

Advocates of minority and women's interests in philanthropy often cite the development of independent funds as optimal for these groups, for several reasons. First, such funds can operate unencumbered by the practical and institutional constraints of workplace fundraising campaigns and community foundation administrative structures. Second, they can better help to develop the base of minority and women's expertise as foundation trustees and grantmaking executives by enabling those groups themselves to control appointments to board and staff, and to manage the growth and distribution of fund endowment assets. Finally, in the process, they can afford expanded opportunities for the field to engage and develop minority and women money managers and professional consultants who are typically underrepresented in the work of mainstream giving institutions.[39]

Regrettably, due to comparatively low levels of wealth and still limited acculturation to philanthropy, most black, Latino, and Asian communities in the United States today remain dramatically underrepresented in the independent fund field. As a practical matter, the capital required to establish and maintain these funds often exceeds the giving capacities of minority donors. In addition, knowledge about the strategies that are most effective in promoting the formation of freestanding giving institutions among these groups is only beginning to evolve. As a result, some observers of the field argue that expanded financial and technical assistance support for minority-focused efforts to establish independent funds is a necessary ingredient in the evolving agenda of established grantmaking institutions concerned about promoting diversity in the independent sector.

Community-Based Philanthropy: Recent Trends, Accomplishments, and Issues Among African-American, Asian/Pacific American, and Women's Groups

African Americans

Although African Americans constitute almost 13 percent of the U. S. population, annual funding of African-American nonprofits represented just 3.4 percent of all foundation grants as recently as 1992. This relative absence of parity between African-American population share and levels of foundation giving targeted to black groups is striking, considering the deteriorating conditions that have afflicted African-American communities during the past decade. Social commentator Jeremy Rifkin, for example, has noted in his widely read book, *The End of Work*, that recent economic trends have fundamentally altered the sociology of America's black community.

> Permanent joblessness has led to an escalating crime wave in the streets of America's cities and the wholesale disintegration of Black family life. The statistics are chilling. By the late 1980s, one out of every four young African American males was either in prison or on probation . . . The leading cause of death among young Black males is now murder [and] 62 percent of all Black families are single parent households.

The socioeconomic consequences of these developments for African-American communities have been devastating. The Black poverty rate is now 28.4 percent, almost three times the average for whites. Unemployment among blacks is nearly 10 percent (compared to just 3.9 percent for whites);[40] and since 1973, real earnings among low-skilled African-American males have declined close to 25 percent (compared to about 14 percent for comparably situated whites).

In order to expand the philanthropic support base committed to addressing these many problems, black communities have developed a number of successful self-help philanthropic institutions in recent years.[41] While a number of African-American foundations and wealthy black independent donors have emerged,[42] much of the philanthropic initiative of African-Americans has developed in the context of community-focused fundraising federations. Instead of targeting large corporate, foundation, and individual donors, these federated institutions focus almost exclusively on workplace giving campaigns as a way of opening up new opportunities for nonwealthy blacks to support programs that address the needs of largely African-American neighborhoods and communities. In essence, these efforts tap the widely underappreciated propensity of African Americans to give to community charities. According to research conducted under the auspices of the Joint Center for Political and Economic Studies, Black Americans are as likely to make charitable contributions as whites, and in comparable amounts, despite having income levels that are lower than whites.

Black community funds provide an alternative to the United Way as a workplace fundraising source for many African-American community groups that were widely felt to have been denied adequate access to United Way funds in the past. According to Emmett Carson, writing in his recent book, *A Hand Up: Black Philanthropy and Self-Help in America*:

> Perhaps the strongest impetus for the formation of these federations was the perceived inequities in allocation of funds by the established federations [and the] belief that newer organizations representing minority groups and nontraditional interests . . . all too often were denied entry to the United Way system altogether, or received too small a share of the funds collected.

The National Black United Fund (NBUF) was formed in 1974 by Walter Bremond as "a black alternative to United Way." Since leading and winning the landmark 1980 legal decision that helped non-United Way federations to participate in the Combined Federal Campaign (the annual fundraising drive held at federal government workplaces), NBUF has grown to include twenty affiliates in eighteen states; and it has gained entry into a wide range of corporate employee giving campaigns at companies such as IBM, AT&T, Bell Labs, Safeway, Nike, and Hughes Aircraft. National Black United Fund affiliates across the country raised an estimated $5.4 million in 1996, with projected fundraising of $5.6 million in 1997 (approximately $267,000 per fund).

Although NBUF affiliates stand at varying stages of organizational development and capacity, at least twelve of these organizations have full-time staff members (the remaining eight operate exclusively through volunteer support). Community engagement is significant in most of the Fund's affiliate states and localities. In some cases, several hundred African-American volunteers are engaged in the fundraising and grant-making activities of NBUF affiliates. Since NBUF's various affiliate funds are governed by all African-American boards and executive staff, black civic participation and leadership development are significant by-products of this work.

Neither NBUF nor its various affiliates maintains an endowment fund; instead, they recycle funds raised each year directly back into African-American community initiatives. In 1993, NBUF and its affiliates raised more than $5 million and gave a combined $3.5 million in grants to nonprofits serving African-American communities. Typically, NBUF and its affiliates directly support groups and activities not considered by more traditional funders, such as training and technical assistance programs targeted to emerging nonprofits and grassroots advocacy groups, as well as local economic self-help business and employment initiatives that benefit predominantly black neighborhoods.

In addition to the NBUF's efforts, other African-American federations, such as the Associated Black Charities (ABC) of New York City, have formed to serve the needs of nonprofit groups working within their local communities. ABC has awarded more than $3.5 million in grants to over sixty member agencies in New York since it was founded in 1982. The United Black Fund (UBF) has operated as a federation of black charities in Washington D. C. since 1969. Unlike the Black United Fund, the UBF partnered with the United Way and became the first black charitable federation to gain entry into the Combined Federal Campaign back in 1973. The UBF also works with the United Way of the National Capital Area to conduct an annual payroll-deduction campaign targeted to private sector employees in the region. In 1990, UBF awarded more than $2.6 million to member and nonmember agencies.

According to several UBF executives and community observers we interviewed in preparing this article, African-American workplace giving institutions have typically made a conscious effort not to solicit grants and donations from large foundations and corporations. In general, fund principals have concluded that dependence on such sources of support, while legitimate for other black groups, would risk diminishing community control of their funding and development. Moreover, exploring and obtaining an expanded engagement with mainstream funders would dissipate already scarce and needed organizational resources, retard community volunteerism in support of their work (by expanding their imperatives to professionalize), and fundamentally contradict their commitment to community self-help and independence.

The predisposition of many black community fund executives effectively to opt out of the mainstream grantseeking arena draws on historical, and arguably unique, strands in African-American community experience and discourse. As one group of eminent black scholars has pointed out:

> The "self-help" tradition is so embedded in black heritage as to be
> virtually synonymous with it. Self-initiated efforts without assistance
> from the larger society—indeed, often in spite of resistance from the

society—have found expression throughout our history in this country. The tradition of building institutions and initiating efforts both to defend [ourselves] and to advance within a hostile society has long been a hallmark of black American life.[43]

Both building on and embodying this tradition, community leaders such as Marcus Garvey and Malcolm X have, to varying degrees, encouraged models of Black separatism. At the same time, the inclination to separatism has competed in the hearts and minds of Black Americans with the more integrationist programs of leaders such as W. E. B. Dubois and Dr. Martin Luther King, Jr., whose social and political views have tended to inform institutional thinking and practice on diversity issues in philanthropy and other sectors of U. S. life.

As we will later see, notions of community separation versus integration as they have been defined within the Black experience—and as they are understood by mainstream funders—often have much to do with how community funds are perceived in the philanthropic field; and this has significant consequences for community-based philanthropic efforts in Latino and other emerging ethnic communities.

Asian/Pacific Americans

While U. S. minority issues have historically been cast largely in terms of Black experiences, the rapid emergence of other large communities of color in the United States in recent decades has begun to expand national attention to the circumstances and needs of Asian/Pacific American groups. The Asian/Pacific American community presently represents only about 3 percent of the nation's population; but it has nearly doubled in size during the past decade and it will likely more than double again, to nearly 8 percent of the total U. S. population, by 2050.

Despite their growing presence in other spheres of American life, Asian/Pacific Americans are largely underrepresented in philanthropic circles. A 1990 survey of seventy-five foundations found that just two had Asian Americans on their boards. The lack of an Asian/Pacific American presence within philanthropic institutions has been matched by extremely low levels of foundation support for Asian-American communities and nonprofits over the years. Just 0.2 percent of philanthropic dollars granted between 1983 and 1990, for example, went to Asian/Pacific American issues and groups.[44] Most of this funding came from just five foundations, and the number of foundations supporting Asian/Pacific American issues and needs has not expanded appreciably since 1983.

Many Asian-American leaders believe this limited support results from a misperception among foundations and other mainstream leaders and groups that Asian Americans do not need charitable help, owing to their widely publicized successes in education and industry. According to *Invisible and in Need*, a recent study supported by Asian/Pacific American foundation professionals to assess the state of Asian/Pacific nonprofits in the United States, "Although the media has portrayed Asian and Pacific Islander ethnic groups as a monolithic 'model minority' that succeeds in spite of societal barriers, this stereotype obscures serious needs among Asian/Pacific Americans." For example, although 17 percent of Asian American and Pacific Islanders in the United States have household incomes greater than $75,000, one in every five Asian-American children grows up in poverty; and public policy research think tank Leadership Education for Asian Pacifics (LEAP) and UCLA researchers report new findings showing that Asian/Pacific Americans, like African Americans, earn 10 to 13 percent less than comparably trained non-Hispanic white workers.

Responding to these circumstances is complicated by the diverse languages, histories, and cultures of the Asian/Pacific population. One of the major factors now affecting the character of Asian/Pacific community development, in fact, is the recent growth of significant refugee populations from nations such as Vietnam, Cambodia, and Laos. In addition, recent years have seen substantial growth in the number of immigrants emanating from Korea, Taiwan, the Philippines, Samoa, and Guam. According to LEAP and UCLA researchers, "From a largely American-born group of 1.5 million in 1970, the Asian/Pacific population has been transformed through large-scale immigration to a predominantly foreign-born population of 7.3 million in 1990 . . ."[45]

While many Asian immigrant groups have come to this country through family reunification allowances under U. S. law and have included highly educated and trained individuals, increasing numbers of Asian/Pacific newcomers consist of highly impoverished refugees who have required substantial public and social assistance. During recent hard economic times, such groups, like other immigrant populations, have encountered increasingly hostile responses to their presence in this country from more established groups concerned about the immigrants' long-term impacts on job availability and the quality of life in the United States.

Although wealthy Asian donors remain relatively underrepresented in overall philanthropic giving and Japanese and other Asian corporations are often criticized for being unresponsive in their giving,[46] Asian/Pacific American philanthropy has responded to changing community realities through a wide range of charitable giving structures. For example, the Council on Foundations' 1993 *Donors of Color* report details the recent development of at least ten Asian/Pacific American special interest funds housed within community foundations. Three of these funds are housed at the San Francisco Foundation, three at the Hawaii Community Foundation, one at the Rockford Connecticut Foundation, two at the Boston Foundation, and one at the Greater Beloit Community Trust of Wisconsin.

Individual donors have also begun to help establish a more developed Asian/Pacific American philanthropic community through the establishment of their own family foundations and giving programs. A 1990 *Foundation News* article, for example, reported that a growing number of wealthy Chinese individuals in the United States have established independent family foundations, controlling assets of more than $50 million. Moreover, the philanthropic largesse of individuals such as Korean American businessman Chong-Moon Lee, who recently committed $15 million to the San Francisco Asian Art Museum, has widely increased appreciation of donor potential within the Asian/Pacific American community.[47]

In addition to these emerging philanthropic efforts, a number of community funds have recently developed to further address the needs and concerns of Asian/Pacific American groups, particularly those operating at the grassroots level. Presently, this field includes the Asian American Federation (AAF) of New York, the Asian/Pacific American Community Fund of San Francisco (APAC), and the Asian/Pacific Community Fund of Southern California (APCF). These funds—each of which is involved in some type of workplace fundraising—attempt to expand the support base for local Asian community groups and to increase Asian-American and Pacific Islander participation in philanthropic decision making. They award grants each year in the range of $100,000 to $150,000.

The APCF—which presently has no endowment campaign in place—supports its grantmaking activities mainly through independent workplace fundraising efforts, often in competition with the local United Way. It supports a broadly diverse affiliate network of sixteen Asian/Pacific community organizations, and also administers a small competitive allocations program targeted to nonaffiliate agencies in the community. The APAC and AAF, meanwhile, have developed in affiliation with local United Ways in their regions and, in addition to participating in workplace campaigns, they attempt to raise grantmaking as well as endowment funds through appeals to foundations, corporations, and wealthy individual donors. The San Francisco fund incorporates fifty-four local affiliate agencies and has conducted surveys to publicly report on the status of Asian/Pacific nonprofits and groups in the regional independent sector.[48] The AAF receives funds from the United Way general pool for regranting to its twenty-eight local member agencies, and its work includes support for a community task force on aging and scholarships designed to expand the local pool of Asian/Pacific American social workers.

Two of these funds have substantially emphasized management training and technical assistance, as well as coalition-building efforts, designed to expand the capacities and impacts of their member agencies and the many ethnic constituencies they represent. In this way, these funds play an important bridging role, not only vis-a-vis foundations and other mainstream institutions, but also within the larger and highly diverse Asian/Pacific American community. A major focus of the community funding and public advocacy produced by these groups relates to the need to expand nonprofit services targeted to Asian/Pacific constituencies, especially bilingual/bicultural services for needy recent immigrants. Basic services for Asian/Pacific groups and newcomer populations are typically underfunded by mainstream institutions. In San Francisco, for example, where Asian/Pacific Americans are 20 percent of the local population (60 percent of which is foreign-born), Asian service agencies receive only 0.5 percent of funds distributed by local foundations and only 6.4 percent of local government block grants.

The board and executive leadership of these funds tends to be exclusively Asian/Pacific American in makeup; and consistent with their community bridging aims, fund leadership typically reflects the broad diversity of ethnic groups within the larger Asian/Pacific community. The quality and level of professional leadership that these funds have attracted, moreover, is impressive and arguably distinctive in the minority workplace giving field. The San Francisco-based APAC Fund board, for example, includes former University of California at Berkeley chancellor Chang-Lin Tien, Yahoo! co-founder Jerry Yang, AirTouch COO Arun Sarin, and GAP community affairs executive Myra Chow; in addition, two CEOs of small, successful Bay Area technology companies and two senior vice-presidents representing a large bank and a utility company also participate as members of the fund's board. In Los Angeles, Warren Furitani, the executive director of the APCF, is a highly regarded former member of the Los Angeles City School Board.

On balance, while Asian/Pacific fund leaders with whom we spoke are concerned about long-term overdependency on mainstream funders, they have been relatively receptive to short-term relationships that help their organizations obtain catalytic start-up and endowment assistance from these sources. For each of these groups, private institutional support has been uneven but growing during recent years. This past year, for example, the APCF—which supports its important work mainly through workplace fundraising—secured more than $100,000 in private support for the first time since its founding in 1991, through grants from funders including GTE and Kaiser Permanente. The San Francisco and New York funds, on the other hand, have experienced greater success tapping mainstream funding, primarily through substantial annual grants derived from their affiliations with local United Ways; but these funds have also developed with meaningful grant assistance from leading private foundations and corporations interested in their work. The APAC fund, for example, generated more than $50,000 in private assistance to support its 1994 start-up budget of approximately $150,000, including grants from the Evelyn and Walter Haas, Jr. Fund, the Levi Strauss Foundation, and Pacific Gas and Electric Company. The New York fund, founded in 1989, generated nearly $250,000 of its $700,000 operating budget for 1995 from private foundation and corporate sources, including The Joyce Mertz Gilmore Foundation, the New York Foundation, and AT&T.

Women

Several grantmaking professionals with whom we spoke see the women's fund movement as a model for community fund development among ethnic and minority constituencies. Women's funds, which trace their roots to the establishment of the Ms. Foundation in 1973 with profits from *Ms.* magazine,[49] attempt to address the continuing neglect by many traditional funders of women and girls. By 1994, there were approximately sixty women's funds in the country with assets totaling over $50 million. The number of funds is estimated to have grown to almost ninety by 1997.[50]

The funds are rooted in a long tradition of women working for social and political reform. According to scholar Marsha Shapiro Rose in a report for *Nonprofit and Voluntary Sector Quarterly*, "For many women, volunteer work was viewed as a necessary part of their social world. Whether motivated by noblesse oblige, family traditions of community service, or a sense of the importance of maintaining class boundaries, women of the upper class often worked in voluntary positions." Although women— especially upper-class women—have made significant contributions to the work of the voluntary philanthropic sector, control over *organized* philanthropic institutions and finances has until recently been left mainly to their fathers, husbands, and other male advisers.

The notion of charity as "women's work"[51] has resulted in relatively high female representation on foundation staffs. According to a recent Council on Foundations report, women made up nearly 76 percent of all foundation staff positions in 1994, up from 60 percent in 1984.[52] And since the 1980s, the growth of women in the labor force and the rise of feminism have contributed to an increase in the number of women running philanthropic programs and organizations. The number of women foundation CEOs has risen from just 27 percent in 1984 to 43 percent in 1994; and women now run some of the nation's leading foundations, including the Ford Foundation, the John D. and Catherine T. MacArthur Foundation, and the Pew Charitable Trusts. But women as a whole remain largely underrepresented on the boards and key committees of mainstream foundations. A 1990 Women and Foundations/Corporate Philanthropy study found, for example, that just 20 percent of the trustees of seventy-five foundations reviewed were women.

Since the early 1980s, women's funds have created a new environment for women's governance in philanthropy. In the management and operation of these funds, "women raise the dollars and decide how they're spent."[53] In essence, women's funds have created a new training ground for female philanthropic practitioners as chief executive officers, program managers, and board members. In addition, women's funds have increasingly focused on and met with success in broadly improving their inclusion of racially and ethnically diverse groups in their appointments and programming.

Many of these diverse new participants in the women's funding field have brought extensive mainstream philanthropic and/or community political experience with them. For example, the San Francisco Women's Foundation is run by Patti Chang, an Asian/Pacific American woman with extensive community and public policy experience, and its board includes Luz Vega-Marquis, a Latina trustee of California's largest private foundation (the California Wellness Foundation) and a former trustee of the Council on Foundations. The Global Fund for Women's new Asian-American executive director, Kavita Ramdas, is a former program executive at the John D. and Catherine T. MacArthur Foundation. And The Women's Fund of the Milwaukee Foundation includes Gwen T. Jackson, an African-American woman who once chaired the Milwaukee Foundation's board of trustees. Leadership of this stature and expertise has substantially advanced the credibility and impact of women's funds.

Meanwhile, serious challenges still confront these groups. A growing concern of women's funds is the apparent lack of a strong correlation between the representation of women in key positions at mainstream foundations and the amount of funds directed by these funders to organizations and programs specifically dedicated to women and girls. Although the dollars awarded to programs for women and girls nearly doubled in the 1980s—as a percentage of total grants from foundations—funding for women's groups was just 5.3 percent of all grant dollars awarded in 1992, up from just 2.9 percent in 1981. According to *Worlds Apart: Missed Opportunities to Help Women and Girls*, these figures illustrate how "funders believe a gender focus is not important, as they think females are adequately served by universal programs."

The case for expanding foundation support targeted to nonprofits that focus on women's and girls' issues would appear to be somewhat compelling. Seventy-five percent of the U. S. population living officially at or below the poverty line today are women and the children in their care;[54] and women continue to experience substantial wage and income discrimination throughout the economy, notwithstanding their expanding presence in and responsibilities at the workplace.[55] Many of the issues seen as funding priorities for women's funds—the breakdown of the family structure, reproductive health, child care, workplace discrimination, and domestic violence—constitute some of the most urgent problems facing the country as a whole; yet still relatively few foundations and corporations support women's groups that are principally engaged in addressing these issues.

To help support expanded philanthropic response to their concerns, women's groups have formed at least seven federations involved in workplace fundraising activities, including: the Women's Fund of New Jersey; the Illinois Women's Funding Federation; the Los Angeles Women's Foundation; the Women's Funding Alliance in Seattle; Women's Way of Philadelphia; the Colorado Coalition Against Sexual Assault; and the Colorado Domestic Violence Coalition. Together, these funds raised $1 million in employee contributions in 1996, an average of approximately $143,000 per fund.

Founded in 1976, Women's Way is the oldest of the women's federations. Allocations to its fifteen member agencies grew to $1 million in 1993; nearly half of this total was raised from workplace solicitation campaigns. Younger women's federations have also begun to successfully tap workplace funding sources. The Women's Funding Alliance in Seattle, for example, raised approximately $270,000 in workplace donations in 1993, while the Illinois Women's Funding Federation raised $150,000 and the Los Angeles Women's Foundation raised $94,000 that same year.

Federation activity is a relatively modest slice of women-focused community funding, however. According to the Women's Funding Network, an umbrella organization for women's funds, most women-targeted grantmaking institutions take the form of independent foundations created and operated by women for women. Independent women's foundations and funds have developed across the country, in states ranging from California and Minnesota to Colorado and New York. Many of the field's leading institutions are working aggressively to develop endowment funds. The Women's Foundation of Colorado, for example, has raised more than $6 million as part of a $10 million endowment fundraising goal for the year 2000.[56] And in 1997, the Minnesota Women's Fund became the first women's fund to surpass $10 million in assets.[57] Other independent women's giving institutions, moreover, have built significant organizational assets, mostly committed to endowments. In Dallas, Kansas City, and New York, for example, women's foundations and funds amassed net assets ranging from $2 million to $7 million in 1994.[58]

Between 1985 and 1992, forty mostly independent women's funds surveyed by the Women's Funding Network awarded grants totaling nearly $40 million. In addition, these funds increased their annual base of donations from $12.6 million in 1991 to $15.4 million in 1992, representing an impressive annual revenue increase of more than 20 percent.[59]

One of the most impressive independent fundraising and grantmaking funds targeted to women has been the Global Fund for Women (GFW). Since its inception in 1987, GFW has provided more than $5.3 million in grants to more than 700 women's nonprofits in 100 countries. In 1994, it gave more than $1 million to some 200 groups, working on issues ranging from domestic violence, to women in the media, to reproductive freedom. Nearly 70 percent of the donations received by GFW (some $2 million annually) are provided by private foundations and corporations; 30 percent come from individuals.[60]

More than just supporting basic service and social assistance programs targeted to women and girls, women's funds substantially promote model interventions and public policy advocacy activities that help to advance women's rights and opportunities. They also supplement their grantmaking activities with investments in a variety of educational and technical assistance programs designed to expand public awareness of women's needs, as well as the institutional capacities of women's and other groups to respond more effectively to those needs. Such programs include workshops on topics such as fundraising and foundation grant-seeking strategies, as well as management assistance efforts targeted to new women's organizations serving emerging groups and needs.[61]

Many leaders of women's foundations and funds express consternation that mainstream private and corporate funders can, but do not, do more to support their efforts. Others express ambivalence about their sense of where they stand with mainstream foundations and corporations. Few, if any, of these leaders see themselves as fully accepted partners in the field of organized philanthropy. It is especially interesting, therefore, that women's foundations and funds are seen by many of the mainstream grantmakers we interviewed for this article as models for minority institutions seeking to expand the philanthropic participation of communities of color.

Several factors account for this perception. The recent successful efforts of women's foundations and funds to substantially include women of color has led mainstream foundation leaders to see these groups as institutions with a broad, multiracial base of community support. The significant mainstream funding experience and civic credibility of many women's fund leaders, moreover, has contributed to the perception of women's giving institutions as entities that substantially know and understand organized philanthropy's leadership and culture—that is to say, its vocabulary, its protocol, and its decision making processes. Finally, many women's foundations and funds appear to have successfully adopted a number of organized philanthropy's standard approaches and systems, including the development of strategic program initiatives, public policy-focused activities, and endowment campaigns.

This adaptation of community initiative to the established standards of the field has helped to enhance women's philanthropy's relative accessibility and comprehensibility to mainstream funders and thus has enabled their funds to achieve a degree of acceptance and centrality in organized philanthropy. As one leading mainstream foundation president we interviewed told us,

> The debates that raged during past decades over the place of women in society and in philanthropy have been resolved . . . Women's funds have shown a great deal of inclusiveness and in many cases are helping to develop a core civic culture that we can all support and share.

By virtue of their tendency to bridge racial and ethnic divides, to attract experienced and reputable philanthropic practitioners, and to incorporate traditional foundation strategies, then, women's foundations and funds have increasingly come to be seen by mainstream foundation leaders to comport with the integrationist culture of organized philanthropy—even though they were designed to address the particularized needs of women and girls and to challenge many existing social and philanthropic conventions.

General Observations

African-American, Asian/Pacific American, and women's philanthropic initiatives have emerged largely in response to a shared sense among these groups of historical exclusion from organized philanthropy's largesse and decision making processes. Each of these groups has drawn on workplace fundraising campaigns, field of interest funds, and independent foundations to pursue its self-help aspirations. Each group, moreover, has incorporated public engagement and technical assistance strategies designed to improve community participation in philanthropy and to augment nonprofit management capacity among its core constituencies. Finally, each group has developed governance structures that overwhelmingly, if not exclusively, reflect its constituency interests and composition.

Notwithstanding these common characteristics, African-American, Asian/Pacific American, and women's groups reflect divergent priorities and preferred methods of operation in important areas. For example, African-American and Asian/Pacific American groups rely much more heavily than women on workplace fundraising models to promote community giving and philanthropic activity in their communities. Women, on the other hand, rely more on the development of independent funding entities to achieve their goals. African-American groups appear to be more ambivalent than either Asian/Pacific American or women's groups about soliciting mainstream foundation and corporate support for both their programs and their pursuit of endowment campaigns. And grant-making priorities seem to vary widely across these constituencies, reflecting their varying issues and needs, with African Americans largely emphasizing economic empowerment issues, Asian/Pacific Americans their pressing social service needs, and women their growing public policy interests on issues such as child care and women's health.

Latino engagement in the community fund field—which we examine extensively below—largely reflects the experiences of all of these groups and the various approaches they have taken to expand philanthropy's reach to women and communities of color. Indeed, our review of Latino groups in the field underscores their placement in the broader movement to promote philanthropic diversity and pluralism through the development of community funds. As such, it underscores many of the challenges and opportunities facing the field generally. At the same time, it highlights important issues that are unique to Latino groups and that warrant special consideration by mainstream philanthropic leaders.

Latinos and Community-Based Philanthropy

Background

The Latino community of the United States, which consists of persons of Mexican, Puerto Rican, Central and South American, and Cuban ancestry, is one of the nation's largest and fastest growing ethnic groups.[62] According to the Census Bureau, there are now more than 28 million Hispanics in the United States, nearly 11 percent of the nation's total population. The Latino population is growing some five times as fast as the non-Hispanic population; moreover, and the Census Bureau projects that it may account for as much as a quarter of national population growth in the next twenty years. By 2010, Latinos will likely constitute the nation's largest "minority" population (U. S. Bureau of the Census, *Statistical Abstract* 1995, 19).

Latino communities face severe socioeconomic difficulties in the United States. Although the percentage of Latinos in the national workforce is high, their incomes tend to be very low. In fact, more than 29 percent of Latino families lived in poverty in 1996, compared to just 8.6 percent of non-Hispanic white families (U. S. Bureau of the Census, *Current Population Survey*). Fewer than 55 percent of Latino adults have a high school education and Latino youth have the highest high school dropout rates in the U. S.[63]

Despite the Latino community's growing share of the American population and of the country's problems, until recently organized philanthropy has largely ignored Latinos. In 1991-1992, the total amount of funds granted by foundations specifically to benefit Hispanic communities and nonprofits constituted just 1.4 percent of all grants awarded, a small increase from the approximately 1 percent of all grants reported for Hispanics in a 1980 study. Roughly three-fourths of all foundation funds directed to Latino groups and causes, moreover, were given by just seven foundations, with half of the total coming from a single source: The Ford Foundation.

While Latino groups have historically given generously to churches and families or individuals in need, such giving has tended to be highly informal in nature. It has tended, largely because of the Latino community's bilingual/bicultural makeup, to be directed to other Latino individuals and groups through noninstitutional sources. Furthermore, due to the relatively low levels of wealth and income among Latinos, giving has tended to be sporadic and uneven. Until very recently, Latinos have not given through community foundations or comparable mainstream funding vehicles. They have only very recently begun to develop independent foundations building on the wealth of the community's small but growing cadre of successful business figures, entertainers, and professionals. In sum, Latinos are largely newcomers to U. S. philanthropy, and their trajectory for growth in the field is limited by an absence of significant wealth and income, and by a relative dearth of institutional vehicles through which to capture and leverage available community giving resources in ways that are culturally acceptable.

To address the U. S. Hispanic community's dramatically expanding needs against this backdrop, various Latino community funds have developed over the last decade in cities across the nation. At present, six such funds are operating in Kansas City, Lorain, Los Angeles, New York, San Francisco, and St. Paul. All but one of these funds have initiated activities only within the last seven years; and four of the six groups have been in existence for six years or less.

Three of these funds primarily operate within the workplace giving arena: the Hispanic Community Foundation of the Bay Area in San Francisco, the Hispanic Federation of New York City, and the United Latino Fund in Los Angeles. The three remaining funds—the Greater Kansas City Hispanic Development Fund, the Hispanic Fund of Lorain County, Ohio, and El Fondo de Nuestra Comunidad in St. Paul, Minnesota—operate as field of interest funds housed at local community foundations. In general, these funds have all sought to increase community and institutional giving targeted to Latino groups. At the same time, they have sought to expand Latino leadership opportunities in areas ranging from grants management and allocations to community research and problem solving.

Since their inception, Latino funds have aggressively sought and attracted a fair amount of corporate and foundation support for their work and development. Supporting institutions have included, among others, the Ford Foundation, the Hall Family Foundation, the Levi Strauss Foundation, the McKesson Corporation, Bank of America, the Greater Kansas City Community Foundation, and the St. Paul Community Foundation, all leading national and regional funders. Notwithstanding these impressive fundraising successes, Latino funds have simultaneously encountered real difficulty in attracting the support of other leading funding institutions concerned about philanthropy and the nonprofit sector. Among such funders—including, for example, the W. K. Kellogg Foundation, the Charles Stewart Mott Foundation, ARCO, the David and Lucille Packard Foundation, the James Irvine Foundation, and the California Community Foundation—Latino funds have presented numerous issues and challenges, questions, and concerns. In some cases, the issues and concerns that Latino and other community funds have raised for these funders relate to procedural or administrative subject matter that lends itself to relatively manageable resolution. In other cases, however, more fundamental, philosophical issues are involved that are more difficult to address.

Overview of Latino Funds

Workplace Giving Funds

Hispanic Community Foundation (San Francisco, California). The Hispanic Community Foundation (HCF)[64], formerly called the Hispanic Community Fund, was created in 1989 to address the perceived lack of philanthropic responsiveness to Latino communities in the San Francisco Bay Area. The HCF was established out of a partnership between the United Way of the Bay Area, the local corporate sector, and local Latino leaders as a way to promote charitable giving in the Latino community; to increase foundation, corporate, and United Way giving and responsiveness to Hispanic community groups; and to conduct research on the needs and capacity of local Hispanic nonprofits.

In 1991, HCF began a three-year assessment sponsored by the Ford Foundation that included a survey of local Hispanic nonprofits and an analysis of Latino donors. The community survey identified education, employment, and health as the three most critical issues facing Latinos in the region and emphasized that the majority of nonprofits felt that it was very important for Latinos to receive services from other Latino agencies, principally because of cultural and linguistic factors.

The donor survey documented the combination of workplace campaign fundraising and individual, foundation, and corporate contributions that supported the Foundation. The United Way campaigns contributed more than $100,000 annually to the Foundation, in addition to approximately $30,000 a year from a Latino donor option program. And each year, a fundraising luncheon hosted by a major corporate CEO raised an additional $75,000 to $100,000 for operations and grantmaking. HCF donors included nine prominent U. S. foundations,[65] nearly twenty large corporate contributors,[66] and approximately 450 individual donors. In addition to its workplace and general fundraising efforts, the Foundation is also beginning a campaign to build its endowment, which presently stands at $100,000.

In 1991, the Foundation's first year of grantmaking, awards of approximately $100,000 were made to Bay Area social service agencies. The HCF has continued to award approximately $100,000 each year to local Latino nonprofits through its RFP grantmaking process. To date, it has made more than $1 million in grants. Awards range in size from $500 to $10,000 and are directed to an average of fifteen Bay Area Latino agencies each year, usually in the program areas of education, youth, and family development. In addition to these grants, HCF has also sought to develop a regional presence by supporting a number of special projects. HCF's most successful special project initiatives to date have included the McKesson Fellowship program, which gives Latino college students hands-on experience in fundraising and grantmaking; and LatinoNet, a community-based telecommunications network that connects Latino nonprofit agencies. Since 1991, the McKesson Corporation has supported nearly a dozen Latino college students in special projects designed to expand Latino community philanthropic activity and nonprofit management capacity. In 1994, LatinoNet became a freestanding national on-line network with major support from the Carnegie Corporation of New York and other private funders.[67]

HCF grantmaking is governed by a ten-member board of trustees, made up primarily of Latinos along with one Asian-American and one Anglo-American member. Past and present board members include prominent corporate and philanthropic leaders such as Douglas Patino, a Council on Foundations and Mott Foundation trustee; Frank Alvarez, a Kaiser Permanente senior executive; Luz Vega-Marquis, a Council on Foundations, California Wellness Foundation, and San Francisco Women's Foundation board member and a former Irvine Foundation senior executive; and Lawrence Baack, manager of government relations at Pacific Gas and Electric Company. The board also retains a number of senior advisors, including Herman Gallegos, a former Rockefeller and

San Francisco Foundation trustee; Tom Ruppaner, President of the United Way of the San Francisco Bay Area; and Kirke Wilson, Executive Director of the Rosenberg Foundation.

HCF has substantial administrative costs, with an annual operating budget of approximately $400,000 in 1995-1996. The Foundation maintains a permanent staff of two, an executive director, and an operations manager (both Latino/a), as well as three part-time consultants (all Hispanic).

Hispanic Federation of New York City. The Hispanic Federation of New York City (HFNYC) was formed as a result of studies conducted in 1987 by the Tri-State United Way with support from the Ford Foundation and a feasibility study commissioned by the United Way of New York City. These reports illustrated the need to strengthen and support local Latino community-based organizations in and around the New York metropolitan area. The United Way of New York City provided an initial operating grant to launch the Federation in 1989 as an umbrella organization to do fundraising for sixty-two Latino health and human service agencies working in the New York area. It is one of seven regional federations, including two other ethnic funds and four religious organizations. While the Federation was able to raise more than $4 million from government and philanthropic sources for its programs, it also identified a need for increased money to build the infrastructure and fund general operating expenses of local nonprofits.

In 1992, HFNYC completed a community needs assessment and added technical assistance to its grantmaking activities. That same year, the Federation entered into a two-year collaboration with the New York Community Trust and the Ford Foundation to allocate pass-through funds to both member and nonmember agencies serving the Latino community. The project generated Latino community-focused grants totaling $450,000. Since the project ended in 1994, the Federation has operated in partnership with the United Way in its workplace fundraising campaigns.

HFNYC is governed by a sixteen-member board that includes a number of highly reputable trustees with prior foundation and corporate experience. The board includes executives such as Rose Birtley of Continental Airlines, Glen Clarke of Avon Products Foundation, Inc., José Torres of Banco Popular, Carlos Morales of Merrill Lynch, and Carlos Santiago of NYNEX.

The Federation uses a multifaceted approach to its work that blends fund development, grantmaking, advocacy, and technical services to strengthen the organizational infrastructure of the local Latino nonprofit sector. The Federation has established various capacity-building interests, ranging from promoting volunteer recruitment to expanding technical assistance in the nonprofit field; and in 1993 it created a fund called the Latino CORE Initiative specifically to support this sort of activity. This initiative was developed in partnership with the United Way of New York City to address infrastructural weaknesses within Latino health and human service organizations that were caused by the scarcity of general operating support. Unlike most philanthropic grants, which are directed towards individual programs, the Initiative focuses on providing Latino agencies with difficult-to-obtain core operating and administrative funding.

Since its establishment, the Latino CORE Initiative has awarded 106 grants totaling more than $2.25 million, primarily to member agencies, including $557,000 in core support grants in 1997. Grants range in size from $1,000 to $50,000 and are awarded through a year-round application process for a diverse spectrum of core support activities. The Federation has funded requests ranging from a handicapped access elevator in a building being acquired by one area Hispanic organization to the start-up of an endowment for another local Latino agency. The Initiative does not maintain an endowment, but it generates substantial operating support through an annual benefit dinner, which raised $380,000 in 1995 and $450,000 in 1996. It also receives funding through affiliated workplace campaigns administered in partnership with the United Way.

To guide its grantmaking activities, and to provide resources and information about the New York Latino community to both Hispanic and non-Hispanic organizations, HFNYC has followed its original 1992 community assessment with annual Latino surveys and a statistical overview report profiling the economic, employment, and housing status of New York City's Hispanic population. Rooted in this understanding of local needs, the allocations and priorities of the CORE fund are decided by an all-Latino advisory committee that includes three members of the Hispanic Federation board of directors, a volunteer from the local Hispanic community, and a representative of the United Way of New York City. The CORE Initiative accounts for approximately a quarter of the Federation's $2 million annual budget and is run by the organization's Director for Programs, one of thirteen staff people at HFNYC.

In addition to its work in the Latino community, the Federation meets periodically with the other local ethnic and religious affiliates of the United Way to pursue common interests and to share information. The Federation is currently considering extending its grantmaking to Latino agencies outside of New York and joining into field of interest funding collaboratives that advance a Latino agenda.

United Latino Fund (Los Angeles, California). The United Latino Fund (ULF) traces its roots to a 1989 study by the Tomás Rivera Center, funded by the Ford and ARCO Foundations, that assessed the needs of the Los Angeles County Latino population. The study concluded that Latinos should be more broadly engaged in setting the agenda and priorities for funding efforts within their own communities. To help achieve this goal, ULF was established in 1990, with $75,000 in initial funding from the Ford Foundation, to develop a program of voluntary giving that would provide support for the needs of grassroots Latino nonprofit organizations (which the study found were not being effectively met by Los Angeles' traditional philanthropic institutions).

To raise and distribute charitable dollars for Latino community groups, ULF set up an innovative RFP grantmaking structure that maintained community control over the grantmaking process. A forty-member Community Planning Council, with a wide cross section of local community leaders, was established to develop ULF's funding priorities and to make allocations recommendations. The Council is made up of approximately fifty-percent Latino/a representatives and fifty-percent African-American, Asian-American, and Anglo-American representatives; half of the Council's members are women. Based on the Council's recommendations, final allocations decisions are determined by the ULF board, which is composed of eight local Latino/a community leaders. The board includes several experienced managers from local corporate and higher educational institutions, including the organization's chairman, Ralph Arriola of Options for Youth—Pasadena, Inc.; Helen Romero-Shaw, an executive at the Southern California Gas Company; and Elva Lima, a public affairs manager at GTE. Throughout the entire grantmaking process, fundraising and allocations are overseen by a staff of three individuals, the president and general manager, a grant assistant, and an administrative assistant (all of whom are Latino/a), as well as numerous active volunteers (both Latino and non-Latino).

The Fund's annual organizational budget totals approximately $260,000, which is raised mostly from workplace solicitations targeted to employees of Los Angeles County, the City of Los Angeles, the Los Angeles Unified School District, the Los Angeles Community College District, Pacific Enterprises, Prudential, Metropolitan Transit Authority, Department of Water and Power, and Mobil Oil Corporation. The Fund is currently working to expand its campaigns to include the Cities of Long Beach, Buena Park, and Pasadena, and private companies such as Kaiser Permanente and Wells Fargo. In addition to these worksite campaigns, ULF has also received contributions from the Ford Foundation, GTE, and the Mattel Foundation. ULF does not maintain an endowment, but raises nearly $200,000 each year through its workplace giving campaigns and general fundraising.

ULF's first workplace campaign began in 1991, when the Fund managed to gain access to the payroll deduction contributions of Los Angeles County employees. Over the next four years, the Fund awarded more than $240,000 in grants to forty-three Los Angeles Latino community-based social service and human care organizations. Instead of directing its funding exclusively to traditional programs, the United Latino Fund provides flexible grants to help meet the specialized needs of new, developing, and established nonprofits working in the local Latino community. Increasingly, these awards have focused on supporting projects in two primary program areas:

1) support systems for families, including programs that provide direct family assistance, as well as employment training, health education, and parenting projects; and

2) policy development activities, including community education and information efforts related to health, literacy, economic development, and citizenship.

In 1995-1996, ULF made grants totaling $56,880 to seventeen organizations with awards ranging in size from $2,500 to $4,000.

ULF also engages in a number of activities to increase the philanthropic expertise and capacity of local Latinos. It has now held two annual board retreats that bring the board together with philanthropic leaders such as Lon Burns, past President of the Southern California Association for Philanthropy and Douglas Patino, President of the California State University Foundation, to train trustees, to increase their understanding of the larger philanthropic and corporate environment, and to reflect on the values, vision, and mission of the Fund. In addition to this work with the board, ULF has developed handbooks to help train volunteers on how to fundraise and manage income, as well as other tasks involved in administering a workplace campaign. Finally, the Fund provides important training and technical assistance to grant applicants at sites throughout the Los Angeles area, holding informational workshops on its funding application process and requirements.

The United Latino Fund has also emphasized the importance of bridging gaps between its work and that of other minority communities. Since its formation, ULF has worked closely with other constituency-based funds such as the Los Angeles Women's Foundation and the Asian/Pacific Community Fund of Southern California, to promote access to new public and private workplace fundraising campaigns.

Field of Interest Funds

Greater Kansas City Hispanic Development Fund (Kansas City, Missouri). The Greater Kansas City Hispanic Development Fund (HDF) is the oldest and perhaps the most successful of the nation's emerging Latino funds. It began in 1984 out of discussions within the Hall Family Foundation about how to more effectively reach Hispanic and African-American nonprofits in Kansas City. The Foundation provided $75,000 per year for three years to support leaders of each community in efforts to direct grants to selected local nonprofits. The success of initial efforts led by Tony Salazar, chair of the Latino working group (and now a California Community Foundation trustee), persuaded the Foundation to pledge an additional $750,000 to help permanently endow a local Hispanic community fund. In order to minimize administrative costs and to optimize its development prospects, HDF was established as a field of interest fund housed at the Greater Kansas City Community Foundation. A subsequent $500,000 challenge grant from the Hall Foundation helped HDF build its endowment to approximately $1.2 million by 1995 with assistance from various corporate, individual, and foundation sources.

One of HDF's significant contributions to the field has been its extensive use of community needs assessments to guide grantmaking allocations. The Fund performed an initial needs assessment of Kansas City Latino neighborhoods in 1988 with support from the Ford Foundation and the Greater Kansas City Community Foundation. This study led to the classification of four major funding priorities, including cultural awareness, community leadership development, human services, and civic participation. A 1995 follow-up study confirmed the initial assessment's findings and updated its documentation of local Latino needs. These instruments, together with supporting community convenings, have expanded the Fund's grantmaking impacts and helped to inform other area funders and civic institutions about Latino community issues.

The Fund has made more than 115 grants over the last fourteen years, totalling more than $850,000, with interest derived from its endowment principal. Grants range in size from $200 to $45,000 and are awarded to Latino community groups in the four program areas identified by its needs assessments. In the process, HDF has supported a broad range of programs in areas including health care, education reform, adult literacy, immigrant advocacy, capital improvements, and various cultural and artistic activities. The Fund was also instrumental in the development of the Greater Kansas City Hispanic Scholarship Fund in 1985, which generated nearly $350,000 in its first six years of operation to help almost 500 Hispanic students attend colleges, including Harvard University, the University of Michigan, Vassar College, New York University, the University of Missouri-Kansas City, and the University of Kansas.

In addition to these funding activities, HDF has helped improve the relationship between the community foundation and the local Hispanic community. While there were no Latino directors on the Greater Kansas City Community Foundation board when the fund started, there are now two, including HDF's board chair, Ramón Murguía. And two additional Latino community advisors now sit on disbursement committees of the foundation. The relationship has also been credited with spurring increased community foundation grantmaking in the Latino community, often as a funding partner of HDF.

While HDF has no permanent staff, it is overseen by a seven-member advisory committee of local Hispanic community leaders. Advisory committee members are responsible for reviewing and approving fund grant awards. They also help to raise additional endowment money for the fund. In addition to Ramón Murguía, a private attorney, the HDF board includes former city councilman Bobby Hernández; Kansas City Power & Light manager Carlos Salazar; and Federal Reserve Bank Board representative Judy Melgoza. A part-time consultant was hired in 1996 to assist the board with fundraising and general administrative tasks.

Numerous observers credit HDF for modeling comparable Latino fund activities subsequently initiated in Lorain, Ohio, and St. Paul, Minnesota.

The Hispanic Fund of Lorain County (Ohio). The Hispanic Fund of the Community Foundation of Greater Lorain County, Ohio, was started with a small contribution in memory of a prominent local Latino leader in 1986, but remained dormant until 1990. Although Lorain's Hispanic population numbers only 12,000 (17 percent of the city's population), the community foundation, mindful of the need to expand its outreach to minority constituencies, convened area Hispanic leaders to develop an endowment to support local Latino community needs. The community foundation pledged $25,000 to match all new contributions to the new Hispanic Fund on a 1:2 basis. Since its creation, the Hispanic Fund has partnered with leaders of a similar community foundation fund targeted to African-American groups and concerns to successfully approach various local corporations for support. Monies jointly raised by the two funds are shared equally between them.

Since Hispanic Fund principals began pursuing community support in 1990, endowment assets have grown to $135,000. To increase awareness and support among Latino community members, the fund has begun a series of community dinners to honor outstanding local Hispanic professionals. It has also begun to publish a community newsletter about the work and interests of the fund.

Each year, the Lorain Hispanic Fund grants 80 percent of investment income from its endowment through an RFP grantmaking process and reinvests the remaining 20 percent. In the last two years, the Hispanic Fund has awarded approximately $8,000 in grants to community groups and individuals, largely for college scholarships targeted to Latino youth and to support the purchase of needed equipment for community facilities. The fund is governed by a board of thirteen trustees—all of whom are Latino/a and a majority of whom are grassroots community leaders. Fund administrative support is provided by community foundation staff.

El Fondo de Nuestra Comunidad (St. Paul, Minnesota). Recognizing the growing impacts of changing demographics in the city of St. Paul, the St. Paul Foundation decided to create the Diversity Endowment Fund in 1994 as a vehicle for increasing minority giving and for building the philanthropic capacity of local communities of color. The Diversity Fund is comprised of four component funds targeted, respectively, to the needs of local Latino, African-American, Asian/Pacific American, and American Indian groups. Each component fund operates separately within the foundation, but participates in joint fundraising efforts designed to support the Diversity Fund generally. To date, a $5 million endowment has been raised for a common fund shared by the four target communities from individual donors and institutions including the Northwest Areas Foundation and the Otto Bremer Foundation.

To establish fundraising and grantmaking strategies for the fund's Latino component, the foundation invited thirteen Latino leaders from the local community to establish an organizing committee. The committee—which soon after its establishment named the Latino fund El Fondo de Nuestra Comunidad (Spanish for "Our Community Fund")—now consists of seven members, including two individuals with significant philanthropic experience: Dr. William A. Díaz, a member of the Council on Foundations board of directors and a former Ford Foundation program officer; and Elsa Vega-Pérez, a program executive at the Otto Bremer Foundation in St. Paul. In addition to funds raised collectively with the other Diversity Endowment Funds, the organizing committee has raised approximately $30,000 for its own endowment. A quarter of the interest from the principal of the common Diversity Endowment fund and all of the interest from the specific fund are available for El Fondo's grantmaking efforts, which focus on nontraditional Latino community initiatives otherwise unlikely to be supported by local or regional philanthropic institutions. In its first two years, El Fondo made grants totaling almost $120,000 in increments ranging from $2,000 to $7,500 to twenty-two organizations supporting neighborhood-based cultural activities and leadership development projects.

El Fondo's grantmaking centers around two guiding principles: 1) to support community self-help initiatives in areas like volunteerism, leadership development, and nonprofit administration; and 2) to promote projects that improve dialogue and access between diverse racial and ethnic groups in and around St. Paul.

Assessment

Latino Funds in Comparative Perspective

To varying degrees, Latino community funds complement and/or draw on the experiences of African-American, Asian/Pacific American, and women's funds. They respond to a felt sense of disconnection from the mainstream philanthropic field and attempt to "add value" to the independent sector by facilitating a closer connection between organized philanthropy and historically underserved constituencies. They utilize a variety of models and strategies that expand community access to needed public information and technical assistance, while promoting grassroots leadership development and volunteerism. And they emphasize support for newer and smaller, community-based nonprofits and initiatives that are typically overlooked or underfunded by mainstream giving institutions.

Like African-American and Asian/Pacific American groups, in particular, Latinos in the community fund arena pay special attention to the institutional capacity-building needs of community-based nonprofit service agencies; and like women's fund managers, Latino community fund managers are increasingly focused on public policy issues and programmatic initiatives of special interest to their core constituencies, particularly in areas like citizenship and education.

While Latino, African-American, Asian/Pacific American, and women's funds share many common traits, however, each of these groups has tailored its various activities to suit the particular needs and realities of its core constituencies. Latino experiences in the field are thus sometimes distinctive from those of other groups in important respects. For example, it is evident that Latino fund structures differ from those typically employed by women. Latinos, like African-American and Asian/Pacific American groups, have tended to emphasize workplace giving and field of interest funds, which appeal to broad, popular support bases of grassroots community donors. Women's funds, on the other hand—possibly owing to the relative proximity of women philanthropists to wealth and the culture of organized philanthropy—have tended to evolve as independent funds with greater access to larger scale donors. In contrast to African-American groups, moreover, which have strongly emphasized independence from mainstream funders, Latino funds are relatively predisposed to seek corporate and private foundation support to help establish and advance their work. In this respect, Latino funds are closer to Asian/Pacific American and women's funds (which, like their Latino counterparts, have each aggressively pursued mainstream institutional support with mixed results).

More generally, Latino groups appear to be distinguishing themselves in the community fund field by virtue of their relative creativity and predisposition to partner with other racial and ethnic funds. Latino funds have introduced important new innovations to the field, including the use of community needs assessments to inform grantmaking strategies and priorities, and the development of on-line communications systems designed to link community nonprofits engaged in similar or related work. They have also shown a comparatively significant propensity to partner with other important constituencies in joint fundraising, planning, and development activities; arguably, only women's groups in the field demonstrate a greater willingness to embrace and incorporate diversity in their governance and programming.

Overall, our research and interviews suggest that Latino funds are neither as widely recognized for their work nor as well developed as women's and African-American community funds. Typically, Latino funds are seen as fairly comparable—if slightly further advanced in their governance and programming—to Asian/Pacific American community funds. Latino and Asian community funds have developed only very recently and in relatively similar ways; accordingly, both constituencies are seen as newcomers to the field and comparisons between them are enhanced by these groups' community-driven concerns about issues such as immigration and bilingual service delivery.

Despite their newcomer status in the field, though, Latino funds, like Asian/Pacific American community funds, are typically seen as legitimate participants in and contributors to the evolving national field of community-based, philanthropic self-help initiatives. Latino funds have begun to attract critical institution building and program development support from leading corporate and foundation funders, and they appear to be pioneering institutional and grantmaking models that could offer valuable replication opportunities in other locations and contexts.

Given these considerations, it is confusing to many Latino fund executives and observers of the field that more private foundations and corporations have not supported the various Latino funds, nor encouraged the field's development and expansion. To better comprehend their concerns, as well as those of Latino fund skeptics and detractors, we turn now to a comprehensive summary of the respective successes and shortcomings that observers of various persuasions attribute to Latino funds.

Successes and Contributions to the Independent Sector

Viewed in terms of the relatively short historical time frame within which Latino community funds have been operating, their evolution and performance during the past decade suggests some important successes and contributions to the independent sector. As we have seen, several of these funds have attracted resources and contributions in the $1 million-$2 million range, a still relatively small but growing portion of which has been generated by individual donors from the community; and with significant matching grant support from mainstream funders, at least two Latino community funds have commenced endowment campaigns that already stand in the neighborhood of $1 million in assets. Most of the funds have tried to incorporate board members and/or advisors that bring established philanthropic expertise to their governance. Almost all of them have developed grantmaking programs informed by community research and needs assessment projects they have supported, often in partnership with mainstream funders. In addition to grantmaking, many of these funds support community education and technical assistance programs designed to expand community awareness and sophistication about grant seeking and grants administration issues. And several of the funds have assembled relatively inclusive community review bodies to guide their ongoing work. Finally, on balance, the funds appear to be directing an important segment of their support to nontraditional groups and projects that are beneficial to grassroots Latino constituencies, which tend to be underfunded or not supported at all by mainstream donors.

Working through various organizational strategies and at varying levels of scale, then, Latino community funds appear to be adding value to organized philanthropy and the larger society—or at least testing new possibilities to do so—in several key areas. In the process, Latino funds are arguably helping to expand philanthropy's relevance and reach in at least the following ways.

Increasing the Quantity, Responsiveness, and Lessons of Charitable Grants to Latino Nonprofits

While there presently exists no definitive evidence to prove the point, Latino funds do appear to be attracting new contributors and new dollars to the field. The Hispanic Community Foundation of San Francisco's 1994 survey of Latino donors, for example, revealed that some 85 percent of all individuals who contributed to the foundation that year also gave to other community nonprofits, strongly suggesting that their contributions to HCF *added to*, rather than diminished, total community giving.[68] More than just expanding the community support base, though, Latino community funds attempt to assist Latino nonprofits and communities in ways that qualitatively differ from the strategies employed by most mainstream funders.

Fund awards are often complemented by technical assistance programs that seek to better position local nonprofits to maximize the effectiveness and impact of their grants. These efforts help to increase the capacity of community groups to both address community needs and to solicit funds from other sources in support of further activities.

In addition to supplementing their giving with extensive technical assistance, Latino funds often provide support with greater flexibility and responsiveness to grassroots community groups than is usually offered through more conventional funders. This allows them to provide "risk capital" to support nontraditional community activities, such as community organizing, voter registration, and immigrant advocacy, and to respond quickly to the needs of local organizations. This flexibility enables them to help develop capacity in newer and smaller community-based organizations that are attempting to respond to the growing Latino population's evolving needs. Latino funds are often able to approve core operating, infrastructure development, and emergency grants to Latino agencies that other funders simply do not or cannot make.[69] As one fund executive we interviewed explained, "Because we know the needs of our communities and our nonprofits, we are able to make grants more effectively."

This proximity to the community also puts the funds in a unique position to experiment with new techniques for working with Latino neighborhood groups. By focusing on nontraditional and innovative investments, Latino funds are exceptionally well positioned to test emerging models and ideas that help to provide lessons for the field about how to more effectively address Latino community and nonprofit needs.

Promoting an Orientation to the Culture of Organized Philanthropy among U. S. Latino Groups

While the U. S. Hispanic community has a long history of mutual aid, Latino giving has in large part tended to be characterized by one-to-one donations to relatives or by gifts to the church. The notion of giving through *organized* philanthropic structures outside of the religious institutional context is new to U. S. Latino groups. One of the critical roles of Latino community funds, then, is to educate Latinos about nonsecular giving and the independent sector, and to encourage their financial support of Latino and other community nonprofit service and advocacy groups. As Latinos numbers increase in American society, it becomes more important than ever to develop an infrastructure that can assist community members to better understand and respond to the culture of organized philanthropy, and that can promote expanded Latino giving and engagement in the field. Community funds represent one mechanism for giving Latinos a community-based means to learn about and support the independent sector.

Expanding Philanthropic Understanding of Latino Community Needs

Latino funds can help to improve organized philanthropy's understanding of Latino nonprofits and their constituencies. Most of these funds have performed extensive community needs assessments and related research to capture the priorities of their local constituencies and nonprofit organizations. Informed by this work, Latino funds have begun to develop more responsive giving strategies that address the particular needs of their funding constituencies. They have also helped significantly to expand the information available to mainstream funders seeking to improve their responsiveness to Latino community issues. Expanding philanthropy's access to information about community-based Latino issues and needs is more important today than ever, as Latino population growth and demographics in the United States underscore a growing diversity within various Latino communities that is neither widely appreciated nor well understood by mainstream leaders and institutions. While the nation's emergent Latino population shares many common tendencies and traits, individual ethnic groups within the larger community—Mexicans, Puerto Ricans, Salvadorans, and Cubans, among others—often have substantially different interests and needs.

Improving Latino Representation in Philanthropy

Latino funds have typically developed with the benefit of board or advisory participation by highly reputable Latino foundation trustees and professionals. At the same time, though, these funds have created new opportunities to identify and develop *emerging* Latino leaders in the field, in areas ranging from fundraising and fund administration to research and nonprofit management. By increasing the number of Hispanics that are able to participate in philanthropy, Latino funds are helping to promote an expansion of the nation's pipeline of Latino philanthropic practitioners. As this occurs, opportunities for organized philanthropy to benefit from the expertise and insights of these individuals—as members of boards of trustees, consultants, and advisors—are dramatically improved.[70]

Facilitating Coordination and Planning Among Latino Nonprofits

Periodically, Latino funds help to bring community nonprofits together to create stronger, more closely linked Latino service and advocacy responses to community problems. Several of these funds have helped, for example, to build community coalitions to support expanded immigrant advocacy, AIDS awareness, and youth education initiatives in Latino neighborhoods and communities. In addition, The Hispanic Community Foundation of the Bay Area's groundbreaking work to develop a regional on-line communications network linking Latino nonprofits (LatinoNet) has helped to establish a national model for expanding agency coordination and planning in large Latino communities. Such initiatives, which help to improve and rationalize community problem solving efforts, are especially important for agencies and funders alike in the current environment of expanding community needs and diminishing support resources.

Issues and Challenges

Despite the reported contributions Latino funds are making to communities and to organized philanthropy in the aforementioned areas, critics and observers of the field have raised a number of concerns that warrant serious consideration. For many foundation and corporate funders, the concerns have served either to discourage their support of the funds' work altogether or to inhibit their support at higher levels. Following are brief reviews of the most significant issues and challenges our research and interviews uncovered with respect to Latino funds.

Insufficient Program Development and Review Systems

Despite their considerable use of community needs assessments and review committees, Latino funds are often accused of paying too little attention to program development and evaluation issues in their grant-making. The funds are largely seen as being too broad in their focus and insufficiently attentive to the kind of strategic grantmaking that significant foundations are increasingly drawn to, in the form of highly targeted programs and initiatives. The funds are also subject to criticism for lacking requisite systems and procedures to accurately measure their community and institutional impacts. Consequently, their actual—as opposed to their publicly asserted—contributions to community and to philanthropy are sometimes doubted.

Substantial Gaps in Community Support

While Latino funds have increasingly engaged Latino—and often-times non-Latino—community members as fundraising and grants review committee volunteers, their civic reach and legitimacy is often questioned. Many observers point to relatively low levels of community donations in support of Latino funds—we estimate an average of only about 10 percent of total budget for the Latino funds we review here. Others question the marginal support and assistance Latino funds have received to date from more established Latino leaders and groups. In fact, for the most part, Latino power brokers from business, government, and large regional and national nonprofits have been conspicuously absent in the work and development of Latino community funds; and relatively little attention seems to have been paid by most of these funds to attract

Latino donors of means, who though still relatively few, are rapidly grow-ing in number.[71] Several foundation executives with whom we spoke expressed the view that before foundations are asked to give to Latino funds, fund principals should first demonstrate the capability of raising money and garnering broad-based leadership from within the Latino community. Many African-American and women's funds, they argue, were initiated through successful community fundraising and organizing pro-jects—rather than grants from large outside donors—that helped to develop a meaningful base of community support for their work.[72]

Leadership Issues

Latino funds are frequently criticized for leadership deficiencies because many of their CEOs and trustees have limited community cred-ibility, management expertise, and/or experience in private grantmaking. Community fund boards often involve local leaders who maintain a close connection with the realities and needs of their communities but lack the vocabulary, sophistication, and reputation to operate effectively within relationship-based philanthropic leadership circles. Several foundation executives who we interviewed for this article expressed surprise (and regret) that experienced Latino philanthropic executives and staff were not engaged more centrally in the development of the various Latino funds. Based on the relative absence of more senior Latino practitioners and advisors in the field, many of these commentators questioned the long-term viability of the funds. While many Latino fund executives and philanthropic supporters agree the leadership criticism is fair, they also feel it is short-sighted. They see the funds as promising and needed mech-anisms to help bolster presently insufficient Latino community capacity to manage and grow philanthropic institutions. As one field observer told us, "While it [leadership] is a problem, it is also one of the reasons why the funds are needed."

Excessive Overhead Costs

One of the biggest issues facing Latino funds that depend heavily on workplace giving is the extensive overhead costs they incur to simultane-ously administer development, grants, and public outreach programs. Typically, the annual operating budgets of these funds far exceed the amount of monies they grant to community organizations, sometimes by a factor of three or four to one. The disparity is normally explainedóat least in large measure—by the substantial non-grant expenditures Latino workplace giving funds commit to community-based technical assistance and education programs that help to acculturate Latino donors and grantseekers alike to the standards and particularities of the field. It is also important to recognize that the small size of Latino funds is a significant factor in the high *percentage* of money expended on overhead costs. Still, legitimate questions are raised about the wisdom and practicality of workplace giving funds customarily spending more money than they are able to commit to community grants each year.

Separatism and Diversity Issues

Probably the most complex challenge to the mainstream fundraising viability of Latino funds involves the question of separatism. As our earlier discussion on African-American and women's philanthropy points up, organized philanthropic leaders tend to favor more integrationist models of community inclusion and to reject strategies perceived as separatist. This is increasingly the case as debate over multiculturalism in American society is producing unsettling divisions in communities across the nation. To their proponents, Latino community funds were established as a means of adding and incorporating emerging constituencies into the mainstream philanthropic and social mix, not to separate them out. Their purpose from the outset has been to provide a targeted mechanism for expanding the philanthropic contributions and engagements of Latino groups. By emphasizing Latino issues and needs to primarily Latino consumers, Latino funds have fundamentally directed their appeal to community self-help and self-interest. Several experts with whom we spoke argue that it is only natural for individuals of all backgrounds to be more inclined to support causes to which they feel a strong personal connection.[73] Latino funds, they say, give Latino donors that sense of connection; in so doing, it is argued, they help to expand the total philanthropic pie, by making the field more relevant and accessible to a community that has not historically been heavily involved in organized giving.

Critics of these funds see their work in another light, however. A number of observers oppose Latino funds precisely for their perceived role in encouraging Latino communities to segregate themselves from mainstream philanthropy and the rest of society. They believe that philanthropy's role in the community should be to identify and support emerging philanthropic models that bring people together around a common civic culture, rather than building up separate and only distantly-connected subgroups. Still other observers express the concern that although foundation-supported community funds help to give the impression that philanthropy is becoming more inclusive and pluralistic, they actually give mainstream institutions an excuse not to diversify their own governance and staffing. One foundation executive we interviewed stated that minority funds, "are an easy 'out' for mainstream funders; they . . . create an illusion of treating exclusion, but in fact they reinforce it by deflecting attention from the need for change within established giving institutions."

More skeptical commentators with whom we spoke outside of the Latino fund arena express doubt that organized philanthropy is truly subject to significant cultural change. Even in the best case, they argue, expanded minority representation in organized philanthropy is no more likely to improve the field's outputs for minority groups than women's ascendance as foundation executives and program managers has improved philanthropic support for women's and girls' organizations during recent years.[74] Latino fund executives take a more moderate stance. They say it is good and essential for philanthropy and for society that foundations and corporations expand Latino representation in their governance and programming. In their opinion, Latino and other minority appointments in the field *do* make an important difference in terms of philanthropy's products and impact. But given the still significant underrepresentation of Latinos in these institutions and the complexities of inspiring rapid change within them, they believe it is unrealistic in the short term to expect established giving institutions to keep pace with growing Latino numbers and needs without the assistance of new, community-based distribution vehicles. In their view, therefore, the Latino fund movement is best seen as a logical and timely complement to the expanding diversity initiatives of mainstream funders.

Latino Funds and Organized Philanthropy: Opportunities and Challenges for the Future

Latino fund executives are not unaware of the various criticisms that have been leveled against their work. Typically they provide reasonable and articulate responses to address the concerns that have been raised. But, on balance, they agree with many of their detractors that much more needs to be done to bolster the funds' institutional shortcomings. They recognize the practical imperative to reach higher levels of scale and impact precisely where their operations are weakest. They also see the need to expand their community-based funding and longer-term independence from mainstream institutional.

To help facilitate their rapid evolution towards that future in the shorter term, Latino fund principals see expanded mainstream foundation and corporate support for their work as key. They are eager to benefit not only from increased corporate and foundation donations, but also from greater access to the expertise of these institutions and their leaders. They feel that augmenting their engagements and partnerships with foundations and corporations can help to provide them with a wider range of resources, knowledge, and technical assistance, all of which are needed to significantly improve their products and impacts. Priority areas for such assistance would include:

- Expanded research on successful fundraising models in Latino communities.
- External evaluation to help the funds better gauge their institutional and grantmaking impacts.
- Challenge grants that would help the funds attract increased project and endowment support from community members and other sources.
- Operating support that would help to improve the funds' administration and systems.
- Staff training and board development assistance.
- Technical assistance that would hone the funds' investment and development strategies, as well as other aspects of their financial management and planning.
- Networking and communications assistance that would assist the funds to exchange important lessons and data, as well as improve their informational reporting to interested external audiences.

• Continuing community assessment projects, that would help to deepen the funds' and other funders' understanding of evolving Latino community needs.

In essence, what Latino fund principals seek is a closer and more purposeful *relationship* with mainstream funders. Unfortunately for these leaders, many aspects of their work and organization preclude foundation executives from seeing them as a comfortable fit with their pragmatic institutional inclinations. As Bruce Sievers has written,

> The modern world of organized philanthropy is, despite the idealism implicit in its name, a world dominated by pragmatism. It is a social activity in which choices are made based on competitive calculations of outcomes in which money and scarcity play determining roles.
>
> In such a world, participants see their role as making decisions among competing priorities by arriving at critical judgments about projected results. Several assumptions guide this decision making: that cost effectiveness ('more product per dollar') is of primary importance; that tangible outcomes are superior to intangible [outcomes]; that [impact] is more important than motivation; and that activities with measurable results (e.g., number of people served) are preferable to those with incommensurable results (e.g., changes in ideas or values).[75]

Taken together, these assumptions constitute what Sievers calls philanthropy's instrumental bias: "an orientation toward the use of the most efficient means to attain objectively measurable results." The bias applies to many sectors of American life, most notably business and science, and it has produced impressive achievements. But in the social domain philanthropy's instrumental bias confronts serious limits, especially in relation to efforts to address social problems which have strong roots in beliefs and values.

On several important fronts, Latino funds contravene standard philanthropic imperatives and assumptions. They are at least as process driven as they are product driven. Their outcomes appear as likely to be intangible as tangible. They are strong on motivation but not yet as clearly strong on impact. And their activities, while sometimes conducive to measurement, tend to focus more typically on nonquantitative concerns.

None of this is to say necessarily that Latino funds will ultimately fail to persuade the major funding partners they wish to attract in greater numbers and in larger ways to support their work. As we have seen,

Latino funds appear to be adding value to philanthropy and/or expanding opportunities for inclusiveness in the field in various ways; and many important foundations and corporations have already funded this work and are satisfied on balance with the results of their investments to date. Still, for the many funders who have not supported the funds, owing to legitimate concerns about their true value added to the field, there remains a large burden of proof to be met that these groups are finally grant-worthy institutions. The general consensus among this group of funders is that Latino funds need to demonstrate greater viability, professionalism, community support, and impact in order to be seriously considered for future funding.

To their credit, Latino fund executives have recently begun to expand their informal communication and engagement with one another, as well as with key foundation executives around the nation.[76] They have begun to acknowledge a need for more strategic and systematic approaches to their development and administration. And they have begun to contemplate ways to better publicize aspects of their collective work and that they offer up real possibilities for long-term value from which funders and society would both benefit.

Formalizing discussions between and among Latino fund principals through the development of a national network of Latino funds would help to improve response to the field's expanding development and coordination imperatives. Similar to the critical convening and information-brokering role that the Women's Funding Network plays for the nation's many women's foundations and funds, a national network of Latino community funds could help Latino fund principals to focus future discussion, exchange, and action around a national body of local initiatives, funding models, and research. It would assist fund leaders in developing more coherent performance measures, goals, and terms of engagement for the field, that specifically relate to deeper knowledge and information about its strengths and weaknesses. And, in the process, such a network would help facilitate more purposeful and fruitful dialogue between Latino fund executives and leading foundation practitioners and corporate gift managers.

Expanded relationships and discussions between these groups would help to accelerate professionalism in the Latino fund field and highlight opportunities to identify and advance effective interventions that improve services and augment participation in grassroots Latino communities. It would also serve to highlight strategies and solutions to address problem areas encountered by Latino funds, which once addressed could substantially improve their performance.

Given the many prospective benefits of this dialogue, it behooves leaders on both sides of the equation to develop more structured venues for interaction and exchange. Periodic conferences, workshops, and other convenings could help to focus the conversation, especially if informed by further research that helps to resolve specific questions and issues beyond the scope of our article. The following section suggests various continuing research topics that should be addressed as this work moves forward.

Continuing Research Questions

Our overview of Latino community funds suggests a need to resolve many issues related to the institutional strengths and weaknesses, as well as the economies and community impact, of these groups through continuing research in targeted areas of inquiry. While we do not pretend that our list is by any means all inclusive, we do believe the questions identified below touch the most critical topics that require additional attention and that reasonably lend themselves to useful analysis of the sort that funders, practitioners, and other interested parties would value. Our questions for further investigation include the following:

1. To what extent, if at all, do Latino funds discernibly help to expand Latino community giving and volunteering?
2. What especially important new lessons or insights have been gleaned about Latino communities and nonprofits from the work of Latino funds?
3. Precisely how extensive are the potential pools of support for these funds among grassroots community members? donors of means? prospective institutional contributors? How might fund access to these donor bases be bolstered?
4. Do the economies of the funds make sense? How might they be improved in ways that maintain consistency with the funds' various objectives and institutional structures?
5. What is the civic value of the funds' products and services? Who exactly do they benefit and how? What activities and refinements would help to augment the funds' value to philanthropy and to their communities?

6.   What concretely are the leadership assets and liabilities of these funds?
7.   Do the funds help to encourage Latino community engagement in the larger society? with other diverse local and national constituencies? How and to what extent?
8.   What do the work and experiences of non-Latino community funds and foundations offer by way of specific lessons that could help to inform and accelerate Latino advancement in the field?

Conclusion

Our assessment of Latino community funds points up a number of areas in which these institutions are either making, or could make, important contributions to society and to organized philanthropy. It also underscores critical challenges and unanswered questions that face the field and that prospectively impede its development and success if not addressed in the near future.

Latino funds are part of an ongoing tradition of community philanthropic self-help in the United States that has inspired important contributions to the independent sector and the nation by many diverse groups and constituencies. Religious communities of Protestants, Catholics, and Jews; late nineteenth century and early twentieth century immigrant groups; African Americans; women; and more recently, Native American and Asian/Pacific American groups, among others, have been central players in this process. Each of these groups has advanced and sustained itself in the United States, often in difficult circumstances, through voluntary, community-based initiatives. Latino funds are contemporary manifestations of the historical impulse among disadvantaged and newcomer populations to build their own philanthropic and community institutions in order to exercise greater control and responsibility over their destinies in America. The development of these funds by grassroots Latino leaders and community professionals reflects a desire and a felt sense of need within Latino communities to promote the public good through Latino community-based philanthropic initiatives.

At the same time that Latino funds draw deeply on historical traditions in America, they also grow out of important new forces that organized philanthropy would arguably do better to embrace than resist. The development of Latino and other constituency-focused funds mirrors a broader trend in our society and in our world towards more democratic and responsive institutional systems and products. Recent events, from the collapse of the former Soviet bloc to the development of the ever-expanding Internet, to the vast proliferation of segmented consumer markets and specialized investment vehicles, all underscore this trend. All across the globe, people and nations are exploring fundamentally new ways to cope with expanding challenges and choices. The old rules are giving way to new rules, still in formation. In the world of business and academia, the phenomenon at issue is known as a *paradigm shift.* A paradigm is a norm that regulates theory and practice in a given area or discipline.

The emerging paradigm in business, government, and society today emphasizes customer choice and satisfaction. According to a recent RAND Corporation report on changing management imperatives, the essential feature of successful organizations in the 1990s is their propensity to devise and perfect techniques that satisfy the shifting needs of heterogeneous consumer markets:

> The old paradigm was grounded on the classical theories of organizations as rational systems whose main purpose is to address problems by reducing the immense number of possibilities . . . to a few clear-cut alternatives. It assumed that markets and consumer demands were basically homogeneous . . . The new management paradigm questions these assumptions.[77]

To be sure, the world is no longer as homogeneous as it once was (or at least seemed to be). In every field, in every discipline, new developments, new institutions, new strategies, and new public claims are reflecting this reality. Organized philanthropy, though less subject to the hard jolts of these unfolding circumstances than business and governmental institutions, is no less susceptible to the changes they are informing. A new role in the community is being defined for organized philanthropic institutions by the growing diversity and segmentation of their client markets, as well as by their self-proclaimed position as community change agents and social venture capitalists.

John Gardner has written and lectured extensively on the nonprofit and voluntary sector's special role as a catalyst for ensuring civic unity as our society becomes more and more diverse, and seemingly more and more divided. According to Gardner, what is essential is balancing the needs of the entire community against the particular needs of disparately-situated subgroups within the larger community by establishing a framework of values and relationships that are mutually reinforcing—"wholeness incorporating diversity." When this balance is struck, even the most diversely-situated individuals operating in their own intimate settings become strong community builders in other settings, for they will have mastered and embraced the essential skills of citizenship—conflict resolution, teamwork, and participation.[78]

In the emerging environment that we face looking ahead to the twenty-first century, foundation and corporate giving institutions have a unique opportunity and responsibility to help acculturate America's growing ethnic populations to philanthropy and the nonprofit sector. They have an opportunity to test promising new models that promote citizenship and civic participation through the meaningful inclusion of diverse constituencies in the field as foundation donors, trustees, staff, and volunteers. While they pursue these aims within their own organizations and traditional fields of engagement, foundations and corporations can also help to promote the development of alternative venues in which newcomers to the field who have the desire but lack the resources and experience otherwise to participate, can contribute time, money, and talent in ways that are meaningful and relevant to the individual as well as to the larger community. Efforts on both fronts are needed and desirable to strengthen philanthropy's present reach and to ensure its continuing viability and relevance for the future.

As the nation's Latino population's numbers and needs increase, Latino community funds are logical vehicles to test for their capacity to meaningfully augment Latino opportunities in and contributions to the independent sector. While the novelty and nature of such work will make some individuals and institutions uncomfortable, the broader opportunities and rewards likely to result from expanded funder engagement with such groups warrant more in-depth exploration.[79]

Notes

[1] The authors wish to acknowledge and thank Dr. Evangeline Ordaz of California State University, Northridge, for her early contributions to the background research for this article.

[2] Gardner, J. W., *Building Community*, Independent Sector, Washington, D. C., 1991, pp. 15-16.

[3] In this article, the terms "Latino" and "Hispanic" are used interchangeably to refer to people who can trace their ancestry to the Spanish-speaking countries of the Americas and the Caribbean. The term "Latino communities" is also used to recognize the perceived heterogeneity among the major Latino national origin populations in the United States.

[4] It is important to note that other community fund models related to important constituencies and fields of interest are not included in this review, including, for example, targeted grantmaking institutions committed to American Indian, gay and lesbian, environmental, and other constituencies and causes.

[5] While we derived essential information from the various sources consulted, we wish to clarify here that we are solely responsible for the article's contents. In addition, it is important to note that in order to optimize the candor and objectivity derived from our interviews, we promised interviewees that their specific comments and observations, even if quoted or discussed, would not be publicly attributed to them.

[6] U. S. Bureau of the Census, *Statistical Abstract of the United States: 1995* (115th edition), Washington, D. C., 1995.

[7] U. S. Bureau of the Census, *Statistical Abstract*, p. 18-19.

[8] Brophy, P. C., "Emerging Approaches to Community Development," *Interwoven Destinies: Cities and the Nation*, Cisneros, H., ed., W. W. Norton & Co., New York, 1993, p. 215.

[9] U. S. Bureau of the Census, *Current Population Survey* (http://www.census.gov/ftp/pub/hhes/poverty/poverty96/pv96est1.html)

[10] U. S. Bureau of the Census, *Current Population Survey*.

[11] Ong, P. and Umemoto, K., "Life and Work in the Inner City," *The State of Asian/Pacific America: Economic Diversity, Issues and Policies*, Ong, P., ed., LEAP Asian/PACific American Policy Institute/UCLA Asian American Studies Center, Los Angeles, 1994, p. 95.

[12] Chavez, C., *Rivers of Compassion: Bridging the Philanthropic Divide*, Working paper, November 1994, p. 2.

[13] Carson, E. D., "Diversity and Equity Among Foundation Grantmakers," *Nonprofit Mangement and Leadership*, vol. 4, no. 3, Spring 1994, p. 331.

[14] U. S. Bureau of the Census, *Current Population Survey*, (http://www.census.gov/population/socdemo/race/black/tabs96/tab01-96.txt)

[15] Carson, E. D., "Diversity and Equity," p. 334.

[16] U. S. Bureau of the Census, *Current Population Survey*, (http://www.census.gov/population/socdemo/hispanic/cps96/tab01-1.txt)

[17] U. S. Bureau of the Census, *Current Population Survey*, (http://www.census.gov/population/socdemo/race/api96/tab01-1.txt)

[18] Carson, E. D., "Diversity and Equity," p. 334.

[19] National Committee for Responsive Philanthropy (NCRP), "More Grantmakers Are Women, Minorities, Says Council Report," *Responsive Philanthropy*, Washington, D. C., Spring 1996, p. 5.

[20] "The Goal of Diversity," *Foundation News*, May/June 1990, p. 9, citing a 1990 report by Women and Foundations/Corporate Philanthropy.

[21] Women and Foundations/Corporate Philanthropy, "The Goal of Diversity," p. 9.

[22] Asian American and Pacific Islanders in Philanthropy (AAPIP)/Leadership Education for Asian Pacifics, "Making the Invisible Visible," Los Angeles, 1996, p. 4.

[23] Bothwell, R., and Priestman, S., *Foundations and Civil Rights*, National Committee for Responsive Philanthropy, Washington, D. C., 1995.

[24] See, e.g., Handlin, O., *The Uprooted* (Second Edition), Atlantic/Little Brown, New York, 1973, pp. 152-179.

[25] See, e.g. Wilson, *et al.*, *The Pursuit of Liberty: A History of the American People* (vol. II), Alfred A. Knopf, New York, pp. 661-662; Scott, A. F., "Jane Addams: Urban Crusader," in Garraty, J. A., ed., *Historical Viewpoints* (vol. 2), Harper and Row, New York, 1975, pp. 152-167; and Handlin, pp. 105-128 and 180-202.

[26] See, e.g., Rose, M. S., "Philanthropy in a Different Voice: The Women's Funds," *Nonprofit and Voluntary Sector Quarterly*, vol. 23, no. 3, Fall 1994, pp. 227-241.

[27] See, e.g., Murguia, R. *Latino Funds in the United States of America: A Review of Models for Philanthropic Resources*, Working Paper, Hispanics in Philanthropy, October 1995, pp. 11-50.

[28] Prior to 1970, the United Way structure operated as a loose association of local United Ways and community chests organized under a trade association called the United Community Funds and Councils of America (UCFCA). In fact, the United Way model and organization date back to 1887, when the first coordinated fundraising campaign for designated local service agencies was organized in Denver.

[29] Bothwell, R. and Delany, D., *Charity in the Workplace, 1997*, NCRP, Washington, D. C., 1998.

[30] See, e.g., Rifkin, J., *The End of Work*, G. P. Putnam's Sons, New York, 1995, pp. 6-7; According to Rifkin, "In the U. S., corporations are [now] eliminating more than two million jobs annually, to support reengineering efforts that promise to expand productivity and company profits. At the same time, public budget pressures are forcing corresponding workforce reductions in governmental agencies;" see also Rifkin, pp. 37-41.

[31] See, e.g., Wilson, W. J., *The Truly Disadvantaged: The Inner City, the Underclass, and Public Policy*, University of Chicago Press, Chicago, 1987; and Sclar, E. and Hook, W., "The Importance of Cities to the National Economy," *Interwoven Destinies: Cities and the Nation*, Cisneros, H., ed., W. W. Norton & Co., New York, 1993, pp. 66-67.

[32] Winters, M. F., *Donors of Color: A Promising New Frontier for Community Foundations*, Council on Foundations, Washington, D. C., 1993.

[33] Span, J. and Springer, C., *The Value of Difference: Enhancing Philanthropy Through Inclusiveness in Governance, Staffing and Grantmaking*, Council on Foundations, Washington, D. C., 1993, p. 49.

[34] See, e.g., Ana Gloria Rivas-Vázquez's article on Latino fundraising in this volume, as well as Carson, E. D., "Valuing Black Benevolence," *Foundation News*,

May/June 1990, p. 40; Span, J. and Springer, C., *The Value of Difference*, pp. 49-50; and Joséph, J. A., *Philanthropy and Pluralism: The Emerging Civic Culture*, Council on Foundations, Washington, D. C., 1993, p. 4. According to Joséph, "It is projected that over the next two decades, between \$6.5 and \$8 trillion of wealth will be passed on from one generation to another." Noted foundation observer Waldemar A. Nielson puts the estimate even higher, at somewhere between \$8 and \$9 trillion. See "The Role of Women in the Future of Philanthropy," The *Chronicle of Philanthropy*, vol. VI, no. 9, February 22, 1994, p. 45. Much of this substantial transfer of assets is expected to be captured by foundations and nonprofit groups in the form of endowments, trusts, and supporting donations.

[35] Lee, R., "The Confucian Spirit," *Foundation News*, May-June 1990, p. 30.

[36] Chavez, Attachment 2.

[37] Rose, pp. 227-241.

[38] "Women's Funds Get 22% Rise in Donations," *Chronicle of Philanthropy*, Washington, D. C., June 15, 1993, p. 7.

[39] See, e.g., Spann, J. and Springer, C., *The Value of Difference*, Council on Foundations, Washington, D. C., 1983, p. 50-52.

[40] Bureau of Labor Statistics, (http://www.bls.gov/news.release/empsit.t02.htm)

[41] See Carson, E. D., *A Hand Up: Black Philanthropy and Self-Help in America*, Joint Center for Political and Economic Studies Press, Washington, D. C., 1993, pp. 42-47. It is important to note that these self-help efforts build on a long tradition of Black philanthropic giving in the United States. The history of African-American giving has its roots in the underground railroad and mutual aid societies that assisted Black slaves, from the 1700s until the end of the Civil War in 1865. According to Emmett Carson, in "Valuing Black Benevolence," *Foundation News*, May/June 1990, p. 37, Black philanthropy after the emancipation was primarily characterized as "philanthropy among friends"; African Americans aided needy members of their own communities, often through the Black church. But after the civil rights movements of the 1960s, Blacks began to develop more formal mechanisms for charitable giving, such as the United Negro College Fund, Associated Black Charities, and the Black United Fund.

[42] A 1993 Council on Foundations listing of African-American foundations and funds in the U. S. placed the number of such institutions at 109; and the scale of

African-American gifts appears to be growing. Entertainer Bill Cosby and his wife Camille, for example, made a $20 million gift to Spellman College in Atlanta.

[43] Carson, *A Hand Up*, "Foreword," p. i, citing the Committee on Policy for Racial Justice, *Black Initiative and Governmental Responsibility*, Joint Center for Political Studies, Washington, D. C., 1987.

[44] Asian Americans and Pacific Islanders in Philanthropy (AAPIP), *Invisible and In Need: Philanthropic Giving to Asian Americans and Pacific Islanders*, San Francisco, 1992, p. 1.

[45] Ong Hing, B. and Lee, R., eds., *Reframing the Immigration Debate*, LEAP Asian/PACific American Policy Institute and UCLA Asian American Studies Center, Los Angeles, 1996, p. viii.

[46] AAPIP and Leadership Education for Asian Pacifics, *Making the Invisible Visible: Strategies to Increase the Participation of Asian/PACific Americans in Philanthropy*, June 1996, p. 6.

[47] Evenson, L., "Sunday Interview: Chong-Moon Lee," *San Francisco Chronicle*, November 5, 1995, p. 3.

[48] See, e.g., NCRP, "Funding to Bay Area Asian Nonprofits Lags," *Responsive Philanthropy*, Washington, D. C., Summer 1996, p. 13, citing findings of the Fund's recent study, entitled "Perception and Realities," an assessment of Bay Area public and private funding allocations to Asian/Pacific nonprofits.

[49] Nielson, W. A., "The Role of Women in the Future of Philanthropy," *Chronicle of Philanthropy*, vol. 6, 22 February 1994, p. 45.

[50] Interview with Carol Mollner, executive director, Women's Funding Network, December 11, 1997.

[51] Odendahl, T., Boris, E. and Daniels, A., *Working in Foundations: Career Patterns of Women and Men*, Foundation Center, New York, 1985, pp. 4-5.

[52] NCRP, "More Grantmakers Are Women, Minorities, Says Council Report," *Responsive Philanthropy*, Spring 1996, p. 5.

[53] Rose, p. 230, citing a pamphlet by the National Network of Women's Funds (now the Women's Funding Network).

[54] The Women's Foundation, *Working Together to Give Life to Dreams* (pamphlet).

[55] According to a recent *Fortune* magazine article, female workforce participation has increased from just over 15 million individuals in 1975 to more than 30 million last year. While some 29 percent of working women who are married now earn more than their spouses, on average, women earn some 33 percent less than male workers. See "Women, Men and Money," *Fortune*, August 5, 1996, p. 60.

[56] Women's Funding Network, *Networthy*, vol. 1, no. 1, Fall 1995, p. 11-12.

[57] Interview with Carol Mollner, executive director, Women's Funding Network, December 11, 1997.

[58] Interview with Carol Mollner, executive director, Women's Funding Network, September 3, 1996.

[59] "Women's Funds Get 22% Rise in Donations," *Chronicle of Philanthropy*, p. 7.

[60] NCRP, "Funder, Activist Sees Women Outside U. S. As Strength of Global Women's Movement," *Responsive Philanthropy*, Washington, D. C., Winter 1996, pp. 9-10.

[61] See, e.g., "Women's Funds Get 22% Rise in Donations," *Chronicle of Philanthropy*; and The Women's Foundation, *Working Together to Give Life to Dreams* pamphlet.

[62] See, e.g., Bonilla, F. and Morales, R., "Restructuring the New Inequality," in *Latinos in a Changing U. S. Economy*, Russell Sage, Newbury Park, N. J. 1993, p. 2.

[63] Cortés, M., "Philanthropy and Latino Nonprofits: A Research Agenda," *Hispanics and the Nonprofit Sector*, Foundation Center, New York, 1991, p. 143.

[64] Information for this organization was drawn from survey responses included in Appendix C of the *Summary Report: Latino Emerging Funds Planning Meeting* (June 6-8, 1996) in Kansas City, Missouri, prepared by Emily McKay of MOSAICA: The Center for Nonprofit Development and Pluralism, based in Washington, D. C.; and Murguia, pp. 12-14.

[65] Foundations contributing to HCF include the Ford, GAP, GTE California, Kaiser Permanente, Levi Strauss, McKesson, Montrose Educational, and Pacific Telesis foundations.

[66] Corporate contributors include AT&T, Chevron USA, Hewlett Packard, Kaiser Permanente, Kaiser Aerotech, Lucky Stores, the Mission Economic and Cultural Association, New United Motors Mfg., the Oakland Athletics Baseball Club, PepsiCo, Pacific Bell, Pacific Gas and Electric, Ross Stores, Safeway Stores, Security Pacific Bank, The Chronicle Publishing Co., Telecommunications Education Trust, and Univision (KDTV-14).

[67] See Hispanic Community Fund of the Bay Area *1993 Annual Report*, p. 9 and Hispanic Community Foundation *1995-1996 Annual Report*, p. 8, Hispanic Community Foundation, San Francisco.

[68] Valdez, A., "A Survey of Donors to The Hispanic Community Fund of the Bay Area," Hispanic Community Fund of the Bay Area, San Francisco, 1994, p. 6. More anecdotal evidence from Kansas City also underscores the point that Latino funds are helping to *expand* community giving. To avoid conflicts between its own fundraising interests and that of other local Latino nonprofits, the Greater Kansas City Hispanic Development Fund refuses corporate and foundation support that would merely rechannel, rather than increase, Latino-focused institutional giving in the community. See Murguia, p. 22.

[69] McKay, E., *Summary Report: Latino Emerging Funds Planning Meeting*, MOSAICA, Washington, D. C., 1996, p. 6. The Greater Kansas City Hispanic Development Fund's informational brochure states the case this way, under a section titled "Responding Quickly to Needs": "[T]he Hispanic Development Fund . . . was the first private funder in the community to focus funds on immigration and amnesty issues, even before recent federal legislation was passed. In addition, the Fund can react quickly as needs arise. When a nonprofit day care facility in the Hispanic community lost its federal funding, the Fund made a commitment within hours that kept the facility in operation." See *Hispanic Development Fund Brochure*, 1990, Kansas City, p. 2.

[70] When the Greater Kansas City Hispanic Community Fund began, for instance, there were no Latinos on the board of the local community foundation. Since the Fund's creation, however, the Greater Kansas City Community Foundation has appointed three highly regarded Latino trustees (two of whom are still sitting) and three Latino community advisors. Virtually all of these individuals were identified through their activities related to the Hispanic Development Fund, and none of them brought any prior mainstream foundation board experience. See Murguia, pp. 36-37; and p. 42.

[71] The early 1980s saw an impressive increase in Latino family income resulting in the expansion of U. S. Latino households with annual incomes exceeding

$75,000, from 20,000 in 1980 to more than 100,000 in 1986. In 1990, moreover, the Council on Foundations estimated the number of U. S. Hispanic households with annual incomes over $50,000 in the range of 500,000. See, respectively, Estrada, L.F., "Hispanic Evolution," *Foundation News,* Washington, D. C., May-June 1990, p. 34, and Joséph, J. A., "Pluralism and Philanthropy: Clarifying the Contradictions," *Ibid.,* p. 75.

[72] On the question of increasing support from community constituents, Latino fund executives argue that their task is discernibly more complicated than that of other groups in the field, due to the lack of an infrastructure and a precedent for promoting organized philanthropic giving in U. S. Latino communities.

[73] See, e.g., Murguia, p. 10. Ramon Murguia explains that Latino community funds have tried to appeal to the community's instinct towards self-help. He writes, "Our fundraising emphasis on a Latino identity is similar to cancer victims giving to support cancer research." Another fund executive we interviewed added jokingly, "It's a lot like going out to eat. You don't go out to a Denny's to go eat an enchilada, you go to a Mexican restaurant." See also, Simmons, R. G., "Presidential Address on Altruism and Sociology," *Sociological Quarterly*, vol. 32, pp. 1-22.

[74] One expert with whom we spoke made the point this way: "To be honest, they [minorities and women that have been brought into the field] have had to adapt to the rules of philanthropy's culture far more than philanthropy has had to accommodate them."

[75] Sievers, B., "Can Philanthropy Solve the Problems of Civil Society" [unpublished], 1994, p 1.

[76] During June 6-8, 1996, with support from the Hall Family Foundation and the Greater Kansas City Community Foundation, leading representatives of the various Latino community funds around the U. S. met in Kansas City to share information and to assess the feasibility of establishing closer ties. The meeting was monitored by several external participants representing leading funding institutions in Chicago, who are interested in the possibility of developing a Latino fund in the Chicago area. At the time of this writing, at least one follow-up telephone conference had been organized to move the group's discussions and planning forward.

[77] Levine, A. and Luck, J., *The New Management Paradigm: A Review of Principles and Practices,* a report to the United States Air Force, RAND Corporation, Santa Monica, 1994, p. x.

[78] Gardner, J. W., *Building Community*, Independent Sector, Washington, D. C., 1991, p. 16 and p. 29.

[79] Since the completion of this article, the six Latino funds described herein have received an important $100,000 grant from the W. K. Kellogg Foundation as a part of its Emerging Funds for Communities of Color Initiative. This one-year planning and networking grant is being used to establish a research and information base on the funds and to develop a collaborative plan for strengthening Latino philanthropy. It will enable the funds to create a structure and process for their ongoing collaboration, to develop a shared base of data and experiences, to document Latino giving and philanthropic involvement in the communities in which their work is concentrated, and to identify individual and joint organizational development needs. This work represents the beginning of efforts to explore new structures and strategies for Latino philanthropy and to increase the capacity of Latino funds as a vehicle for both involving Latinos in philanthropic efforts and increasing the availability of resources targeted to Hispanic community needs (*Proposal for a Planning and Networking Grant for Collaborative Development of the Latino Funds*, Proposal to the W. K. Kellogg Foundation, June 1997).

Bibliography

Asian Americans and Pacific Islanders in Philanthropy (AAPIP), *Invisible and In Need: Philanthropic Giving to Asian Americans and Pacific Islanders*, San Francisco, 1992.

AAPIP and Leadership Education for Asian Pacifics, *Making the Invisible Visible: Strategies to Increase the Participation of Asian Pacific Americans in Philanthropy*, June 1996, p. 6.

Bonilla, F. and Morales, R., "Restructuring the New Inequality," in *Latinos in a Changing U. S. Economy*, Russell Sage, Newbury Park, N. J., 1993.

Bothwell, R. and Priestman, S., *Foundations and Civil Rights*. National Committee for Responsive Philanthropy, Washington, D. C., 1995,.

Brophy, P. C., "Emerging Approaches to Community Development," *Interwoven Destinies: Cities and the Nation*, Cisneros, H., ed., W. W. Norton & Co., New York, 1993.

Carson, E. D., "Valuing Black Benevolence," *Foundation News*, May/June 1990.

Carson, E. D., *A Hand Up: Black Philanthropy and Self-Help in America*, Joint Center for Political and Economic Studies Press, Washington, D. C., 1993.

Carson, E. D., "Diversity and Equity Among Foundation Grantmakers," Nonprofit Management and Leadership, vol. 4, no. 3, Spring 1994.

Chavez, C., *Rivers of Compassion: Bridging the Philanthropic Divide*, Working Paper, November 1994.

Cortes, M., "Philanthropy and Latino Nonprofits: A Research Agenda," *Hispanics and the Nonprofit Sector*, Foundation Center, New York, 1991, p. 143.

Estrada, L. F., "Hispanic Evolution," *Foundation News*, Washington, D. C., May-June 1990.

Evenson, L., "Sunday Interview: Chong-Moon Lee," *San Francisco Chronicle*, November 5, 1995, p. 3.

Gallegos, H. and O'Neill, M., "Hispanics and the Nonprofit Sector," *Hispanics and the Nonprofit Sector*, Gallegos, H. and O'Neill, M., Foundation Center, New York, 1991, pp. 1-13.

Gardner, J. W., *Building Community*, Independent Sector, Washington, D. C., 1991.
de la Garza, *et. al*, *Latino Voices: Mexican, Puerto Rican, and Cuban Attitudes Toward American Politics*, Westview Press, Boulder, Colorado, 1992.

Handlin, D., *The Uprooted*, 2nd Ed., Atlantic/Little-Brown, New York, 1973.

Joseph, J. A., "Pluralism and Philanthropy: Clarifying the Contradictions," *Foundation News*, Washington, D. C., May-June 1990.

Joseph, J. A., *Philanthropy and Pluralism: The Emerging Civic Culture*, Council on Foundations, Washington, D. C., 1993, p. 4.

Kroll, J., "On A Steady Course—Upwards," *Foundation News*, Council on Foundations, Washington, D. C., May-June, 1992.

Lee, R., "The Confucian Spirit," *Foundation News*, May-June 1990, p. 30.

"Women's Funds Get 22% Rise in Donations," *Chronicle of Philanthropy*, Washington, D. C., June 15, 1993, p. 7.

Levine, A. and Luck, J., *The New Management Paradigm: A Review of Principles and Practices*, A Report to the United States Air Force, RAND Corporation, Santa Monica, 1994.

McKay, E., *Summary Report: Latino Emerging Funds Planning Meeting* (June 6-8, 1996 in Kansas City, Missouri), MOSAICA: The Center for Nonprofit Development and Pluralism, Washington, D. C., 1996.

Murguia, R. *Latino Funds in the United States of America: A Review of Models for Philanthropic Resources*, Working paper, October 1995.

National Committee for Responsive Philanthropy (NCRP), "Corporations Increasingly Turn to Non-United Way Charities," *National Committee For Responsive Philanthropy Special Report*, Washington, D. C., Fall 1992, p. 7.

NCRP, "Local Alternative Funds in 1993 Employee Giving Campaigns," *Responsive Philanthropy*, Fall 1995.

NCRP, "Activists, Governor in New Jersey Launch New Women's Federation," *Responsive Philanthropy*, Fall 1995, pp. 7-9.

NCRP, "United Ways Grew By 1 Percent . . .", *Responsive Philanthropy*, Washington, D. C., Winter 1996, p. 7.

NCRP, "Funder, Activist Sees Women Outside U. S. As Strength of Global Women's Movement," *Responsive Philanthropy*, Washington, D. C., Winter 1996, pp. 9-10.

NCRP, "More Grantmakers Are Women, Minorities, Says Council Report," *Responsive Philanthropy*, Washington, D. C., Spring 1996, p. 5.

NCRP, "Funding to Bay Area Asian Nonprofits Lags," *Responsive Philanthropy*, Washington, D. C., Summer 1996, p. 13.

Nielson, W. A., "The Role of Women in the Future of Philanthropy," *Chronicle of Philanthropy*, vol. VI, no. 9, 22 February 1994, p. 45.

Odendahl, T., Boris, E. and Daniels, A., *Working in Foundations: Career Patterns of Women and Men*, Foundation Center, New York, 1985.

Ong Hing, B. and Lee, R., eds., *Reframing the Immigration Debate*, LEAP Asian Pacific American Policy Institute and UCLA Asian American Studies Center, Los Angeles, 1996.

Ong, P., ed., *The State of Asian Pacific America: Economic Diversity, Issues and Policies*, LEAP Asian Pacific American Policy Institute/UCLA Asian American Studies Center, Los Angeles, 1994.

Rifkin, J., *The End of Work*, G. P. Putnam's Sons, New York, 1995.

Roane, K., "United, the Alternatives Stand," *Los Angeles Reader*, November 27, 1992, p. 4.

Rose, M. S., "Philanthropy in a Different Voice: The Women's Funds," *Nonprofit and Voluntary Sector Quarterly*, vol. 23, no. 3, Fall 1994.

San Francisco Hispanic Development Fund, *Hispanic Development Fund Brochure*, Kansas City, 1990.

San Francisco Women's Foundation, *Working Together to Give Life to Dreams* (pamphlet).

"Women, Men and Money," *Fortune*, August 5, 1996, p. 60.

Sclar, E. and Hook, W., "The Importance of Cities to the National Economy," *Interwoven Destinies: Cities and the Nation*, Cisneros, H., ed., W. W. Norton & Co., New York, 1993.

Scott, A. F., "Jane Addams: Urban Crusader," in Garraty, J. A., ed., *Historical Viewpoints* (vol. 2), Harper and Row, New York, 1975, pp. 152-167

Sievers, B., "Can Philanthropy Solve the Problems of Civil Society" [unpublished], 1994.

Simmons, R. G., "Presidential Address on Altruism and Sociology," *Sociological Quarterly*, vol. 32, pp. 1-22.

Span, J. and Springer, C., *The Value of Difference: Enhancing Philanthropy Through Inclusiveness in Governance, Staffing and Grantmaking*, Council on Foundations, Washington, D. C., 1993.

U. S. Bureau of the Census, *Commerce News*, Washington, D. C., October 4, 1993.

U. S. Bureau of the Census, *Statistical Abstract of the United States: 1995* (115th edition), Washington, D. C., 1995.

Valdez, A., "A Survey of Donors to The Hispanic Community Fund of the Bay Area," Hispanic Community Fund of the Bay Area, San Francisco, 1994.

Wilson, W. J., *The Truly Disadvantaged: The Inner City, the Underclass, and Public Policy*, University of Chicago Press, Chicago, 1987.

Wilson, *et al., The Pursuit of Liberty: A History of the American People* (vol. II), Alfred A. Knopf, New York, pp. 661-662.

Winters, M. F., *Donors of Color: A Promising New Frontier for Community Foundations*, Council on Foundations, Washington, D. C., 1993.

Women's Funding Network, *Networthy*, vol. 1, no. 1, Fall 1995, p. 11-12.

"The Goal of Diversity," *Foundation News*, May/June 1990, p. 9, citing a 1990 report by Women and Foundations/Corporate Philanthropy.

"Number of Poor Americans Rises for 3rd Year," *Washington Post*, October 5, 1993, p. A6.

Current Issues Affecting U. S. Hispanic Foundation and Nonprofit Directors/Trustees: A Survey of the Field

Diane Sanchez and Rosie Zamora

Introduction

This article examines the evolving opportunities and challenges confronting Latino trustees of independent sector institutions, including private and community foundations in particular. It builds on thirty structured interviews with a representative sampling of individuals belonging to the current U. S. field of approximately 250 Latino trustees of leading foundations and nonprofit organizations. Overall respondents expressed optimism about the future prospects of U. S. Latinos on boards of major philanthropic institutions. However, respondents agreed they face more challenges and benefit from fewer support systems than their mainstream counterparts due to several factors, including their limited numbers and their sense of special responsibility to represent Hispanic concerns in controversial areas such as immigration, bilingual education, and civil rights.

The pages that follow track the study's background and its major findings, including the demographic characteristics and institutional affiliations of respondents, the factors contributing to their appointments to foundations and other boards of directors, the special challenges they believe they confront in philanthropy, and emerging issues and opportunities shaping the future of the field. Although the study builds on more limited prior surveys by Hispanics in Philanthropy (HIP) to gauge Hispanic trustee issues, it constitutes the only major inquiry to date that we are aware of.

Background

In 1995, Hispanics in Philanthropy convened a conference in Santa Fe, New Mexico. The theme for the conference was "Democratizing Institutions & Communities: The Role of Philanthropy and the Nonprofit Sector." One of the workshops was a session held exclusively for Latino trustees of foundations. The session was to provide a forum for informal exchange among those who are trustees at corporate, private, and community foundations. The dialogue among the trustees was both candid and rich. Many of the participants expressed how grateful they were to have this unusual opportunity to hold such a dialogue. This was, perhaps, the first time that a group of Hispanic foundation trustees came together in an exchange relating to their experiences as trustees.

The discussion was guided by an informal agenda that covered issues such as developing new leadership, getting Latino trustees interested in joining affinity groups such as HIP, and balancing responsibilities between foundations and the community. In the introductory part of the discussion, we found that a number of the foundation trustees were also board members of for-profit corporations.

The discussion focused on strategies to increase Latino leadership participation at foundations and how to leverage this participation to increase opportunities for Latinos to become board members of for-profit corporations. There was a clear realization that Hispanics in either of these roles have unusual opportunities to influence other policy and decision makers, and to network for both personal and community gain.

In the discussion, most of the trustees agreed that the civil rights movement had been instrumental in opening up possibilities that had previously not existed for all minorities. However, the trustees in general also agreed that their individual appointments to boards had a great deal to do with their ability to fit into the specific organization's culture and to deliver on the specific goals of the organization.

A concern was raised about the need for greater effort to recruit and develop new leadership at all levels, both in Hispanic organizations and in larger community institutions. Participants acknowledged that while

Latino participation on foundation boards has meaningfully expanded in recent years, such participation remains low in relation to the Latino community's growth and increasing national significance.

We know from research that participation and leadership in community organizations boosts the electoral involvement of Latinos, even more than it promotes Anglo political participation.[1] We also know that community organizations typically provide core vehicles for Latino civic education and empowerment. Community organizational participation is thus strategically critical[2] to not only having the Latino point of view heard, but also in helping Latinos to realize their broader leadership potential.

The Latino population currently totals around 29 million, which is roughly 10 percent of the U. S. population, and is growing faster than any other ethnic or racial group. On average, we are seven years younger than the median age for the general U. S. population and we are estimated to have annual buying power of nearly $350 billion.

The 1980s were dubbed "The Decade of the Hispanic" with the notion that Latinos, both in terms of numbers and participation, would become a prominent force in U. S. society. As the century approaches its end, however, many of us have yet to experience any sense of "arrival" into the mainstream. Among continuing obstacles to national Latino advancement are the highly diverse circumstances and experiences that separate the various Latino subgroups across the nation, as well as lingering institutional barriers to participation in key sectors of U. S. life. HIP's preliminary surveys of Latino foundation trustees suggested that Latino independent sector leaders might begin to address these challenges by focusing on issues that cut across race, class, and regional lines in such a way as to unite our disparate communities. One issue that galvanized strong consideration was citizenship. It was felt that citizenship and participation in the democratic process could be a rallying cry for bringing both foundations and corporate Hispanic leaders together to discuss common agendas and goals for generating more generous funding targeted to Latino nonprofits across the United States.

A second cross-cutting issue related to the role of Hispanics as current and potential donors to community-based nonprofits and giving institutions. As Latinos are becoming a significant portion of the U. S. population, their participation in philanthropy in terms of giving is increasingly important to the continued stability and growth of the sector. Research from the Tomás Rivera Policy Institute (TRPI) has shown that there is no significant difference between U. S.-born Anglos and U. S.-born Mexican-Americans on the key dimensions that tend to characterize charitable donors, i.e., birthplace and education level. Clearly, immigrants have lower rates of participation in organized giving and volunteering than do native-born individuals, but TRPI's research suggests that these behaviors are learned and incorporated generally within one generation. This points to a tremendous potential for Latino donors to shape the work and values of U. S. philanthropy and communities in the twenty-first century.

To test these early survey results with an eye to developing appropriate program responses, HIP instituted a follow-up research program aimed at compiling more in-depth information about Latinos who serve on corporate and foundation boards and the issues they feel are important both to the organizations whose boards they serve on and to the Latino community as a whole. More than thirty extensive semi-structured interviews were conducted by the Houston, Texas-based Telesurveys Research Associates with Hispanics who currently serve on leading nonprofit boards, including corporate, foundation, and/or educational institution boards. The research was accomplished under the direction of Hispanics in Philanthropy board member Rosie Zamora, president of Telesurveys Research Associates, and Diane Sánchez, principal of the Oakland, California-based consulting firm Sunset Associates. The goal was to gain insights into the demographic characteristics of Latino trustees, including their educational and professional backgrounds, as well as to assess the factors that contributed to their appointments to various boards. We also wanted to explore their personal experiences in serving on boards and any obstacles they perceived to effective board service. Finally, we surveyed them on their perceptions of current and future issues and opportunities affecting the Hispanic population and society as a whole. This article reflects the results of our inquiry.

Methodology

The initial phase of this research project involved information gathering designed to identify the current universe of Hispanic board members. This process, which relied on information provided by the membership of HIP, resulted in the identification of 250 potential respondents who serve on foundation, corporate, and/or educational institution boards. A random sample of thirty individuals was drawn to represent geographic, gender, and organizational diversity among Hispanic directors and trustees. Telephone interviews, which generally lasted somewhere between twenty and forty minutes, were conducted between October 1996 and January 1997 with all thirty sample subjects. All the interviews were conducted using a largely open-ended interview instrument that was designed to collect quantitative as well as qualitative data.

As would predictably be the case with any group of busy professionals, arranging time with these individuals for our interviews sometimes proved to be tricky. We had hoped to conduct significantly more interviews, but given our limited resources and time, we were not able to do so. Consequently, our universe of interviews cannot technically be considered to constitute a statistically significant sample. However, we feel that information derived from the interviews that were conducted paints an interesting and telling picture of the field that certainly should be the basis for more expansive future inquiries. It should be noted that research interviews like these have been conducted in the past with African-American board members; however, to our knowledge, the present study constitutes the first time any such research has been targeted to Hispanic board members.

Background Data Related to Our Survey Pool of Interviewees

Demographic Characteristics

With a mean age of forty-eight, the Latino board members we interviewed are somewhat older than the Latino population as a whole. With eight in ten indicating they were born in the United States, they are also more likely to be native-born than the Hispanic population as a whole. Approximately half of the individuals we interviewed were of Mexican descent, two in ten were of Puerto Rican descent, with one in ten being of Cuban descent.

Significantly, almost 37 percent of our respondents were raised in predominantly non-Hispanic neighborhoods, compared to some 44 percent who grew up in almost exclusively Hispanic areas. Approximately two in ten, or 19 percent of our respondents, indicated that they grew up in areas that were largely Hispanic with some representation of other racial and ethnic groups.

Board Experience and Qualifications

Two-thirds of those we spoke with indicated that they had extensive experience in serving on boards of Hispanic/Latino organizations and/or mainstream organizations prior to their present board appointment. They tend to be both professionally distinguished and to have strong histories of community involvement. They also tend to be well educated and are likely to be in the same professions as their Anglo counterparts.

Participants brought a wide range of professional skills and qualifications to their board service. More than half responded that they had experience in finance and fiscal management; 20 percent had legal experience; 20 percent had academic experience; and 40 percent had experience in human services or human relations. In addition, a number of respondents indicated that they had extensive experience in filling volunteer and/or staff functions in the organizations on whose boards they served, or in similar organizations prior to their current board appointment.

Factors Leading to Board Appointment

When asked why they felt they were selected to serve as trustees in the field, a majority indicated that specific expertise facilitated their selection to the board. In addition, many of them were known by other board members. Most were aware that their ethnic and cultural background may have had a bearing on their selection to the board, particularly on boards that had an express interest in reflecting more ethnic and racial diversity. Knowledge of and involvement in the Hispanic community were considered primary factors in their selection. Many were known for their community work or had worked previously with key members of the current board in other organizations. Some comments regarding their appointments included:

- "Because I am brown and I have been an executive director for a nonprofit and that is what they were looking for."

- "First of all, because I was Hispanic and secondly because I had a financial background."
- "They see what's out there in the community, and they want some balance."
- "You are there to provide [ethnic] representation, though you're not really asked to do that."
- "More because of my skills—they were already diversified."
- "If I hadn't been Hispanic, I would not have been considered to begin with."

Although many acknowledged that the desire to diversify the board was a factor in their appointment, it was not seen by most as the primary reason for their selection. Still, most of our interviewees willingly acknowledged that Latinos continue to be highly underrepresented on foundation and other nonprofit boards and that their appointments were important in this context.

Perceived Factors Affecting Hispanic Underrepresentation on Boards

With Hispanics representing ten percent of the national population, but less than one-half of one percent of foundation and corporate board members, we asked our participants to provide opinions as to why this is the case. The primary reasons stated generally revolved around lack of mainstream institutional awareness of suitable Hispanic candidates for these positions. It was also pointed out that candidates with sufficiently high profiles to be obvious selections were asked by large numbers of organizations to be on their boards, thus having the effect of placing a tremendous burden on them individually, as well as closing off opportunities to equally qualified, but perhaps less known candidates. Since the concepts of "fit" and "comfort level" (that is, finding people who are reflective of the values and, in many cases, economic levels of those who would be their peers on boards) is so important to leaders and institutions in the field, some of those we interviewed felt there exists a "closed shop" atmosphere where current board members recruit and select only people they know, thus making the possible candidate pool a reflection of their work or social contacts, rather than of the actual pool of qualified Hispanics in the population. Relevant comments on this topic included:

- "Many philanthropic foundations or boards are made up of the very wealthy and are very well known people . . . We are not at that socio-professional level."

- "It's a matter of economics . . . they tend to look for money people who can contribute monetarily. Hispanics tend to be lower income and lower in education."

- "It's a matter of who you know and how you know them. Hispanics are not developing these kinds of relationships. It's not just a lack of qualification, but rather a lack of network, so that people think of you when something comes up."

- "It's a closed group where board members select other board members who are like them."

- "Hispanics are not culturally attuned to these boards. They come from national cultures where foundations did not exist because we relied on other resources such as churches, or *el jefe* or *el patron,* who took care of things."

- "We have not been doing a good job when it comes to promoting our own kind. We have plenty of qualified candidates, but we do a bad job of noticing and promoting them within our own community. Also, we have not educated those Hispanics who have come to this country in the past twenty years to prepare them to serve on boards."

Almost half of our survey respondents have been asked by the institutions they represent to help in the recruitment of Hispanic staff or board members. Almost three-quarters of those who had been asked indicated that they have experienced some success in their efforts. Although the inclusion of Hispanics into the recruitment and selection process can clearly broaden the potential pool of candidates, strategies that are primarily driven by the social and business connections of these individuals alone are typically limited. This points to the need to expand the base of information available to institutional leaders in the field about emerging and/or otherwise nontraditional Hispanic candidates. The majority of respondents we interviewed felt that there is especially great need for the identification of qualified Hispanics who are both frequently in touch with the community and who have the professional skills that most boards seek.

Current Issues

Institutional Governance

When asked what important issue or issues their board had been working on in the past six months, respondents frequently mentioned planning for the future. Other respondents spoke of refocusing, attempting to target funding, and organizational restructuring. Those serving on foundation boards indicated that their board was increasingly concerned with identifying the critical needs of the community, and realigning funding processes and strategies to reflect those needs. Other issues mentioned included focusing on grassroots empowerment, examining how best to support programs for women, discussing alliances with other groups, and rethinking funding processes. These issues were seen as relating to the general direction their boards or foundations were planning for the future, and all of our respondents felt they were actively involved in these plans.

Perceived Issues Affecting Hispanic Communities

Respondents were asked what issues they feel are most critical to Hispanics in the United States. Although respondents cited a range of problems and issues, more than half indicated that education is the most critical issue for Hispanics. Legal and illegal immigration issues were also mentioned by a substantial number of respondents. Comments included:

- "Education is critical. We have less and less who are going to college."
- "The breakup of the extended family is hurting the essential makeup of Hispanic life."
- "Immigrant bashing—making Hispanics the scape-goat for all the problems."
- "The new generation of Hispanics have to be trained. The anti-immigration move affects you no matter how long your family has been in the United States. We have to get off of the bottom of the economic ladder."

To determine perceptions of the relative importance of various concerns affecting American society as a whole, respondents were asked to rate lists of national and local problems on a ten-point scale. These issues are presented below in their order of importance based on the average ratings of respondents.

Issues of Concern	
10 = Most Important	
NATIONAL ISSUES	
Job Opportunities	7.73
Parenting	7.43
Racial/Ethnic Conflicts	7.28
Health Treatment	5.69
Illegal Immigrants	4.89
LOCAL ISSUES	
Access to Higher Education	8.87
Bilingual Education	7.83
English Only	7.77
Community Development	7.17
Citizenship	7.10

Consistent with the concerns indicated in their comments, respondents provided the highest average ratings on issues involving Hispanic access to higher education. Respondents also expressed concern about the future of bilingual education and the English Only movement that appears to be gaining momentum throughout the country. The general hot button issues that have had wide national coverage—employment, parenting and race issues—also capture the attention of Hispanic leaders, but for different reasons. Lower on the list of issues, interestingly, are those related to health care, AIDS, and illegal immigration in the United States—all issues that substantially affect Hispanics.

When asked what their boards are doing to address the problems, most indicated that their institutions have supported organizations and programs that address at least some of them. However, most also indicated that many of the problems identified in our survey were not part of the mandate of their organizations.

Agency Effectiveness in Meeting Hispanic Needs

Respondents were asked to rate how major nonprofit agencies that receive the bulk of their funding from corporate and foundation gifts are doing in effectively serving the needs of Hispanics in the United States. Significantly, ratings of fair or poor outnumbered excellent or good ratings by two to one.

When respondents were asked specifically in what ways major nonprofits were doing an excellent/good job, their comments included:

- "They have identified the needs of the Hispanic population they serve and are attempting to address [the] problems."
- "The United Way is the primary source of funding to Hispanics, and the YMCA is involved in the community."
- "The Boy Scouts and Girl Scouts are bringing more Hispanics on staff to help with Hispanic issues."

Two-thirds of our respondents indicated less than positive feelings toward major public and private agencies due to the belief that most of these institutions have not spent sufficient time building relationships with the Hispanic community. The most serious criticism of major nonprofits involved their tendency to continue favoring groups and programs they supported long before there were Hispanics or other minorities in the community, rather than reallocating resources to meet changing population characteristics and needs.

- "Most funders and the nonprofits they support do not serve Latino groups in proportion to their population or needs, it seems. Most of the youth programs are formed in churches which are not in Hispanic communities, for example, and these are funded."
- "Funders have a tendency to look at the racial/ethnic makeup of the board and to fund in that percentage. They make . . . speeches about reaching deeper into our communities, but there is no action."
- "There is very little effort by service agencies to reach the Hispanic community with mental health problems. This is due to lack of outreach."
- "There is a tendency among foundations and mainstream nonprofits to stay away from controversial issues, and immigration organizations appear to be controversial."

- "There is just not enough allocation of funds and diversification of staff in the field to meaningfully address our needs."
- "Some programs which service Hispanics without Hispanics on their board do not understand our needs, or even seem to care about the Hispanic community."

The almost universal expression of our respondents that funding is not aligned with expanding Hispanic community numbers and needs is significant. Part of the problem is that the Latino trustees we surveyed by and large sit on boards where they are the only Latino community representative. Thus, while their placement does perhaps meet the institution's need to appear and feel that it supports diversity, it may not translate into significant tangible change in funding or benefits for Latino communities.

Emerging Issues

Respondents were asked what issues they felt would most impact all Americans, Hispanics as well as non-Hispanics, in the year 2001. Issues and concerns mentioned most frequently included education and access to higher education; hunger and poverty; job skills, opportunities and security; and empowerment of individuals for upward mobility. Comments that follow suggest serious concerns for the future.

- "I think the biggest problems will be lack of preparation of the workforce."
- "Class struggle will consume most of us. The rich are going to get richer and the poor poorer."
- "The change in the global economy will [especially] impact the Hispanic population in the U. S."
- "If we do not have the education we cannot move forward in this country."
- "Keeping up with technology. If Hispanics cannot do this, they will be left behind."
- "Keeping strong family ties is critical to the well-being of the Hispanic community."
- "[Major economic and] political tensions . . . are going to be created between African Americans and Hispanics."
- "Redistricting after the year 2000 will be a major issue."

Corporate Board Member Views and Comparisons

When addressing the opinions of Latino foundation trustees who are also members of corporate boards, some differences emerged. Like their foundation counterparts, Latinos on corporate boards tend to be older than the average age of Latinos in the population as a whole, and they are, as their counterparts on foundation boards, typically from more privileged backgrounds and professions. They tend to move easily between Hispanic and Anglo communities, having had strong assimilation experiences at work or in their communities. Some of those interviewed had been referred or suggested for corporate board membership by non-Latino colleagues they met while serving on foundation or other important community boards. A majority felt that the primary reason for their appointment to a corporate board was their reputation and qualifications in their professional field. They felt these attributes were being utilized to the fullest by their corporate board, though generally, unless asked to be part of a search committee for a new CEO, they had no responsibility for the selection or promotion of staff. Many of them were the firm's only Hispanic board member, yet they were almost never asked to provide the Hispanic position or perspective on issues relating to the overall community in any formal sense. Where corporations had giving programs that involved board committees, some Latino board members had the experience of being involved at that level.

The corporate boards in this country that are the most ethnically, racially, and gender diversified serve consumer products companies, banks, and educational institutions, as well as firms in selected, regulated industries such as gas and electric utilities and, in some cases, telephone companies. Most of the corporate trustees we interviewed represent companies that fall in these categories. When asked about the issues they thought were most critical to Hispanics in the United States today, the corporate trustees we surveyed provided answers quite similar to their foundation counterparts. However, unlike their foundation counterparts, the companies whose boards they served on were not involved with community issues, except through their corporate foundation or community giving program.

Those who serve on corporate boards that support corporate giving programs or foundations expressed that there has been some recent retrenchment in these areas, owing to significant downturns that have significantly diminished the money available for corporate giving.

Closing Thoughts

Our research did not cover a statistically significant sample nor was it as broad as we had originally intended. The problems of obtaining access to board lists, securing time from busy interviewees, as well as project resource constraints necessitated that we limit our survey. However, we found remarkable similarity between the concerns raised by those we did speak to and the concerns of another group of Latino trustees convened at HIP's 1995 Santa Fe meeting.

Although there have been important increases in Latino political participation and general institutional opportunity over the last decade, Latinos on foundation and corporate boards are still quite rare, less than one-half of one percent of the overall universe of board level appointments in the U. S. While affirmative action gains of the 1960s and 1970s added African Americans to foundation and corporate boards and helped to forge an African-American funding agenda, a similar process has yet to occur for Latinos. We need to make it happen now.

Without scheduled conferences and necessary meetings that create access to each other and our respective insights, Latino trustees and emerging community leaders will be constrained from efforts to build linkages that leverage influence in the field. We need to establish a framework and agenda to initiate such exchanges. Additional research on the experiences and attitudes of Latino foundation and nonprofit trustees, moreover, is also needed to help inform and direct future leadership convenings and initiatives in the field. Finally, continuing efforts by groups such as Hispanics in Philanthropy to expand needed knowledge and dialogue related to Latino trustee resources are also needed. Leading donors and independent sector institutions can and must expand their support for Latino trustee-focused convenings, research, and support programs. By doing so, they will increase Latino contributions to philanthropy and strengthen the field's relevance and impact.

Notes

[1] See, e.g., de la Garza, Rodolfo, "Explorations into Latino Voluntarism" in this collection.

[2] See Espinoza, Galina, "Five U. S. Stocks With Latin Heat," *Money* magazine, December 1997, p. 142.

Part III

Promoting Social Investment in Latin America:
Emerging Issues and Lessons

Women, Fundraising and the Third Sector in Mexico

Rosa María Fernández Rodríguez, Griselda Martínez Vázquez,
Sara Elena Pérez Gil Romo, Cristina Zepeda,
Centro Mexicano para la Filantropía

Introduction

In the last decade, Mexico has faced one of the most severe economic crises in its history. During this period the national debt rose to $180 billion and federal revenues for social services decreased from 49 percent to 29 percent of the total budget. Parallel to this process, the Mexican independent sector has developed new strength. According to data collected by Centro Mexicano para la Filantropía (Mexican Center for Philanthropy—CEMEFI), there are now more than 3,500 nongovernmental organizations (NGOs) in the country doing community work and many more that have not been officially registered.

Without a doubt, the nonprofit sector has increasingly contributed to the promotion of socioeconomic development in Mexico; nevertheless, it faces enormous challenges, given Mexico's recent difficulties. To further strengthen its impacts, it is essential to address one of the sector's principal problems: the lack of financial resources.

Women have been developing an especially important role within these organizations in recent decades and have been modeling great efficiency in fundraising and grantwriting directed to social and community projects. Unfortunately, owing to a significant dearth of research and data on the subject, relatively little is known about the motivations, leadership, and impact of women in the field.

The limited information about the role of women in Mexico's Third Sector has motivated this research project by CEMEFI with the support of Hispanics in Philanthropy. Its goal is both to honor the history of women in the community-building field as well as to motivate other women to become part of this movement.

The data we provide herein on women's participation in third sector organizations in Mexico is mainly based on interviews with 42 leaders of women-run and women-focused community agencies. These data and our corresponding analyses are sure to contribute to greater awareness and support among international foundations, multilateral organizations, corporations, individuals, and Mexican government agencies interested in supporting the critical work in which women leaders and groups are engaged. Expanded knowledge about women's roles and their participation in philanthropic organizations should also encourage a greater awareness among Mexican women themselves about the public value and importance of their work.

The article is organized in various sections designed to accomplish the following specific objectives:

1. to describe the evolution of Mexican women's participation during recent decades in fundraising for third sector institutions;
2. to describe the macrosocial factors that have influenced these women and their participation in such institutions;
3. to present a socioeconomic and cultural profile of Mexican women who participate in fundraising;
4. to examine the types of institutions in which these women are participating;
5. to examine the impact of women's participation on nonprofit institutions based on interviewees' perceptions; and
6. to describe the obstacles confronted by women in their fundraising endeavors.

Background

Efforts to strengthen civil society in Mexico and Latin America began during the 1960s in a context of great political upheaval and civic participation. This decade marked a substantive change in notions of civic and social responsibility, going beyond the exclusively charitable realm. Participation, and the social, economic, and political development of the country, were presented as important new objectives. Clearly this constituted a major change in our society and established a new context and imperative to address social problems and challenges.

Women's participation in Mexican social life promoted especially great transformations towards the end of the 1960s. The contemporary feminist movement, like the student and hippie movements, questioned the social values rooted in a traditional social structure that did not accept cultural diversity. In the case of women, questioning their traditional roles as mothers and wives as a predetermined destiny took root during these tumultuous times.

This cultural phenomenon coincided with the development of a federal education policy committed to mass education at the beginning of the seventies that supported cultural questioning of women's historically subordinate role and created possibilities for women to acquire professional degrees. All of this supported the construction of new female identities and life aspirations. These changes in female social and political standing have influenced the way in which contemporary Mexican women participate in the third sector. Middle- and upper-class women as well as those belonging to religious groups increasingly participate in social labor designed to improve Mexican community life. They mobilize and allocate charitable contributors of basic life necessities (food, medicine or clothing) on behalf of groups with very little resources. They also find themselves engaged as volunteers in health, education, and antipoverty institutions. Frequently, they manage and staff NGOs that are active in these and other altruistic pursuits.

Rooted in the cultural modernization process initiated at the end of the seventies, and supported by the establishment of new sociocultural relationships, important new forms of women's participation in the third sector, especially in fundraising, have emerged. As time goes by, greater women's participation can be observed in organizations dedicated to social welfare activities that transcend altruism and charity and that promote instead fundamental social and cultural change through fundraising and the leadership of community development and policy institutions.[1]

Women's participation in decision making processes in public and private institutions is a very recent social phenomenon. Very little information is available about women in high administrative positions that allows us to discern the particular characteristics, leadership styles, decision making qualities, and impacts of their work in institutions and communities.

The female identity appears in fact to substantially influence new and more participative forms of third sector activity, especially in the area of fundraising. We consider three specific centers of Mexican women's participation in the third sector as staff and/or financial supporters of nonprofit institutions. They consist of:

1. Middle- and upper-class Mexican women with a strong family tradition in philanthropy who typically support more established and conservative charities and religious communities.
2. Women supporters and volunteers of institutions that promote social change and civil and human rights with an eye to reforming political, social, and economic realities in Mexico.
3. Women professionals in the third sector who are struggling to expand the human, financial, and material resources available to the institutions, communities, and causes they represent, whether more conservative or progressive in nature.

To examine both the particularities and the commonalities related to these centers of women's participation in philanthropy, we begin with a general overview of the third sector in Mexico, its makeup, its essential elements, and its recent evolution. In a second part of the article, we generally address gender roles and issues in the field. The last section of the article covers our core research objectives, methodologies, findings, and conclusions.

Mexico's Third Sector: An Overview

In Mexico, as in other countries, the notion of the third sector is a concept familiar to only a very limited number of people. When we refer to the third sector, therefore, many individuals may lack a clear definition of its objectives and makeup. A clarification of our meaning is thus in order.

When we address organized, private, and voluntary activities that focus on social and not-for-profit goals we are referring to the third sector. The third sector distinguishes itself from the commercial sector (market) and the public sector (state) by establishing as its main goal the private pursuit of the common good through nonpartisan initiatives and institutions that address basic health and human needs at the community level absent financial profit. For the purposes of this article, then, the third sector is defined as not-for-profit private institutions engaged in the provision of social assistance and/or the promotion of social development opportunities. Among these institutions we find nongovernmental organizations (NGOs), charitable institutions, philanthropies, not-for-profit organizations, and various related groups promoting social welfare and economic development, civil and human rights, and public health, education, and engagement activities. All of these agencies are usually defined under the umbrella of nongovernmental organizations; however this concept covers just one part, perhaps the most public segment, of the third sector.

Another related term sometimes used to describe the third sector is the Greek-based word *philanthropy*, which embodies at least aspects of each of the following definitional qualities:

> An efficient mode for private fund distribution, volunteerism, and the creation of community investment models that promote more balanced and harmonious social realities.

> A voluntary commitment of people, institutions, and their collective resources to social, economic, and community development.

> A set of nonpaid private actions oriented toward the expansion of social capital and community welfare.

Among the various factors that shape and influence the work of third sector organizations in Mexico today we find:[2]

Increasing Heterogeneity: Expanding population diversity requires increased institutional attention to the needs and circumstances of certain minority groups. The diversity of Mexico's population is mainly based on religious affiliation, ethnicity, age, gender, geography, and socioeconomic class. Given the growing scarcity of Mexico's public resources to satisfy all social demands, there are certain groups whose needs can be addressed only by third sector organizations whose assistance supplements limited government support.

Diminishing State Welfare: Mexico's third sector thrives in inverse proportion to the availability and accessibility of government social welfare assistance. Given the need to reduce public expenses stemming from the nation's recent economic crisis, many federally-administered social welfare programs are disappearing, and organized philanthropy is being called upon to help fill the void.

Persistent Development Needs: The level and kind of third sector activity in any nation will vary according to national development needs. While Mexico has made great developmental strides in recent decades, it remains a largely rural, impoverished, and underdeveloped society. This explains why in Mexico, like other developing countries, third sector organizations are overwhelmingly committed to rural assistance and poverty reduction programs.

Mexico's Third Sector in Historical Perspective

The history of institutions providing social assistance in Mexico can be divided into three distinct periods.

Colonization

This initial period was characterized by a strong religious influence in the creation of institutions of social assistance. It began with the creation of the Hospital de Jesús in 1524 and ended in 1860 when liberal politicians in favor of secularizing church property took control of the national government. During colonization, Mexico's principal leadership centers were the Spanish Crown and the Catholic Church. The Church created schools to promote conversion, centers to feed people, and hospitals.

Secularization

Mexico's second major phase of social welfare management was characterized by a strong state presence in the field; it lasted for the better part of a century, beginning in 1860 with the fall of colonization and ending in 1960 with the advent of Mexico's contemporary third sector institutions. In 1861, Mexico's central government nationalized all church property, including properties owned by the leading Catholic institutions contributing to social welfare. After the Mexican Revolution (1910-1920), state control over social welfare was consolidated in various public agencies committed to poor people's needs. The Church did, however, retain practical control of its institutions of social welfare, such as orphanages, hospices, clinics, and schools. The combined consequences of Catholic Church and state domination of Mexican social welfare until the 1960s were substantial and largely negative. These included:

A weak civil society resulting in a very small number of organizations independent of the state.

A profoundly paternalistic culture with a strong emphasis on central authority and control.

A low level of private sector participation in social welfare institutions.

Modernization

This period, commencing in the 1960s and continuing to the present, is characterized by a strong participation of independent, community-based nonprofits in the treatment of social needs. Economic circumstances exacerbated poverty and social inequality during the 1960s and 1970s. In response, many public advocates and community groups demanded a transformation of Mexico's economic and political structures. The Catholic Church, after the Second Vatican Council, commenced important new advocacy programs on behalf of the nation's poor. Liberation Theology began influencing people's actions. These social forces promoted the emergence of two types of NGOs dedicated to marginalized groups:

1. Grassroots organizations favoring the elimination of poverty through fundamental political and economic reforms, and the advancement of new empowerment strategies targeted to popular education, economic cooperatives, and community action agencies.
2. Organizations created by corporate leaders and groups to provide succor and assistance to the poor and needy without any corresponding goals regarding economic and political change.

Between 1980 and 1990, Mexico's economic problems increasingly placed in question the nation's capacity to support continued welfare state policies and practices. In response, nonprofit institutions began to diversify. Some older charitable organizations began to develop increasingly strategic community development activities. Institutions already involved in development work focused increasingly on new areas such as human rights and environmental justice. Important new organizations were necessarily created to confront emerging problems such as AIDS and the preservation of Mexico's rich cultural heritage. And large private foundations emerged.

Current Assessment of the Third Sector in Mexico

Two factors especially affect nonprofit sector development in Mexico today: the recent crisis in the political system and continuing, acute economic challenges.

In the context of Mexico's deepening political and economic turmoil in recent years, nonprofit institutions have become an essential vehicle for public participation in community governance and systems reform. Out of necessity, this development is receiving growing support among government leaders themselves. Government spending for social programs, for example, decreased from 40 percent of Mexico's total budget in 1980 to 29 percent in 1992; and 50 percent of the Mexican population still lives in poverty. To address the many challenges resulting from all of this, government officials are compelled to encourage expanded third sector problem-solving initiatives. However, the response capacity of civil institutions is limited, given the still very small number of nonprofit organizations in the country. The Mexican Center for Philanthropy has identified only 2,362 such organizations in a country whose population exceeds 180 million individuals. Of these organizations, 23.2 percent work in education, 21.8 percent in welfare, 20.6 percent in health, 17.9 percent in development, 6.9 percent in human rights, 5.3 percent in ecology, 2.7 percent in art and culture, and 1.7 percent in science and technology.

Of the 2,362 organizations we reviewed, 50 percent were located in the Federal District, 9.7 percent in the state of Jalisco, 4.1 percent in the state of Guanajuato, 3.4 percent in the state of Mexico, and the rest, 32.8 percent, were distributed among Mexico's other states and regions. A total of 999 institutions in this universe specifically defined their target population: 55.8 percent of these groups worked with children, 16.4 percent with youth, 14.1 percent with women, and 13.7 percent with elders.

Specific Areas of Activity for Nonprofit Organizations in Mexico	
ART AND CULTURE	Sacred art, secular art and culture, sociocultural activities, museums, sports.
DEVELOPMENT	Managerial and/or technical assistance, neighborhood associations, job counseling, saving co-ops, housing, cooperatives, indigenous, rural and urban community development, industrial development, political education, women's rights, retired citizens.
ECOLOGY	Water and air pollution, environmental education, animal rights, reforestation, waste management, resource management, environmental management, parks.
EDUCATION	Literacy, scholarships and grants, job skills, centers for documentation, workshops and training, special education, religious education, technical education, integral development, cultural exchange, learning methods, preschool, elementary, secondary, and postsecondary education.
HEALTH	Drug and alcohol addiction, visual impairment, family medicine, mobility impairment, surgery, intensive care, disabled individuals, medical specialties, hospitals, physical therapy, general medicine, deafness and hearing loss, nutrition and hygiene (preventive medicine), family planning, emergency services, rehabilitation, mental retardation, AIDS, Down's syndrome.
HUMAN RIGHTS	Legal counsel, "disappeared," homosexuals, migrants, political prisoners, prisoners, refugees, torture victims.
SCIENCE & TECHNOLOGY	Technical assistance, basic, social, and biological sciences, development of technology.
WELFARE	Homeless shelters, elder homes, services to the homeless, services to the poor, services for children, health services, hospices, youth homes, child care centers, general social welfare.

(Source: CEMEFI, *Directorio de Instituciones Filantrópicas 1995-1996*, Mexico.)

Major Categories of Nonprofits in Mexico

For purposes of analysis, the nonprofit institutions we reviewed for this study can be conceptualized as falling into three major categories, taking into account their historical roots, priorities, and organizational makeup:

Service Institutions: Typically, these are older organizations with as much as one hundred years of experience. They tend to prioritize services targeted to low income and disabled people. Most of them have deep religious roots. They generally are legally organized as private service institutions, qualifying automatically as tax-exempt institutions.

Development NGOs: These groups, typically created in the 1960s, tend to promote community-based efforts designed to increase jobs and income for very poor people. Because their legal structure usually takes the form of informal civic associations, they often do not qualify for tax exempt status under Mexican law.

Emerging Nonprofits: Important emerging groups have evolved during the last ten years to address other social issues not attended by Mexican service institutions, development NGOs, or government. Typically, their issues and interests relate to ecology, human rights, and the preservation of Mexican cultural heritage. These organizations are organized either as tax-exempt organizations or nonexempt associations.

Main Problems of All Nonprofit Organizations in Mexico

Lack of Financial Resources: Most Mexican organizations face serious financial challenges. Numerous factors account for this.

1. Large corporations generally channel their donations exclusively to tax-exempt organizations, but because many Mexican charities are nonexempt, they are typically excluded from receiving corporate support. The main areas supported by Mexican corporations are health, education, and ecology (Fernández 1993).
2. There presently exist very few Mexican community foundations dedicated to the accumulation and public allocation of charitable donations. Consequently, these sources of income are largely inaccessible to all but a small handful of Mexican nonprofit organizations (CEMEFI 1995).
3. Individual donations made directly to Mexican nonprofit institutions are generally few in number and small in amount. Individuals who do give directly to nonprofits prefer to gear their resources to health and education institutions that support service-oriented programs and projects.

Foreign foundations operating in Mexico are an important source of income for NGOs: fully 10 percent of all CEMEFI member nonprofits received foreign financial support in 1990; and in 1993, North American foundations alone distributed 150 grants in Mexico for a total of $22 million. However, despite the growing desirability and importance of these external financial resources, they are typically accessible to relatively few nonprofits and they are increasingly a source of competition among Mexican NGOs.

Low Level of Professionalism: The level of efficiency of Mexican non-profit institutions is very uneven. Relatively few organizations in the field operate efficiently and with capable personnel. Most of these organizations, in fact, lack personnel who bring professional nonprofit management experience. They also typically lack strong boards of directors (CEMEFI 1990).

Another significant problem inhibiting professionalism in the field is the lack of coordination among philanthropic institutions. In Mexico, there are few umbrella organizations. Unfortunately, among those that do exist, there is little integration of effort and much unnecessary duplication.

The Mexican nonprofit community also suffers from a dearth of institutions that offer quality consulting services and technical assistance on legal, managerial, financial, and information issues (CEMEFI 1990). Such gaps in field capacity and activity are continuing sources of concern to the health and vitality of Mexico's independent sector.

Insufficient Research Infrastructure and Data: The current infrastructure for research on Mexico's third sector can not adequately assess the wide variety of problems that the field faces. There is consequently very little statistical data available to quantify and characterize the Mexican nonprofit sector. There is also a lack of information about third sector employment, income, and other contributions to the Mexican Gross National Product. This lack of information on the sector makes it difficult for nonprofit institutions to exercise greater influence on public policy making that could enhance the sector's future development (CEMEFI 1990).

Women's Presence in Third Sector Organizations: Equality Versus Difference Theory

To assess female participation in third sector management and fundraising in Mexico, it is helpful to look first at emerging theoretical frameworks of gender roles and women's studies that facilitate understanding of women's changing circumstances and experiences in different social spheres. Two different feminist discourses on womanhood have recently dominated discussion of these topics: the first focuses on equality and the second on difference.

These theoretical discourses have as points of departure, two different conceptions of being a woman in contemporary society. What is constant is both groups' agreement that society has defined masculinity and femininity in opposition, with the feminine being defined as a negative perspective.[3] There is also agreement that social relationships are hierarchical, based on sexual difference, with women playing a subordinate role in relationship to men.

What distinguishes equality advocates from difference advocates are their divergent responses to these shared understandings of the problems women face in society. Generally speaking, equality advocates have defined an action agenda geared towards incorporating women as equals into the extant institutional and social order historically defined and led by men. Difference advocates, on the other hand, concentrate mainly on defining a fundamentally new shape of gender relations that allows society to project a new feminine identity. This emerging split in feminist conceptualization explains why both in feminist theory and praxis leading figures have been searching for an answer to the fundamental philosophical question: What does it mean to be a woman today? Feminine identity has been traditionally defined in relation to women's reproductive role in society, and therefore women's identity has fixated on the equation woman=mother. To be a woman, and therefore a mother, in contemporary Western society has its representation through a set of ideological stereotypes of motherhood in both the private and the public spheres. These stereotypes are culturally assigned to women, even if patriarchy justifies them as natural attributes. Among these attributes we typically find altruism, dedication, nurturing, and generosity. We also assume a tendency among women to seek personal fulfillment through service to others, mainly the men in their lives—fathers, brothers, husbands, and sons.

The emergence of difference theory suggests, however, that gender construction is in transition. Within this context, difference research considers that the incorporation of women into the labor force, their professional education, and reproductive choices are processes that support the construction of new gender identities and therefore contribute to the establishment of new social relations between the sexes. These considerations open the possibility for women who so choose to create their own (i.e., alternative) identities. To capture the social change dynamic in this redefinition of female identity, it is necessary to avoid looking for evidence of women's subordination at every turn, without denying its existence.

In fact, changing notions of gender are inevitable, even in extremely male-dominated societies like Mexico, with the progressive presence of women in the public sphere, their high degree of participation in the economy, and their growing political influence. It is also important to note that changes in gender culture are expressed not just in the quantitative participation of women in all spheres of society but also in the qualitative contributions to institutions and society that highly qualified women invariably make as they advance.

The growing presence and leadership of women in Mexico's third sector, especially in executive staff and fundraising positions, establishes a significant trend in the field, even if the number of women in these positions is still very limited. According to the *Directorio de Instituciones Filantrópicas* published by CEMEFI,[4] in 1990 there were 608 registered institutions of which 187 were directed by women (31 percent). In 1996, CEMEFI registered 2,364 organizations of which 812 (34.3 percent) were directed by women. Given this growth in women's leadership at the present time of significant restructuring and redefinition in Mexican society it is important to know more about women's aspirations in the field, their perceptions about their role in shaping the sector's development, and their experiences as nonprofit managers and fundraisers.

Are these women inclined to adapt a more equality-based focus relative to their male counterparts, or are they instead more inclined to embrace a difference focus? What characteristics among these women, if any, appear to distinguish them? Finally, what can or should leaders and institutions concerned about the vitality of Mexican philanthropy be doing to support the development and success of these women? These are the essential questions covered in the balance of this article.

Key Objectives and Research Questions

Our essential goal in pursuing the research that informs this article was straightforward: to describe how women's participation in nonprofit management and fundraising has evolved during the last ten years, from the perspective of fifty representative female practitioners. Beyond this basic goal, our inquiry was informed by several specific objectives. These included the following:

To establish a socioeconomic and cultural profile of women participating in nonprofit fundraising.

To determine the major social, economic, political, cultural, and ideological factors influencing women's participation in the field.
To describe the types of institutions in which these women are active.

To assess the impacts of female participation on third sector institutions as perceived by interviewees.

To identify the major obstacles faced by women in their management and fundraising activities.

The corollary questions we wanted to pose with an eye to achieving our objectives included the following:

How have women's roles in management and fundraising at third sector institutions changed during the last ten years?

Who are the women principally involved in this work in Mexico?

Which factors have mostly influenced their engagement in the sector: economic, sociocultural, educational, ideological?

What is the profile of the institutions where these women are mainly active?

What aspects of third sector institutional activity have been impacted most by women's participation?

What are the main obstacles women face in this work?

Methodology

Research Characteristics

Our research was mainly designed to measure and assess data relative to our key objectives and questions under current circumstances rather than in global, historical terms. It was designed to be both *descriptive* and *analytic*, given that it attempted to establish associations between variables (i.e., qualitative interviewee responses) and static indicators (i.e., quantitative data derived from the field).

Selection of Subjects

Using CEMEFI's *Directorio de instituciones filantrópicas 1995,* 812 women-directed institutions were identified in CEMEFI's total member base of 2,364 institutions. From that grouping, fifty organizations and their chief executives were selected for follow-up interviews and study in simple random form.

Hypotheses and Assumptions

To inform and organize our research, we sought to test some specific hypotheses and assumptions related to each of our main areas of interest. Our major hypotheses and assumptions were:

Profile of Women Participating in Third Sector Organizations

1. In general, Mexican women who participate in third sector organizations are characterized by a largely religious orientation, a privileged socioeconomic class assignment, a college-level educational background, a strong family philanthropic tradition, and middle-age status.
2. In contrast, women who specifically affiliate with social development organizations tend to be greatly influenced by feminist ideology, to come from middle-class families, to have a graduate or professional degree, and to be younger than their counterparts in the larger field.

Factors Contributing to Women's Participation in the Third Sector

1. The increased participation of women in the third sector has been influenced by macrosocial national processes.
2. Women are especially participating in third sector organizations given the lack of action by the state in favor of marginalized groups.

Profile of the Institutions Where Women Participate Most

1. Women primarily participate in health and educational institutions that serve poor women and children.

2. Borders between charitable institutions and those that promote social development are becoming blurred. The tendency is increasingly to provide both types of services.

The Impact of Female Participation in Third Sector Institutions

1. Women have become professionalized in fundraising and fund management.
2. The role of women in third sector organizations is being transformed from social assistance to social development.
3. Changes in women's roles within the third sector find their origins in the contemporaneous feminist movement.

Obstacles Women Face in Fundraising

1. Women's advancement in the field is significantly influenced by traditional perceptions of women's roles.
2. Women nonprofit managers who do fundraising break with traditional stereotypes of female roles in Mexican society.

Data Collection Instrument

A questionnaire was constructed with sixty-two open and closed questions addressing our proposed objectives, as well as our hypotheses. The questionnaire was divided into six categories:

1. Subject's profile;
2. Description of subject's ideology;
3. Subject's opinion about women's role in nonprofit organizations;
4. Institutional description of program priorities and training opportunities;
5. Description of sources of financial support; and
6. Description of nonprofit challenges in fundraising.

Data Collection Process/Timeline

We assigned four interviewers to collect our requested information. These individuals located and made first contact with our designated subjects; described to them our research rationale and solicited their collaboration; and conducted confidential one-on-one interviews with forty-two of the fifty subjects we targeted, following our standard instrument. The period in which the interviews took place was July-October, 1996.

Data Analysis

Data analysis took place in the following manner: data collected from closed questions were analyzed by the statistical program SPSS, and standard derivatives from our open questions were transcribed, codified, and edited. Following is a summary of our "Findings," including tables, narratives, and comments on salient information derived from our interviews.

Findings

Evolution and Awareness of Mexican Women's Participation

Sixty-seven percent of our interviewees declared having information about the role women have played in nonprofit fundraising in Mexico during the last ten years. When asked about what this role has been, their answers varied. Some did not answer or answered only vaguely (e.g., "very interesting"). Others provided elaborate explanations. It is important to note that these more elaborate responses were not always a strict description of women's roles but also covered other issues, such as women's goals and the importance of women's participation in the field. Examples of some of the answers expressed during our interviews follow below:

"Our role is very important. It is not easy to give away our time. We are more sensitive [than men] and have a better disposition to do things."

"We have opened a road that did not exist before. Women are demonstrating greater capacity and characteristics that enable them to do things better than men."

"[Women] have played an important role because they have opened new financial sources; they are imaginative, creative, sensitive."

"We have to break the limitations. This is very important. We should take over some of the space men have because we are more sensitive."

"[Women's role is] very important. Women have taken over greater responsibility than men in fundraising."

Many of our interviewees related women's changing roles in nonprofit organizations to larger political issues and trends:

> "Today, women have a wider and more public participation in Mexican social, economic, and political life."

> "Women have moved from playing a social assistance role towards empowerment through advocacy on political and economic issues."

> "[Women's role is to bring forward] their consciousness and to exercise women's rights; to promote social and political participation of women."

> "We have changed; now we are empowered. There was an advance with the feminist movement and now we are part of a citizen's movement. We intend to propose public ethics and changes in the law. We are taken into account by the government."

> "Now women do not just participate, but [we also] organize. Therefore it is easier to defend our rights."

> "Women naturally take charge of executive functions in addition to the formulation of projects for fundraising. We are the ones who organize events and manage the resources."

The aforementioned observations were often mixed with those accompanying our question "What have been the most influential factors affecting changes in women's roles during the last ten years?" In addition to describing the perceived reasons for these changes, our interviewees made frequent reference again to fundraising. The predominant response was related to women's training, preparation, and professionalization. In other words, interviewees principally attributed recent changes in women's roles in the nonprofit sector to the availability of women's training and professional development opportunities in fundraising and other areas. Considering these observations, we conclude that education is a fundamental factor in women's professional development in the field. Let's look at some of our interviewees' specific comments:

> "Women have become more educated and professionalized."

"Fundraising has become more competitive; therefore we need to professionalize it. Universities are [now] offering diploma programs and women are enrolling in them."

"Women are more and more trained and they want [to exercise] social leadership."

"Until recently [female] participation was subordinated to that of men. Now, given [our] preparation, [women] have a protagonist role."

Interviewees agreed that Mexican women play more productive roles in the third sector today. They occupy directorships. They exercise leadership in key staff positions. There is a more open field for women as they have moved from caretaker to advocacy roles.

Subjects Profile

In this section, some of the main characteristics of the forty-two interviewed subjects are described and analyzed. As noted in Table 1, the largest percentage of our interviewees fell into the 36-50 age category, 26 percent in the older than 50 category, and just 12 percent in the younger than 35 category. It is important to note that most women in the 18-35 age category work for social advocacy institutions, whereas women over 50 were almost equally divided between religious institutions (5) and community service nonprofits (6).

Table 1 Age		
AGE	NUMBER	PERCENT (%)
36-50	26	62
51 or more	11	26
18-35	5	12
Total	**42**	**100**

More than half of the women we interviewed are married (57 percent), about a quarter (21 percent) are divorced, and the rest are either single, in partnerships, or widowed (Table 2).

Table 2 Civil Status		
CIVIL STATUS	NUMBER	PERCENT (%)
Married	24	57
Divorced	9	21.5
Single	4	9.5
Partnered	3	7
Widow	2	5
Total	**42**	**100**

When looking at religious affiliation (Table 3), we observed that most of these women (fully 67 percent) professed to be Catholic; but more than a quarter (31 percent) self-identified as agnostic and one called herself "Guadalupana."

Table 3 Religious Affiliation		
AFFILIATION	NUMBER	PERCENT (%)
Catholic	28	67
Agnostic	13	31
Guadalupana	1	2
Total	**42**	**100**

Table 4 reflects the distribution of interviewees' educational attainments. Most of the women we interviewed held a college or postgraduate degree in the social sciences, mainly in anthropology and sociology. Twenty-nine out of forty-two women we studied (69 percent) had a professional degree, leading us to believe that a significant number of Mexican women with professional degrees are participating in third sector organizations. It is logical to assume, moreover, that high levels of schooling prepare these women for decision making positions within their institutions.

Table 4
Degree of Schooling

SCHOOLING	NUMBER	PERCENT (%)
Professional	16	38
Specialization	6	14
Technical Degree	5	12
Master's Degree	4	10
Ph.D.	3	7
High School	2	5
Teaching Certificate	2	5
Diploma program	2	5
Other	2	4
Total	**42**	**100**

Only twenty-two of the women in our pool were asked specifically about the kind of academic institutions they attended (Table 5). Of these women, 41 percent went to private universities, mainly Universidad Iberoamericana de México, and 32 percent attended public universities, including Universidad Nacional Autónoma de Mexico, Escuela Nacional de Antropología e Historia, and Universidad Autónoma de Mexico, among others.

Table 5
Type of University Attended

TYPE OF UNIVERSITY	NUMBER	PERCENT (%)
Private National University	9	41
Public University	7	32
Private Foreign University	3	13.5
Did not answer	3	13.5
Total	**22**	**100**

When asked (Table 6) about their socioeconomic class, most (55 percent) of the women we spoke to classified themselves as middle class, followed by those who considered themselves upper class (38 percent). These outcomes were not surprising, given that women with a high degree of professionalization and decision making authority are expected to belong to the middle and upper classes in Mexico.

Table 6 Socioeconomic Class		
SOCIOECONOMIC CLASS	NUMBER	PERCENT (%)
Middle	23	55
Upper	16	38
Low	2	5
Did not answer	1	2
Total	**42**	**100**

As can be observed in Table 7, most of the women we interviewed occupied the highest staff positions within their organizations. They were executive directors, program directors, and development directors. This was consistent with our objective of interviewing women nonprofit executives in order to learn about their perceptions of women's roles in third sector organizations and fundraising.

Table 7 Position in the Institution Where They Work		
POSITION	NUMBER	PERCENT (%)
Board President	17	40
Executive Director	12	29
Vice-President	3	7
General Manager	2	5
Treasurer	1	2
Other	7	17
Total	**42**	**100**

Sixty-four percent of our interviewees described their work as voluntary. The significance of this resides in the assumption that people with a high degree of professionalization and responsibility would normally characterize their work as salaried or otherwise paid. Our interviewees' responses illustrated the relatively slow pace of change relative to female professional identity in the field.

Social, Economic, Political, Cultural, and Ideological Factors Motivating Women's Participation

Among the factors motivating these women to work in private non-profit organizations, "social concerns" occupied first place with 58 percent. Twenty-two percent identified family culture, while 18 percent identified religious conviction (Table 8). (Because many interviewees selected multiple factors in this category, our baseline totaled 55 responses.)

Table 8 Reason for Interest in Philanthropy		
REASONS	NUMBER	PERCENT (%)
Social concerns	32	58
Family culture	12	22
Religious conviction	10	18
Transcendence and self-realization	1	2
Total	**55**	**100**

To learn how long our interviewees had been involved in not-for-profit activities (Table 9), we asked respondents to identify the year they became involved in philanthropic pursuits. Twenty-nine percent identified the period between 1981 and 1985, 21 percent the period between 1986 and 1990, and 14 percent the period between 1991 and 1995. This means that a clear majority of these women started to work with third sector institutions only within the last fifteen years. It is important to note here that the modern peak of third sector organizational development in Mexico occurred during the 1980s, especially after the 1985 earthquake when civic participation increased in large numbers nationwide. Therefore, it is congruent that so many of the women we interviewed began to participate in the field during this period.

Table 9		
Year in which They Became Involved		
Year	**Number**	**Percent (%)**
Before 1970	8	19
1971-1980	7	17
1981-1985	12	29
1986-1990	9	21
1991-1995	6	14
Total	**42**	**100**

Among the ideological factors (Table 10) influencing these women's participation in third sector institutions, most (42 percent) of our respondents identified "civic consciousness" as being the most influential. Religious and socialist ideology followed with nearly one-fifth (17 percent) of our respondents identifying these as most influential. Feminist ideology occupied third place among respondents (13 percent). (Again, because numerous respondents listed multiple influences, our baseline totals exceed the actual number of women we interviewed.)

Table 10		
Ideology that has Influenced the Most in Their Philanthropic Labor		
INFLUENCING IDEOLOGY	**NUMBER**	**PERCENT (%)**
Civic Consciousness	22	42
Religion	9	17
Socialist	9	17
Feminist	7	14
Religion/Civic Consciousness	2	4
Moral Consciousness	1	2
Liberal	1	2
Humanist	1	2
Total	**52**	**100**

To gain some insight into the impact of women's rights struggles on Mexico's third sector, the women we surveyed were asked about their degree of involvement in this work (Table 11). Nearly half of the women we interviewed did not respond to our key questions in this area. But some 54 percent of those who did respond appear to perceive themselves as active, versus 29 percent who responded negatively. However, the percentage of interviewees who self-identified as being actively involved in the women's movement increased to 63 percent when interviewees were asked to associate their participation in women's rights activities with their participation in a women's institution (compare Tables 11 and 12, respectively.)

Table 11
Active Participation in Women's Rights Struggles

ACTIVE	NUMBER	PERCENT (%)
Yes	13	54
No	7	29
Did Not Answer	4	17
Total	24	100

Table 12
Participation in Women's Organizations

PARTICIPATION	NUMBER	PERCENT (%)
Yes	15	62.5
No	9	37.5
Total	24	100

In an attempt to learn more about these women's motivations for engaging in third sector leadership, we decided to ask them about the social, economic, and political events marking the beginning of their participation in private nonprofit organizations. Events mentioned most frequently were the 1985 earthquakes (22 percent) and the 1995 Mexican economic crisis (20 percent). The student movement of 1968 and the women's movement followed. The recent Chiapas rebellion together with "nothing specific" occupied fourth place. As can be observed in Table 13, besides the aforementioned events, the interviewees mentioned other informing influences, such as chronic population health problems and government corruption. (Again, because interviewees identified multiple influences in this category, our baseline responses exceed the number of women in our pool.)

Table 13		
Mexican Social or Natural Phenomenon Influencing Participation		
PHENOMENON	NUMBER	PERCENT (%)
1985 Earthquakes	13	22
Economic and Political Crisis	12	20
1968 Student Movement	8	13
Feminist Movement	8	13
Chiapas Rebellion	4	7
None	4	7
Natural Disasters	2	3
Others	9	15
Total	**60**	**100**

It was not possible to decipher an agreement among our interviewees who referenced feminism as an influence as to what the feminist movement is. One respondent suggested it has to do with "the social and political consciousness of women" and another mentioned it in relationship to the emergence and presence of certain important female figures.

In sum, except for four women who responded that "no event" influenced their decision to participate in third sector organizations, the rest were moved by socioeconomic and political factors. The following are some examples of what our respondents reported:

"Being a witness to the marginalization of a large segment of the Mexican population made me start taking action."

"Every [problem] that affects Mexico and Mexicans hurts and it is my concern."

"[I was moved by my] contact with rural communities, their marginalization, social injustice, and the need for liberation."

"When I learned about poverty and marginalization in Oaxaca, I began to do community work in more than 250 municipalities."

Interviewee Institutions, Fundraising and Other Involvements, and Job Training Opportunities

Sixty-seven percent of our interviewees' employment institutions (16) were founded after 1980 and just two of them before 1940. The rest, according to interviewees, date their origins between 1950 and 1955, with one exception dating to 1970. Of all the institutions represented, 62 percent are registered as nonprofits, 33 percent are registered as private assistance institutions, and 2 percent as trust funds.

Table 14 below describes the missions of interviewees' organizations: 27 of them (64 percent) defined those missions as social action and 29 percent as social welfare. However, 7 percent consider that they are involved in both. The rest of the institutions represented in the pool are involved in missions varying from education and civic participation to health and the arts.

Table 14
Institutional Orientation

INSTITUTIONAL ORIENTATION	NUMBER	PERCENT (%)
Social Action	27	64
Social Welfare	12	29
Social Action and Welfare	3	7
Total	**42**	**100**

All the institutions represented in our study were classified (Table 15) according to their financial resources, with foundations not surprisingly manifesting the greatest share of resources in the field (48 percent), community service agencies securing second position (36 percent), and organizations providing services to the third sector placing third (16 percent).

Table 15
Type of Institution in Relationship to their Financial Resources

TYPE OF INSTITUTION	NUMBER	PERCENT (%)
Foundation	20	48
Community Service	15	36
Services to Third Sector	7	16
Total	**42**	**100**

Among the services these institutions provide (see Table 16), education and health were especially salient (49 percent between the two). Human rights, community development, and welfare followed. (Here again, because our 42 respondents frequently cited multiple services, our baseline exceeds our total interview pool in this category.)

Table 16
Services Provided by the Institution

SERVICES	NUMBER	PERCENT (%)
Education	24	26
Health	22	23
Human Rights	12	13
Community Development	11	12
Welfare	9	10
Ecology	5	5
Art and Culture	4	4
Political Rights	4	4
Others	3	3
Total	**94**	**100**

Our interviewees reported that 55 percent of their institutional projects were concentrated in urban zones, 12 percent in rural areas, and 33 percent in both. Only 33 percent of the respondents' institutions considered it a priority to change the geographic areas in which they worked in the near future. Very few of these institutions, moreover, mentioned any desire to work in regions at a distance from their central office location.

On the other hand, when asked, most of these institutions admitted some interest in areas such as Chiapas, Oaxaca, Guerrero, and the metropolitan zone of Mexico City, because they were the locations with the greatest indices of poverty and marginalization. Only one interviewee responded that her organization was thinking of undertaking project explorations in regions devastated by natural disasters.

The populations served by respondents' institutions are overwhelmingly comprised of women; only 6 percent of these institutions provided services exclusively for men. The remaining 94 percent served predominately female populations of varying ages, whether from urban, rural, or indigenous areas. (Because various respondents cited multiple populations as their focus, our baseline in this category also exceeds our total interview pool of 42.)

Table 17
Populations Served by Respondents' Institutions

POPULATION	NUMBER	PERCENT (%)
Women, Youth, and Girls	12	23.5
Indigenous Women	9	17.5
People in General	9	17.5
Women	6	11.5
Girls and Boys	5	10
Indigenous People	4	8
Men	3	6
Peasant Families	2	4
NGOs	1	2
Total	**51**	**100**

Impact of Female Participation on Mexico's Third Sector According to Areas of Greatest Participation

Women's leadership in some nonprofit areas, such as health and education, is especially pronounced in Mexico. Human rights and community development follow in order of salience. Some of these areas, of course, have been labeled "home extensions," as in the case of health and education, where women have traditionally exercised leadership. (Because almost all of our interviewees cited multiple areas in which they are most active, our baseline data in this category exceeds our total interview pool of 42.)

Table 18
Areas Where Women are Most Active According to Interviewees

AREAS	NUMBER	PERCENT (%)
Education	17	24
Health	15	21
Human Rights	7	10
Community Development	7	10
Welfare	6	8
All Areas	6	8
Children, Women, and Elders	4	6
Advocacy	3	5
Others	6	8
Total	**72**	**100**

The third sector is not an exception in relationship to how feminist thought has become relevant in many activities and projects. Sixty-four percent of our interviewees expressed some knowledge of feminism, and an even higher percentage of these women (67 percent) noted feminism's influence on their actions. Finally, nearly 40 percent of our subjects indicated an opinion that feminism has positively influenced their institutions.

Those women who registered positive feminist influences on their institutions were asked to explain their responses in detail. Responses cited opportunities for some female employees to the recent introduction of women-focused public policy projects and convenings.

Interestingly, only two of our respondents mentioned feminist aspirations as the main reason for supporting women in philanthropy. The vast majority of our respondents saw it differently. One respondent noted, for example, that, "The thought is a double-edged sword and not practical at all." Another mentioned that, "The philosophy is good, but the praxis is bad, maybe because of ignorance, lack of resources, education, etc." (It is important to note that many of the respondents' assertions about feminism's limits reflect some confusion about the relationship between philosophy, movement, and praxis.)

We asked interviewees whether their organizations had changed priorities in relationship to certain population groups over time and learned that more than half (52 percent) had not modified their priorities. Of the institutions that had made changes, their modifications typically related either to the populations served or the areas of work that established their substantive program priorities. Interviewees who referred to changes in population priority especially noted expanding interest in: women cancer patients and their caretakers, adolescent girls, children and teenagers, people with disabilities, indigenous people, and victims of natural disasters. It is important to note that many institutions included in our study that focus on children are considering incorporating mothers as a core focus of attention in the future. Regarding changes in program priorities, respondents mainly cited education and health as new areas, while some mentioned environmental education.

Seventy-five percent of our interviewees reported that they had been involved in fundraising. When asked about their specific functions in this area, many of them addressed general institutional activities instead of personal activities. Bazaars, film premieres, balls, and fairs were the favored fundraising activities of respondents' institutions. However, it was mentioned that some institutions were increasingly focusing on establishing and maintaining relationships with national and international foundations to support the design and implementation of new projects, including various training workshops and consulting efforts designed to assist women's and other community groups' development capacities.

Thirty-five of the forty-two (64 percent) women we interviewed mentioned attending fundraising training. Table 19 shows how workshops and seminars have been utilized.

Table 19 Type of Training Received in Fundraising		
TRAINING RECEIVED	NUMBER	PERCENT (%)
Workshops	16	46
Seminars	8	23
Courses	5	14
Diploma Programs	4	11
University	1	3
Others, Financial Experience	1	3
Total	**35**	**100**

Table 20 reflects the surprisingly large percentage of training recipients who have received instruction at the national and international levels.

Table 20 Origin of the Training Institution		
TRAINING INSTITUTION	NUMBER	PERCENT (%)
National	15	44
International	6	17
National and International	5	15
Did Not Answer	8	24
Total	**34**	**100**

As we mentioned earlier, attending workshops was the most common training method utilized by interviewees, followed by seminars. Various institutions provided these trainings: The Junior League; Espiral; Asociación Civil; Salud Integral para la Mujer; and Secretaria de Desarrollo Social. The diploma program of the Universidad

Iberoamericana de México, however, was the most recognized program among our respondents.

While our survey did not delve specifically into the quality of these programs, informal interviewee feedback suggested to us that the training available to them was relatively expensive and sporadic. It also suggested that interviewees were hungry for additional opportunities to attain deeper training in the field and to network more extensively with their counterparts across the nation. Presently, opportunities of this sort are few and far between in Mexico, however.

Impact of Female Participation on Fundraising According to Institutional Type and Financial Resources

Twenty-six percent of the third sector institutions whose executives we interviewed integrated their initial capital with individual donations, followed by foundation grants (20 percent), mostly from international grantmaking institutions. Across time, individual donations diminished and grants from national and international foundations increased. Income generated by fees for service constituted only a modest share (4 percent) of these institutions' total income. (Because respondents cited multiple sources of institutional support, our baseline in this category exceeds our total interview pool of 42.)

Table 21
Integration of Initial Endowment and Actual Income of Respondent Institutions

INITIAL INSTITUTIONAL CAPITAL	INITIAL CAPITAL		ACTUAL INCOME	
	Number	Percent (%)	Number	Percent (%)
Individual	21	26	19	19
International Foundation	16	20	19	19
Corporation	11	13.5	15	15
National Foundation	10	12.5	13	13
Government	6	8	10	10
Family	5	6	5	6
Multilateral	3	4	3	3
Staff	3	4	2	2
Banks	2	3	4	4
Volunteer Work	1	1	1	1
Events	1	1	3	3
Fees and Services	1	1	4	4
Embassies	0	0	1	1
Total	**80**	**100**	**99**	**100**

One of the most important ways in which to ensure the success of third sector institutions is the implementation of successful new fundraising methods. We asked our interviewees about what their organizations were doing or considering in this area. We observed a wide variety of responses. The most popular methods reported for expanding organizational funds were the selling of products such as new and used clothing, books—especially cookbooks—Pope John Paul II gold medals, and art work; also popular were fundraising events, including auctions, raffles, concerts, balls, and film premieres.

One group of women mentioned were generating income by consulting with new and emerging groups in the field requiring technical assistance. Other respondents cited the development of microenterprise loan funds and various fees for service efforts. Two of the institutions we reviewed reported a lack of need to raise funds because patrons sent them resources periodically without solicitation.

Thirty-four percent of the institutions whose executives we surveyed were small organizations with budgets below one million pesos. These institutions typically experienced serious financial problems. They rarely had the resources or contacts to access the select circles of funders that must be tapped if nonprofits are to survive and grow in Mexico. In addition, all of the (14) organizations falling into this category were dedicated to social action, generally one of the more difficult areas for fundraising in philanthropy.

Table 22
Institutional Annual Budget (in Mexican Pesos)

ANNUAL BUDGET	NUMBER	PERCENT (%)
Less than 1 million	14	34
More than 1 million	18	42
5 - 10 million	4	10
More than 10 million	2	5
Variable	1	2
Did Not Answer	3	7
Total	**42**	**100**

When asked about the types of relationship, interviewees consider most helpful to their institutional fundraising efforts, most mentioned personal relations, as described in Table 23.

Table 23 Relationships Used in Fundraising		
RELATIONSHIP	NUMBER	PERCENT (%)
Personal	17	41
Institutional and Personal	14	33
Institutional	10	24
National Fundraising	1	2
Total	42	100

Challenges Faced by Mexican Nonprofits Seeking Financial Resources

Mexico's continuing economic problems make it more and more difficult for nonprofit research, service, and advocacy groups to find financing for projects and administration.

When our respondents were asked whether the economic crisis has increased their institutions' financial problems, 52 percent responded affirmatively and 40 percent negatively. An exacerbating circumstance appears to be a general decline in foreign sources of support in Mexico, which until recently have established a critical base of nonprofit fundraising. Many believe this decline to be related to political or ideological considerations. The following are examples of this possibility as expressed by two of our interviewees:

"The image of Mexico as a developed country, that [former Mexican president] Salinas de Gortari promoted abroad, encouraged many countries to withdraw their financial support."

"[Foreign funders often] reject our proposals based on ideology. AID [the Agency for International Development] has declared that in 1998 U. S. funds will be reduced. International funders are tired of how the [Mexican] public sector [mismanages] aid, and they do not make a distinction between government and nonprofit organizations."

Most of our interviewees agreed that to contend with these circumstances, Mexican nonprofits need to increase their competitiveness by demonstrating more efficiency and creativity in their work and by engaging more staff in paid positions dedicated to fundraising.

The Mexican nonprofits that, according to these women, are not in financial crisis are those which have established a variety of mechanisms: commercialization of products, national campaigns, revenue-generating fees for service, fixed term investments, membership dues, and financial trust instruments, among others. Eighty-eight percent of our interviewees reported that women executives have played an important role in managing those institutions that are experiencing the fewest financial problems in Mexico's independent sector.

Obstacles Women Face

Most respondents answered negatively when asked whether women face special hardships in nonprofit fundraising. They observed, for example, that women "use their relationships [more efficiently than men];" "they are as capable as men"; "women know [best] how to communicate the importance of supporting an organization"; and "[women] are treated with [special] respect." Only one of our respondents noted that women are not given as much credit as men because "there is machismo and a generalized idea that women are incapable as administrators."

Tables 24 and 25 present the advantages and disadvantages women and men face when fundraising, according to our interviewees.

Table 24
Comparative Advantages of Men and Women When Seeking Financial Resources, According to Interviewees

WOMEN	MEN
Better personal relations	Moral consistency
Resort to feelings and intuition	Wider networks
More initiative and dedicated	It is part of his business
Greater time availability	They are in the money business
More passionate	More assertive
More emotional	More studious
More persuasive and persistent	More talented
Acquire dignity by asking others for help	Bigger thinkers
More able	Being men
More creative	More ambitious
Inspire more confidence	More authoritative
More seductive	More confident and self-assured
Better trained	Know how to ask and apply pressure
More committed	

Clearly, perceptions about the advantages and disadvantages men and women face when fundraising on behalf of third sector organizations are closely linked with traditional gender perceptions. The persistence of these traditional notions may inhibit women's advancement in the field, even as they are evidently progressing by artificially diminishing their self-confidence. Respondents' perceptions of socially ascribed roles, for example, frequently comprehended the public domain as men's domain and men's ability to navigate it more effectively than women as a fundraising disadvantage for women. Our respondents especially interpreted men's knowledge of the financial world as a disadvantage for women in the field, who tend to lack such knowledge. Of course, sexist policy and practice more than any intrinsic difference between the sexes likely account for these perceptions (or misinterpretations as the case may be).

Table 25
Disadvantages Men and Women Confront when Seeking Financial Resources, According to Interviewees

WOMEN	MEN
None	Easier to say no
More easily embarrassed, shy	Lack of time
More scattered	Too much pride
Weaker	Not trusted
Difficult relationship with money	Lack of contact/commitment
Lack of professionalism	re: community projects
Lack of managerial experience	Lack of creativity
More divided	Lack of sensitivity
Low self-esteem	Shyness
Sexual harassment/discrimination	Lack of interest
More family problems, being mothers and wives	Lack of persistence
	Too competitive

Summary

Women's Evolution in Fundraising

Most of our interviewees expressed the view that women's participation in fundraising for third sector organizations is evolving. This evolution is defined as women moving from an essentially "assistance"-

focused position to one allowing them to exercise management and leadership prerogatives over key functions in organizational governance, fundraising, and fund granting.

Interviewees identified the degree of schooling as the most relevant factor affecting female participation in philanthropy and other social realms. Another factor that was not explicitly addressed during our interviews, but that we consider especially relevant based on our observation was these women's celebration of their evolving identity. This new identity, which positions Mexican women for the first time as leading nonprofit managers and as fundraising decision makers, dismantles the old stereotype of women as mere caretakers.

Interviewees' Profile

Our profile of women participating in third sector organizations is highly heterogeneous. In pursuing our research, we considered two types of philanthropic organizations in which women are present: those that engage in social welfare and those that engage in social action. We expected to observe real differences between these two sets of women. Our results do not confirm our hypothesis. There does not exist a definite profile that allows us to differentiate the women who participate in each of these two types of organizations.

The basic profile of interviewees participating in social welfare organizations is as follows: 55 percent are between 36 and 50 years of age, and 36 percent are over 50; 64 percent have graduate degrees; 55 percent come from upper-class backgrounds and 45 percent self-identified as middle class; 64 percent are motivated to work in philanthropy due to social or political considerations, while 36 percent identified family tradition and religious conviction as their main motivating influences.

Most of the women we interviewed who work in third sector organizations that focus on social action identify feminism as a major influencing factor in their lives. Fifty-seven percent identified themselves as middle class while 29 percent identified with the upper class. Most of these women were between 35 and 50 years of age.

Social, Economic, Political, Cultural, and Ideological Factors Motivating these Women's Participation in Third Sector Activities

Among the factors identified as having the most influence on these women's initial participation in third sector organizations were the earthquakes of 1985, the economic and political crises of 1988 and 1995, the student movement in 1968, the feminist movement, and the 1994 Chiapas rebellion. These responses essentially underscore how Mexican women involved in the third sector are acting on their social consciousness and responding to real as well as perceived state limitations to act on behalf of marginalized populations.

Institutional Makeup; Population Groups and Geographical Areas Served

Most of the organizations whose leaders we surveyed are relatively younger institutions formed since 1981. On balance, they direct their resources and attention mainly to education (26 percent) and health (23 percent), and groups that can be labeled "vulnerable": children, the poor, women, and indigenous populations, in particular.

The women we interviewed participated in institutions that can be characterized as either social action or social welfare institutions. Social action institutions seek to modify extant structural conditions that contribute to larger social problems, while social welfare organizations tend to focus on the resolution of immediate problems. However, in reality, we observed that there is very little that actually distinguishes between the work of these two types of nonprofits in Mexico. In effect, both types of organizations have as a common goal the meaningful improvement of conditions for all Mexicans, with a special emphasis on the most marginalized groups in Mexican society.

Impacts of Female Participation on Mexico's Third Sector Institutions

Our research attests to the fact that Mexican women have recently become more professionalized in fundraising and fund administration. Fully 64 percent of our interviewees have received training in these areas. However, as our earlier comments suggest, the training and networking opportunities available to these women appear to be thin. Training is critical to emerging nonprofit leaders in countries like Mexico, where NGOs depend heavily on support from international foundations located in the Netherlands, (NOVIB), Germany (Neuman, Friedrich Ebert), and the United States (Ford, MacArthur, Rockefeller, Kellogg). These foundations, as leading global institutions, require certain standards in project and proposal development that are essential to comprehend and master for their major programs and initiatives.

When looking at the fundraising methods utilized by the women we interviewed, most of them are very traditional: bazaars, raffles, film premieres, and balls. We identified the emergence of some new methods, such as consulting and fees for services; however, these newer, revenue-generating approaches remain scant.

Overall, the growing participation and initiative of women in the field appears to be expanding the sector's base, as well as its orientation to grassroots empowerment and reform efforts. What impacts these factors will have in the long term remains to be seen.

Obstacles Faced by Women

The obstacles faced by Mexican women engaged in nonprofit management and fundraising activities are informed both by lingering societal biases, as well as related self-perceptions about traditional roles and responsibilities among these women themselves.

At first blush, our interviewees did not consider that any obstacles existed for them as nonprofit managers and fundraisers. However, when pressed to consider the various advantages and disadvantages facing women and men in the field, they perceived significant differences traditionally ascribed to gender identities. As often as not, these perceptions worked to the disadvantage of our interviewees.

Conclusions

Based on our extensive review of the issues, we close with the following recommendations to leaders of grantmaking institutions. Our hope is to inspire these institutions to more concerted action and investment in the field-based structures and supports needed for enhancing the reach and impact of female nonprofit executives and fundraisers in Mexico and other Latin American countries.

1. Expand funding support for more responsive development training and technical assistance efforts targeted to women-run and women-focused nonprofit groups.

    While nonprofit ·development training and technical assistance efforts do exist in Mexico, they do not appear to be sufficiently accessible to needy women's groups and their leaders to establish a critical mass of value to women in the field or to the larger community. They are only infrequently offered and relatively unaffordable to many. Such programs tend, moreover, to occur as one-time or otherwise fleeting experiences rather than as ongoing or more intensive undertakings; and they typically cover superficial rather than in-depth subject matter.

    Foundations would do well to support more accessible and intensive development training and technical assistance programs targeted at women nonprofit professionals and women-run agencies. Such programs could focus on more applied activities and needs of participants and more structured curricula geared to expand competencies that are increasingly required in real-life organizational management, administration, and fundraising. They could also support stipends and scholarships based on need, to make training more economically accessible.

2. Support networking and exchange opportunities for female nonprofit executives and development directors.

    Female nonprofit executives and development directors in Mexico and Latin America would benefit immensely from expanded opportunities to network and to exchange learning and experiences. Funders could facilitate this level of networking and exchange by making grants to support structured conferences, seminars, and fellowship exchange programs targeted at women. Such programs could focus on expanded interaction between various Mexican women practitioners themselves, between these women and their counterparts in other Latin American countries, and/or between Latin American women and their counterparts in industrialized nations such as the U.S. and Germany.

    Such investments would significantly expand the base of knowledge and expertise available to Mexican women engaged in nonprofit management and fund development. Networking opportunities would also contribute to relationship building of potential value to the field as well as leadership development among participants.

    Presently, few opportunities of this sort are available to Mexican women executives in the independent sector.

3. Commission additional research on women's work and professional development needs in latin american nonprofit management and fundraising.

This article represents a beginning, not an end. It is a direct response to the incredible dearth of practical research that exists on female nonprofit executives and fundraising in Latin America. Much more research and field monitoring is warranted to facilitate more responsive private grantmaking directed at these women's special needs and potential. More longitudinal foundation research and evaluation support would significantly help to augment the currently thin information base on women's nonprofit management and fundraising in the region.

Notes

[1] Alberto Melucci signals that a main characteristic of new movements that emerged in the seventies was the deployment of their resources to encourage social change beyond conventional political discourse. Such new social movements sought long-term change towards a culture of solidarity and participation for the common good. *"Collective action is separating more and more from the political form, common to the traditional oppositional movements, to [seek change] in the cultural field."* Alberto Melucci, "El reto simbólico de los movimientos contemporáneos"(The Symbolic Challenge of Contemporary Movements) en *Sección Política del Nacional* (Political Section of the National) Mexico, no. 14, August 10, 1989.

[2] Salamon, Lester M. and Helmut K. Anheier. *The Emerging Sector: An Overview.* The Johns Hopkins Comparative Nonprofit Sector Project Studies, USA, 1994.

[3] Catalá, Magda. *Reflexiones desde un cuerpo de mujer* (Reflections from a woman's body). Barcelona, Editorial Anagrama, 1983. This author considers that the feminine ideal is opposed to the masculine one, women being a reflection of everything that men are not, or want to be. She proposes that women try to think like men but adapt actions and perspectives based on feminine realities and experiences.

[4] Centro Mexicano para la Filantropía (Mexican Center for Philanthropy), *Directorio de Instituciones Filantrópicas 1995-1996*, Mexico, 1995.

Bibliography

Aguilar, Arriola, Guevara N., y Hernández C. "Sociedad civil. Organizaciones no gubernamentales." *Transición a la democracia*, México City, Miguel Angel Porrúa, 1994.

Fernándes, Ruben César. "Private but Public: The Third Sector in Latin America." *Citizens: Strengthening Global Civil Society*. Washington, D. C., Civicus, World Alliance for Citizen Participation, 1994.

Fernández, Rosa María. "Las medianas empresas y las instituciones no lucrativas en México," Centro Mexicano para la Filantropía, Mexico City, 1995.

Fernández, Rosa María y Jorge Villalobos. "Las organizaciones del Tercer Sector y transitión democrática", Mexico City, mimeo, 1990.

Fernández, Rosa María. "Las fundaciones norteamericanas y las instituciones no lucrativas en México", Mexico City, Centro Mexicano para la Filantropía, 1993.

Foro de Apoyo Mutuo. "Organismos no gubernamentales. Definición, presencia y perspectivas", Mexico City, UNICEF, 1995, pp. 24.

"Memoria. 1er. Seminario sobre la situación y perspectivas de las instituciones privadas de asistencia, promoción y desarrollo social en México", Mexico City, Fundación Alondra, I.A.P. 1990.

Johns Hopkins International Philanthropy Fellows. "Los organismos no lucrativos y el desarrollo: el reto y la oportunidad", Mexico City, julio 1996.

Joseph, James A. "Evolución de las perspectivas de la filantropía y el bien público", San Francisco, California, mimeo, 1995.

Joseph, James A. "El papel de la filantropía en la sociedad actual. Una alocución dirigida a promover el diálogo internacional", Mexico City, Universidad Iberoamericana, 1992, mimeo.

Lopezllera Méndez, Luis. "Sociedad civil y pueblos emergentes. Las organizaciones autónomas de promoción social y desarrollo", Mexico City, Promoción del Desarrollo Popular, A. C. e Instituto Latinoamericano de Estudios Transnacionales, 1987.

Martínez Vázquez, Griselda. "Los retos de la mujeres ejecutivas ante los nuevos liderazgos", *Nueva Sociedad*, Venezuela, núm. 135, enero-febrero 1995, pp. 126-137.

Martínez, Griselda y Rafael Montesinos. "Mujeres con poder. Nuevas representaciones simbólicas", *Nueva Antropología*, Mexico City, UAM y GV editores, núm. 49, marzo 1996, pp. 81-100.

Melucci, Alberto. "El reto simbólico de los movimientos contemporáneos", *El Nacional Política*, Mexico City, 10 de agosto de 1989.

Salamon, Lester M. *America's Nonprofit Sector*, Baltimore, 1992.

Salamon, Lester M. y Helmut K. Anheier. *The Emerging Sector: An Overview*. The Johns Hopkins Comparative Nonprofit Sector Project Studies, Baltimore, 1994.

Salamon, Lester M. y Helmut K. Anheier, "En busca del sector no lucrativo I: cuestión de las definiciones", *Umbral XXI, El desafío del Tercer Sector*, Mexico City, Universidad Iberoamericana, marzo 1995, pp. 7-25.

SEDESOL, *Memoria del primer encuentro*. ONG's acción transformadora, Jalisco, 1993.

Thompson, Andrés A. *El tercer sector en la historia Argentina*. Buenos Aires, CEDES, 1995.

Thompson, Andrés A. "¿Qué es el tercer sector en la Argentina? Dimensión, alance y valor agregado de las organizaciones sin fines de lucro?", Buenos Aires, CEDES, 1995.

The Social Involvement of Corporate Foundations in Argentina

Elba Luna

Introduction

This article examines the activities of emerging corporate foundations in Latin America, focusing in particular on recent developments in Argentina. Its main purposes are: to promote dialogue between corporate donors and their grantees in Latin America; to shed light on the field of corporate philanthropy, which is largely unfamiliar to the general Latin American public; and to identify aspects of corporate giving in the region that might be improved. The article is critical in nature, notwithstanding corporate philanthropy's many important contributions to worthy groups and causes in Latin America, based on the assumption that practitioners can benefit more from constructive criticism than from an affirmation of institutional strengths.

The article, based on an extensive review of giving practices at thirty institutions, begins with a brief overview of Argentina's corporate philanthropic sector, the various groups and causes that have been its focus in recent years, and the specific types of investments that characterize the sector's work. Thereafter, it analyzes corporate foundations' motivations and objectives, and offers various observations and recommendations designed to strengthen corporate philanthropy's development and social impact in Argentina.

In Latin America and Argentina in particular, the collective imagination is often tinged with prejudice towards philanthropy. Donors and recipients alike are suspected of less than pristine motives that include tax evasion on the part of donors and improper uses of funds by nonprofits. Much of the sector operates under a cloud of mystery, therefore, which promotes and flames public misconception about corporate philanthropy's value to society.

Inspired by the need to broaden public appreciation of philanthropy in Argentina and encouraged by the expanding role of corporations in financing and overseeing programs and initiatives in the social arena, this study seeks to encourage more transparent and strategic practices among corporate foundations in Argentina. Our objective is to constructively challenge corporate donors in Argentina and elsewhere in Latin America to improve the sector's public visibility, impact, and accountability.

Background

Corporate foundations are independently-incorporated institutions created and financed by a business to support donations to philanthropic groups. As such, they constitute third-sector organizations, which are typically characterized by their orientation to the common good, nonprofit status, and nongovernmental, nonsectarian and nondenominational charitable activities.

Corporate foundations can be of two types: those that are independent, owing to endowment support and resulting dividends from an individual entrepreneur, a family, a corporation, or a corporate group; or foundations that are dependent on funds received periodically from a founding corporate entity. Both of these foundation types, together with programs developed by individual corporations, form what is known as the field of corporate philanthropy.

International experience indicates that since the "boom" decade of the nineteen-sixties, independent foundations have represented the most widespread mode of corporate philanthropic activity. More recently, studies done in the United States show that while corporate philanthropic activity continues to function at a high level of energy and vitality, it is undergoing a process of revision, propelled mainly by the need to assure a positive impact, both in the philanthropic sense and in relation to corporate image. A downward trend in amounts donated and a greater preoccupation with program outcomes are some of the indices marking the field's evolution.

In Argentina changes related to re-democratization have initiated a multipronged reform process. These changes include the rapid privatization of publicly-owned companies, the opening of the economy to expanded domestic and international competition, increasing regional integration, more stringent public budget controls and tax enforcement, and consolidation and restructuring of public internal and external debt.

This scenario simultaneously poses renewed possibilities and new exigencies (or at least exigencies of a different kind) in relation to those which have operated during the last few decades. Without a doubt, one of the major challenges of the present arrangement is the necessity to reestablish competitiveness, most notably through improved productivity and continuing innovation.

While many debate whether these changes will exert sufficient impact to create a path of consolidated growth for the Argentine economy, the modifications already taking shape are undeniably profound. These modifications speak to everyone of a new economic order based on market forces, a stark contrast with earlier national policy.

The successes of privatization and the open market have brought corresponding undesirable effects as well—for example, a growing gap between rich and poor, and what has been called "savage" capitalism.[1] These outcomes contradict democratic ideals based on increasing levels of civic participation. Ultimately, the challenge appears to be multifaceted in nature: how to reach a level of development that simultaneously assures economic sustainability and wide social participation in the development of civil institutions that better advance citizen rights and opportunities.

In this context, the corporate sector must reposition itself to become not only more competitive but also more humanized in order to meet changing social norms, expectations, and needs. Social responsibility can be expressed in many ways—in actions within the corporation or via initiatives directed to external constituencies through socially-focused funding, advocacy, and related strategic alliances. This review of corporate philanthropy in Argentina suggests that Argentine practitioners would gain social relevance and standing by experimenting more aggressively with this range of social responsibility options.

Corporate Philanthropy in Argentina

Philanthropy in general has a long history in Argentina. Its first manifestations came during the colonial period of the late eighteenth century, when the Catholic Church and various ancillary institutions played an important role. At the beginning of the nineteenth century, a wave of liberation movements took hold in Argentina and other Latin American nations. The first attempts at institutionalizing philanthropic and nonprofit activity in the region stem from this era. The Society of Saint Vincent de Paul and the Beneficent Society of Buenos Aires emerged as leading institutions through which members of high society transferred economic and human resources to poorer sectors.

The beginning of the twentieth century witnessed the appearance of mutual aid societies, cooperatives, and other organizations that were primarily established by and for immigrants. The subsequent advent of public health care and social security eventually replaced earlier initiatives, with the State assuming a central position as social provider, mainly in league with various national guilds and trade unions.

In more recent years, philanthropy has become a practice that broadly extends to Argentina's corporate sector. Of one hundred large corporations consulted for this study, for example, 85 percent stated that they participate in some form of activity in this field. New corporations are increasingly being added to this proliferation of philanthropic business initiatives, helping to sustain Argentina's base of annual donations, notwithstanding cutbacks by many more established corporate donors.

Argentine corporations manifest a high preference for channeling resources directly to nonprofit agencies, especially those engaged in social service delivery. The majority use this route exclusively, whether through a dedicated foundation or a corporate contributions program, because they consider it the most effective way to address community needs. Some corporations, however, particularly those that focus their philanthropic largesse on employee or industry groups, incorporate operating foundations that administer and oversee assistance initiatives targeted specifically to these more internal constituencies.

Whatever their operational preferences, corporate foundations increasingly confront strong public pressure for funds, accompanied by a large number of unsolicited requests. This growing pressure on corporate donors is informed by a number of factors. These include expanding dislocations in the economic realm, increased poverty, reductions in state funding, and related dramatic growth in nonprofit activity. Each year, on average, corporate donors in Argentina now typically receive more than one hundred proposals. With only minor exceptions, most of these institutions are not sufficiently structured or staffed to manage this volume. Moreover, most do not appear anxious to consider additional proposals especially since Argentine corporations generally do not publicize their philanthropic programs nor their donations.

Corporate philanthropic decisions are, in general, the domain of directors or managers of human relations, institutional relations, or marketing departments in Argentina, and only in very few cases do corporate trustees or CEOs become involved. Grantmaking professionals are involved even less. At the same time, the administrative aspects of corporate funding programs are minimally developed, involving a small number of nonspecialized personnel who typically lack the norms and standard criteria for decision making.

As a result of all of this, corporate philanthropy in Argentina supports relatively little public discourse or scrutiny related to policies and practices that shape the independent sector. It tends to focus on more charitable, rather than more strategic grants. And it typically inspires public uncertainty about its value added to society's most needy groups.

Fortunately, among a growing handful of corporate giving institutions a new approach to philanthropy is emerging. Embodied mainly in the work of corporate foundations, this new approach coincides with the resurgence of democracy and private initiative throughout the region; and it addresses many of the shortcomings of more established approaches in the field.

Corporate Foundations in the Social Field

Corporate foundations that focus on social action constitute a relatively new phenomenon in Argentina. Some precursors did exist in the 1960s, but it was at the end of the 1970s that the bulk of these organizations came into being.

Table 1
Corporate Foundations Active Today According to the Decade Founded

FOUNDING DECADE	PERCENTAGE (%) STILL ACTIVE
1960s	14
1970s	28
1980s	30
1990s	28
N=33	

Fuente: datos de Grupo de Analisis y Desarrollo institucional y Social (GADIS) 1997

Typically, these institutions are characterized by:

- More targeted and proactive community grantmaking.
- A discernible investment focus on such areas as education, youth, and health.
- A strong balance between grants to support foundation-adminis tered initiatives and programmatic grants.

The corporate foundations reviewed for this study tend, accordingly, to concentrate on fewer, more discrete funding categories than corporations. Education, for example, which is supported by no less than 86 percent of the corporate foundations studied, constitutes the principal target for these institutions' programmatic work. Fifty percent of these foundations work simultaneously in the areas of health and education, and 30 percent target health, education, and culture.

Table 2		
Donations according to type of program		
CONTRIBUTIONS PROGRAMS	CORPORATE FOUNDATIONS (%)	CORPORATIONS (%)
Programmatic Grants	52	28
Operating/Foundation- administered Grants	48	72

Source: GADIS 1993/97

These data suggest that corporate foundations do constitute a mechanism capable of exercising greater professionalism in corporate philanthropy and expanded reach in needy communities. Notwithstanding these indications, however, even Argentina's more progressive corporate foundations simultaneously share many of the tendencies embodied in their more conventional counterpart institutions in key areas. For example, fully 52 percent of these foundations direct their funds to communities located near their companion facilities or those of their suppliers, even though community needs may be much greater in other locations.

Table 3 Corporate Funding According to Beneficiaries	
GROUP	**PERCENTAGE (%)**
Children	24
General population	15
Youth	14
Organizations	14
Employees	6
Women	3
Native populations	3
Disabled	3
Elderly	3
Source: GADIS 1997	

The majority of Argentine corporate foundations reviewed for this study, moreover, lacked distinction from other corporate giving institutions relative to important giving preferences. For example, like corporate contributions programs, these funders typically distribute both cash and in-kind gifts, without demonstrating a preference for either means of support. While this may merely reflect the desire to maximize institutional flexibility in the field, it might as likely indicate corporate foundation ambiguity about how to most effectively target resources.

Table 4
Businesses and Corporate Foundations
According to Type of Donation Made

TYPE OF DONATION	FOUNDATIONS (%)	CORPORATIONS (%)
Only in-kind	22	10
Only cash	22	13
Both	56	77

Source: GADIS 1993/97

Finally, virtually all of the corporate foundations reviewed for this study closely tie their grantmaking to their core business activity: for example, bank foundations tend to support economic development and micro-enterprise; oil companies tend to focus on the environment; while cement companies typically support community housing and construction. While these are worthy investments that make business sense, they do not necessarily ensure optimal response to society's most pressing needs.

Table 5
Corporate Foundations According to Program Area

AREA	PERCENTAGE (%)
Education	86
Arts & culture	65
Health	57
Environment	18
Business	14
Housing	8
Communication	8
Small business	7
Social welfare	4
Agriculture & ranching	4
Development	4
Evangelical (religious)	4

Source: GADIS 1997

Corporate foundations in Argentina currently funnel a yearly average of one million pesos (i.e., about one million dollars U. S.) into their social investment programs, a figure that roughly matches the amount that Argentine corporations donated five years ago. These donations are made in countless small amounts (an approach similar to that of corporate contributions programs), with few donations ever exceeding 10,000 pesos (i.e., about $10,000 U. S.). One of the major reasons corporate foundation donations have remained static in recent years in Argentina is because the overwhelming majority of these institutions' grant budgets are annually dependent on corporate profitability. In fact, 91 percent of the corporate foundations reviewed for this study are budget-dependent on the vagaries of each year's corporate profits and losses. Only 9 percent of these institutions are endowed.

Among corporate foundations reviewed for this study, whose grants budgets are tied to company profitability, fully 25 percent have recently suspended grants to social programs citing the negative effects of recent economic pressures on their business. This figure would actually approximate 50 percent if we considered those corporations that have reduced their philanthropic programs during the past five years.

The bulk of corporate foundation donations in Argentina are oriented in general to institutions that are more traditional or "known" entities, including socially prestigious institutions, whose members in many cases belong to the same circle of friends, colleagues, or families as corporate principals and/or their major stockholders. Corporate foundations also typically support community-based institutions that provide basic social services (schools and hospitals), as well as religious institutions that serve needy individuals and constituencies.

NGOs that benefit from this largesse are principally focused on providing basic community goods and services in health, education, and related fields: they emphasize direct assistance at low levels of technical complexity. They constitute the group of organizations initially formed by colonial society and later invigorated by various immigrant groups. Ultimately, these organizations received philanthropic support from society's higher echelons, especially from wealthy females, who largely comprise their boards of directors and volunteers. Although there are no reliable data available, it is estimated that more than 5,000 organizations of this type are presently active throughout Argentina.

Social justice organizations and legal defense funds that center their activities on monitoring state actions, and responding to human, civil, and consumer rights concerns have not been targeted by corporate philanthropy. Although such organizations have only recently appeared on the scene, their activities have attracted much publicity. In many cases, these groups have managed to attract the support of prominent personalities from the arts, the church, and academia. These organizations, however, are only very slowly entering the circle of corporate philanthropy in Argentina.

Table 6 Type of Organizations Receiving Funds		
TYPE	CORPORATION (%)	FOUNDATION (%)
Traditional or known entity	92.5	95
Religious organizations	65	85
Neighborhood organizations	50	50
State institutions	82.5	50
Individuals or families	35	50
Labor institutions	27.5	6

Source: GADIS, 1993/1996

Corporate Motivation and Social Innovation in the Field

There is a growing tendency toward institutionalizing corporate foundations in Argentina. This is especially the case among larger, more important companies. While only 2.5 percent of Argentina's 1,000 principal corporations currently support foundations, 40 percent of the nation's largest twenty companies by sales volume do so.[2] The tendency to adopt this institutional form of community giving raises the question: Will Argentina's emerging foundations expand or inhibit social innovation and modernization? The core motivations of corporate leaders and institutions will shape how this question is addressed in the years to come. At present these motivations are still being articulated and assessed. Opportunities to expand profits and market share offer an immediate base of incentive for corporate expansion in the philanthropic field. On the other hand, more long-term social development and social investment considerations offer an alternative outlook. This social development and investment ideal is gaining wider appeal at the close of the twentieth century, both in and outside of Argentina. In fact, more and more leading thinkers and practitioners embrace it. According to Mizrahi (1994), for example, "the philanthropic effort of foundations, especially those with a corporate base, ought to focus on how to open up opportunities for people . . . And solutions ought to be considered in a manner that reinforces this objective."[3]

This view encourages corporate leadership to ascribe to corporate philanthropy the same importance and seriousness as other areas of corporate activity, in order to realize the maximum impact possible for every dollar invested, consistent with values of justice and equality of opportunity. This brand of leadership is of necessity more innovative and disposed to explore beyond the constraints of conventional rules of operation. It encourages initiative and decision making practices that promote these values by supporting people with the calling and commitment, as well as the vision and personality, to transcend traditional directives and assumptions. Unfortunately, traditional philanthropic leadership in Argentina's corporate sector too often suffers from institutional inertia, a lack of confidence in innovation, and a fear of taking on additional tasks. Recent testimony of the president of one of the nation's oldest corporate foundations indirectly illustrates the point, acknowledging that for many years his organization simply "followed a routine in its funding practices." (GADIS, pg. 135.) Reflecting upon the limits of this approach, the foundation president commented further that corporate philanthropy ought to reflect the social conscience of the corporate group it represents at the same time that it demands a fair return on its investment. Implicit in these observations is a recognition of the need for corporate giving institutions to exercise more dynamic investment practices that promote important social values and public impact.

Corporations that act in this way do not expect direct or short-term benefits. According to a recent study done in the United States, corporations that act in compliance with a sense of social responsibility are among the field's most generous donors: they maintain their donation levels even in periods of commercial crises; they spend a considerable time choosing the organizations and the causes they support; they give to causes in which their core business has a special interest; and they want to know that their donations have positively impacted beneficiary organizations and constituencies.

Too few corporate foundations in Argentina emulate these practices. Most such institutions are exclusively driven by "what's good for business." Their funding is unduly motivated by opportunities to increase sales and short-term profits, improve public image, and establish a competitive edge. Corporations with funding policies of this sort are typically characterized by a high level of interest in how other businesses of similar types are doing, and their donations fluctuate in relation to economic conditions, the level of public recognition they receive for their grant-making, and the public salience of potentially negative reaction to corporate decisions and/or practices.

Notwithstanding all of this, it is curious to note that Argentine corporations typically list "philosophical reasons" as their inspiration for creating foundations, and give relatively low priority to operational and business considerations. Similarly, they overwhelmingly site corporate social responsibility (as opposed to profitability) considerations as their main reason for making grants.

Table 7 Reasons for Creating a Foundation	
REASON	PERCENTAGE (%)
Philosophical	62
Operational Considerations	22
Community Support	16
Source: GADIS, 1996	

Table 8 Principal Reason for Making Donations	
REASON	PERCENTAGE (%)
Corporate Social Responsibility	82
Employee Morale/Support	12
Company Image	6
Source: GADIS, 1996	

Conclusions

During the past two decades Argentine corporate foundations have become more publicly visible. These emerging institutions appear to present promising and needed vehicles for expanding social investment and well-being in Argentina. Unlike their analogs in more developed nations such as the United States, however, corporate foundations in Argentina frequently lack a strategic focus extending beyond immediate business interests. They also tend to be slow to professionalize and to innovate;

and they typically demonstrate reluctance to advance needed social change activities.

These tendencies in Argentina's corporate philanthropic field are unfortunate, given Argentina's persistent social problems and its considerable reform needs related to re-democratization and market liberalization. Much more can and must be done by more forward looking leaders in the field to address these considerations. More research and assessment that would expand the base of knowledge relevant to reform strategies and restructuring opportunities for the field would be helpful. This study, therefore, should be considered merely a beginning, rather than an end. Its core data set, though relatively small, and its essential findings establish a baseline for further inquiry. Argentina's corporate foundations and other interested philanthropic groups have a logical interest in supporting this work. Key areas of concentration would include:

Comparative Studies

Given the limited cumulative experiences of corporate foundation leaders and institutions in Argentina, comparison with leaders and institutions in other countries could be key to increasing Argentine practitioners' knowledge base regarding best practices in the field. In addition, such comparison could help to establish a basis for more direct exchanges between Argentine corporate foundation principals and their counterparts in other countries, particularly the United States, where corporate foundations constitute a highly developed field.

Model Program Research

Argentine corporate philanthropy practitioners would benefit immensely from research on model programs impacting important areas of community and independent sector need. Such research would help to establish standard benchmarks for institutional performance and practice in important substantive and procedural areas, such as civic participation and social justice, foundation management, and endowment building.

Other Initiatives

In addition to expanded research, Argentine corporate foundations would benefit considerably from experimental initiatives targeted to professional training for practitioners, the need for new reporting practices designed to expand public awareness regarding giving procedures and priorities, and the development of new information exchange and conferencing opportunities for Argentine and other Latin American foundation executives. Such initiatives, coupled with the additional research recommended herein, would help dramatically to facilitate needed movement and improvement in the field.

Notes

[1] According to an article in *The New York Times,* Friday, February 6, *capitalismo salvaje* is the sudden, radical application of free market policies personified by the United States in nations such as Argentina and others in Latin America that have little recent history with economic competition and free markets.

[2] See listing of major Argentine firms in *Mercado* magazine, Buenos Aires, June 1997.

[3] See Mizrahi, Roberto, *Changes in Funding Styles: Donations versus Social Investment,* Buenos Aires: GADIS, Working Document Series Number 14, 1994.

Bibliography

Bettoni, Analía y Graciela Vázquez. *Aproximación al estudio de las actividades filantrópicas empresariales en Uruguay.* ICD, mimeo, Montevideo, 1995.

Campoamor, Diana. "El voluntariado, la filantropía y la acción comunitaria en EEUU", en Elba Luna comp. *Fondos privados, fines públicos. El empresariado y el financiamiento de la iniciative social.* GADIS, Buenos Aires, 1995.

Esquel Group Foundation. *Civil Society, State and Market: An Emerging Partnership for Equitable Development.* Washington, D. C., mimeo, 1993.

Fundación Juan Minetti. *Directorio de Fundaciones.* Provinica de Córdoba, Argentina, 1997.

GADIS/PNUD. *Fondos privados, fines públicos.* "Fundaciones empresarias en campo social en Argentina", Buenos Aires, 1997.

Grupo de Analisis y Desarrollo Institucional y Social (GADIS) Directory of Argentinean Corporate Foundations. Documentation series Number 4, Buenos Aires, March 1994.

Luna, Elba. *La filantropía empresaria en Argentina.* GADIS, Serie Estudios Nro. 7, Buenos Aires, 1994.

Majul, Luis. *Los dueños de la Argentina I.* "La cara oculta de los negocios". Editorial Sudamericana, Buenos Aires, 1992.

Majul, Luis. *Los dueños de la Argentina II.* "Los secretos del verdadero poder". Editorial Sudamericana, Buenos Aires, 1994.

Mizrahi, Roberto. *Los cambios en los estilos de financiamiento.* "Las donaciones vs. la inversión social", GADIS, Serie Documentos de Trabajo Nro. 14, Buenos Aires, 1994.

Roiter, Mario. "El mercado de la beneficencia. Algunas evidencias sobre las características empresaria y pública en Argentina". UNICEF Argentina, s.f. (mimeo).

Roiter, Mario M. "La Razón social de las empresas. Una investigación sobre los vínculos entre empresa y sociedad en Argentina". CEDES, Documento 115, Buenos Aires, 1996.

Ruétalo, Jorge. *La visión de los empresarios sobre su papel como impulsadores del desarrollo social.* SADES, Montevideo, 1995.

Tercer Sector. Año 1, números 1, 2, 3. Fundación del Viso, Buenos Aires, 1994.

Thompson, Andrés. "El tercer sector en la historia Argentina". Documento CEDES 109, Serie organizaciones no gubernamentales y filantropía, Buenos Aires, 1995.

Toro, Olga Lucía y Germán Rey editores. *Empresa Privada y Responsabilidad Social.* Centro Colombiano de Filantropía, Asociación Nacional de Industriales, Fundación Social, Bogotá, 1996.

UNICEF. "Mobilizing Corporations to Eradicate Child Labor in Brazil". A study of strategies developed by the Abrinq Foundation for Children's Rights, Sao Paulo, 1996.

Velez, Restrepo. *Compromiso Social y Liderazgo Empresario.* Fundación Corona, Bogotá, 1994.

About the Contributors

Diana Campoamor

Diana Campoamor is president of Hispanics in Philanthropy (HIP), a national organization of staff and trustees of foundations that advocates for increased philanthropic support to Latino communities. Prior to joining HIP, she was a director for the Mexican American Legal Defense and Educational Fund (MALDEF) and for the Shallon Foundation. Ms. Campoamor has a B.A. in sociology, has completed extensive graduate work in Latin American Studies from the University of Florida, and has an M.A. from the School of Communication at the University of Miami. Her columns on education, immigration, and other topics have appeared in the *New York Times*, the *San Francisco Chronicle*, among other news media. Ms. Campoamor is a member of the Board of Governors of KRON-TV, the NBC affiliate in the San Francisco Bay Area and serves on the board of the Council on Foundations, among others.

Michael Eduardo Cortés

Michael Cortés is Codirector of the University of Colorado Latino Research and Policy Center. He is also a member of the faculty of the University's Graduate School of Public Affairs, where he teaches courses on public policy, organization theory, and nonprofit organizations. He also directs the School's Program on Nonprofit Organizations. He holds an M.P.P. and Ph.D. in Public Policy from the University of California at Berkeley, and an M.S.W. in Community Organization from the University of Michigan. Dr. Cortés is one of the founders of Hispanics in Philanthropy and serves on various government and private boards and commissions. He has been a research and management consultant to private foundations and nonprofit organizations throughout the United States.

William A. Díaz

William A. Díaz is a Senior Fellow at the University of Minnesota's Hubert H. Humphrey Institute of Public Affairs where he is responsible for a program of research, teaching, and writing on the relationship between public policy, philanthropy, and the nonprofit sector. Prior to joining the Institute, Dr. Díaz was a Ford Foundation program officer. While at Ford, he developed a special foundation initiative concerning the Hispanic population which is described in the publication "Hispanics: Challenges and Opportunities." He is a nationally recognized expert on the Latino population in the United States. Dr. Díaz has served as a consultant to The Ford Foundation, Aspen Institute, and the Hispanic Policy Development Project. He is a trustee of the Puerto Rico Community Foundation and a director of Hispanics in Philanthropy. Dr. Díaz received a Ph.D. in political science from Fordham University.

Rodolfo de la Garza

Rodolfo de la Garza is currently a professor in the Department of Government at the University of Texas at Austin, where he is also the Mike Hogg Professor of Community Affairs. He serves as Vice President and Director of Research at the Tomás Rivera Center and holds a Ph.D. in Government from the University of Arizona. Dr. de la Garza has been the principal investigator and project director for numerous research projects, including the "Latino National Political Survey" funded by The Ford Foundation and others. His publications are numerous as well, including "Mexican Immigrants, Mexican Americans and American Political Culture," published as part of the volume *Immigration and Ethnicity: The Integration of America's Newest Arrivals* and several articles on Latinos and the 1990 and 1992 elections.

Sara Elena Pérez Gil

Sara Elena Pérez Gil graduated as a nutritionist from La Escuela de Salud Publica de México and has a degree in Sociology from the Universidad Nacional Autónoima de México. She has written numerous articles for various publications devoted to maternal and infant health issues.

Gabriel Kasper

Gabriel Kasper is an independent consultant who has reviewed and published various studies for private and nonprofit clients on topics including organizational reengineering, community and economic development, and utility deregulation. A graduate of Wesleyan University and UC Berkeley, he is currently working as a project associate with the Berkeley Community Fund.

Fujia Lu

Fujia Lu is a Ph.D. candidate in the University of Texas at Austin Government Department.

Elba Luna

Elba Luna received her doctorate in sociology from the University of Buenos Aires and currently directs GADIS, the Institutional and Social Analysis and Development Group in Buenos Aires. She works as a consultant for the Interamerican Development Bank, the NGO Association of Brazil, and is vice president of the Bueno Aires Regional NGO Forum.

Henry A. J. Ramos

Henry A. J. Ramos is Principal of Mauer Kunst Consulting, a Berkeley-based private consulting group that specializes in strategic planning, product development, program evaluation, and research activities targeted to business, foundation, and nonprofit institutions. His current and recent clients include Levi Strauss & Co. and the Levi Strauss Foundation (for which he managed the Project Change Anti-Racism Initiative); the California Wellness Foundation; and the California Endowment. Mr. Ramos is a graduate of the University of California at Berkeley and Harvard University, where he earned degrees in political economics, law, and public administration. He is founding editor of the Harvard Journal of Hispanic Policy, a former Robert Bosch Foundation fellow in Germany, and a past member of the professional staffs of The Ford Foundation and The James Irvine Foundation.

Ana Gloria Rivas-Vázquez

Ana Rivas-Vázquez is the vice president for External Relations and Development at St. Thomas University in Miami, Florida. Prior to that, she worked with the Dade Community Foundation. She also practiced law and worked as a journalist. She is a member of Hispanics in Philanthropy as well as other volunteer and professional organizations. Ms. Rivas-Vázquez received a M.A. from Georgetown in Liberal Studies and graduated with honors from the University of Miami School of Law.

Rosa Maria Fernández Rodríguez

Rosa Maria Fernández Rodríguez is a researcher at the Mexican Center for Philanthropy (CEMEFI) in Mexico City where she has completed several research projects, including: Corporate Philanthropy in Mexico, A Profile of Mexican Foundations, Citizen Involvement in Philanthropy in Mexico City, and North American Foundations and Nonprofit Organizations in Mexico. She graduated with a degree in sociology from the Iberoamerican University in Mexico City.

Diane Sanchez

Diane Sanchez is Principal of Sunset Associates, human resource and organizational development consultants in Oakland, California. She works extensively with globalization issues, consulting with clients in Asia, with the European Commission, and with organizations throughout North America that include Fortune 500 corporations, start-up companies, nonprofit and government agencies. She is a member of the Northern California NAACP Legal Defense Fund and is a board member of the Spanish Speaking Unity Council and the East Bay Community Foundation, where she also served as chair. Ms. Sanchez is also a member of Hispanics in Philanthropy.

Arlene Scully

Arlene Scully has worked for three years at Hispanics in Philanthropy as a Project Consultant, primarily for the research project. Prior to coming to San Francisco, she directed an adult education program in Connecticut where she was also a member of a statewide committee to coordinate job training and education for welfare recipients returning to the labor market. Active for many years with antiracist organizations in Connecticut, Ms. Scully also volunteered at Curbstone Press helping select and edit manuscripts from the U. S. and Latin America. Ms. Scully has a B.A. from the University of Connecticut in English and Sociology and has completed coursework at that University toward a degree in public administration.

Griselda Martínez Vázquez

Griselda Martínez Vázquez is a researcher and professor at the Universidad Autónoma Metropolitana-Xochimilco, Departamento de Producción Económica. She has a Ph.D. in Anthropology.

Rosie Zamora

Rosie Zamora is president and CEO of Telesurveys Research Associates, an opinion research firm with offices in Houston, Austin, and Chicago. The company specializes in the design and implementation of full service research and evaluation programs for organizations in the public and private sectors in the U.S. and Latin America. She is the executive director of Legal Strategies, a multidisciplinary consortium which provides litigation research services throughout the United States. Ms. Zamora serves on the board of regents for Texas Southern University and on the board of directors of the Association of Governing Boards of Universities and Colleges, the Houston Endowment, Inc., and Hispanics in Philanthropy, among others.

Cristina Zepeda

Christina Zepeda is currently the vice president and executive director of Semillas, Sociedad Mexicana Pro Derechos de la Mujer, a nonprofit organization that assists women. She has a degree in economics from the Universidad Nacional Autonomidad de México and has participated in many national and international seminars as a presenter. Ms. Zepeda was recently an exchange fellow to the United States, sponsored by Hispanics in Philanthropy with support from the W. K. Kellogg Foundation.